# Semiotics, Communication and Cognition 1

*Editor*

Paul Cobley

Mouton de Gruyter
Berlin · New York

# Culture and Explosion

*by*
Juri Lotman

*edited by*
Marina Grishakova

*translated by*
Wilma Clark

Mouton de Gruyter
Berlin · New York

Mouton de Gruyter (formerly Mouton, The Hague)
is a Division of Walter de Gruyter GmbH & Co. KG, Berlin.

Translated from the edition: Lotman, J. M. 2004. Kul'tura i vzryv. In Juri Lotman, *Semiosfera*, 11–148. St. Petersburg: Iskusstvo-SPB.
First published as: Lotman, J. M. 1992. *Kul'tura i vzryv*. Moscow: Gnozis.

On corrections included in the 2004 edition, see p. 685 of 2004 edition.
Footnotes: T. K. – T. D. Kuzovkina (from 2004 edition).

♾ Printed on acid-free paper which falls within the guidelines
of the ANSI to ensure permanence and durability.

*Library of Congress Cataloging-in-Publication Data*

Lotman, IU. M. (IUrii Mikhailovich), 1922–1993.
  [Kul'tura i vzryv. English]
  Culture and explosion / by Juri Lotman ; edited by Marina Grishakova ; translated by Wilma Clark.
    p. cm. – (Semiotics, communication and cognition ; 1)
  Includes bibliographical references and index.
  ISBN 978-3-11-021845-9 (hardcover : alk. paper)
  ISBN 978-3-11-021846-6 (pbk. : alk. paper)
    1. Semiotics.    2. Culture – Semiotic models.    3. Semiotics and
literature.    4. Semantics (Philosophy)    5. Semiotics and the arts.
  I. Grishakova, Marina.    II. Clark, Wilma, 1964–    III. Title.
  P99.L6713    2009
  302.2–dc22
                                                          2009027049

ISBN 978-3-11-021845-9 hb
ISBN 978-3-11-021846-6 pb

ISSN 1867-0873

*Bibliographic information published by the Deutsche Nationalbibliothek*

The Deutsche Nationalbibliothek lists this publication in the Deutsche
Nationalbibliografie; detailed bibliographic data are available in the Internet
at http://dnb.d-nb.de.

Cover design: Martin Zech, Bremen.
Printed in Germany.

# Contents

# Translator's preface

## *Wilma Clark*

The genesis of this English translation of Juri Lotman's last work *Culture and Explosion* was in a conversation with his son, Professor Mikhail Lotman, and Professor Kalevi Kull and Professor Peeter Torop in a meeting which occurred at the 1st International Conference on Semiosphere in Sao Paolo in August 2005. Whilst there were already, at that time, a growing number of translations in other languages, most notably Estonian, Italian and Spanish, it was acknowledged by many of the prominent semioticians present that the time was ripe for an English translation of *Culture and Explosion*, deemed to be one of Lotman's most important and key works.

Lotman's tastes were eclectic and wide-ranging and he was a prolific writer. The Russian edition of *Culture and Explosion* (*Kul'tura i Vzryv*) was published in 1992 shortly before his death in October 1993 at the age of 71. At the time of his death, he had over 800 articles and books to his name. Whilst his key interests lay in literature and in particular, the works of Pushkin, Lotman's writings reflected a wide ranging interest in a variety of subjects from information and systems theory to aesthetics, poetics, art, cinema, mythology, history and, of course, culture. Many of these themes are addressed in *Culture and Explosion,* which represents Lotman's culminating thoughts on his life's work, dedicated to the development of a semiotic theory of culture.

As a student of philology in Leningrad in the late 1930s, Lotman was inevitably influenced by the 'great names' of Russian formalism: Eichenbaum, Propp, Tynyanov, and Jakobson. However, in this present work, whilst acknowledging the debt of contemporary semiotics to formalism and traditional structuralism, he clearly distinguishes between the atomistic nature of the 'closed, self-sufficient, synchronically organised system; isolated not only in time, between past and future, but also in space' of these earlier traditions and the holistic, open, modelling systems theory approach of the Tartu school, as well as his own commentaries on semiosphere and, in this volume, the explosive processes of cultural development.

Lotman's early studies at Leningrad State University were, in fact, interrupted by the Second World War, in which he served from 1940–1946, as a result of which he only managed to complete his studies in 1950. Thereafter, he moved to Estonia where he worked first of all as a teacher of Russian language and literature at Tartu Teacher Training College. He obtained a lectureship in the Department of Russian Language and Literature at the University of Tartu in 1954, attaining full professorship and becoming Head of Department in 1963.

The 1960s were a prolific period for Lotman and the Tartu school and it is in these early beginnings that we trace the origins of a theoretical framework based on the concept of secondary modelling systems (semiosic models described as being 'beyond natural language' – which itself was treated as a primary modelling system) as a basis for the semiotic analysis of culture. The origins of this framework are located in a symposium held in Moscow in 1962 (at which Lotman was not himself present) upon which the Tartu school subsequently built a series of summer schools dedicated to the study of semiotics, with a particular focus on modelling systems and the development of a typology of culture. The summer schools were organised by Lotman from 1964, and the first of these took place in Kääriku, Estonia in August of that year. In the same year, Lotman launched the semiotics journal, *Sign Systems Studies* (*Trudy po znakovym sistemam*).

Beyond the 1960s, Lotman's work on the development of a semiotic theory of culture can be traced in a number of texts, of which *Culture and Explosion* is the final chapter. The preceding texts include *Theses on the Semiotic Study of Culture*, *On the Semiosphere* and the collection of articles revised and presented in *Universe of the Mind*. In these texts, Lotman moves inexorably forward from the concept of culture as a secondary modelling system to its immersion in semiotic space (the *semiosphere*) – viewed as a reservoir of dynamic processes with explosive potential.

Lotman, together with his colleagues Uspensky, Ivanov, Toporov and Piatigorsky produced *Theses on the Semiotic Study of Culture* (Lotman et al. 1975 [1973]), a conceptual framework for the systemic and semiotic analysis of culture as a 'metasystem' in 1973. Arguably, the origins of Lotman's later development of the concepts of semiosphere and explosion are to be found here. He coined the term *semiosphere* in 1984, in an article published in *Sign System Studies* entitled 'On the semiosphere' (Lotman 2005 [1984]) in which he elaborated his interest in the spatial modelling of culture as an inextricably intertwined hierarchy of sign systems immersed in semiotic space. These initial explorations are further elaborated in *Universe of the Mind* (Lotman 1990) which drew out the salient features of the semiosphere, including the key concepts of core, periphery and boundary, alongside the notion that the sign systems of culture formed part of a semiotic continuum, dispersed in a multi-levelled, multi-dimensional semiotic space. The conceptual framework elaborated in the notion of the *semiosphere* and foregrounded in *Universe of the Mind* highlights and anticipates the complex systemic contradictions and tensions which frame

Lotman's final reflections on the nature of 'culture' and the potentials of 'explosion' explored in the current volume.

*Culture and Explosion* opens with the paradoxical question of how a system (here, the system of culture) can develop and, at the same time, remain true to itself.

In 'Statement of the problem', Lotman draws attention to the relational aspects of his semiotic theory of culture and the notion that culture is not a 'closed' system but, rather, proceeds to a process of self-description only in terms of its relation to the extra-system, which he describes, here, as 'the world beyond the borders of language'. This positioning of culture as but one element within a polylingual semiotic reality is used to introduce the notion of dependency and reciprocity between co-existent systems, neither of which – alone – can wholly reflect the 'space of reality'. This inadequacy points to the 'necessity of *the other* (another person, another language, another culture) and thus produces the need for a form of translation to be effected between systems and at the same time reflects the multilayered complexity of semiotic space and the tensions and boundaries that are generated between the disparate systems that occupy it.

Lotman continues this theme in Chapter 2 where he uses Jakobson's communication model to elaborate on these notions of tension and translatability in the lingual spaces of communication. Differentiating between 'code' and 'language', he suggests that the former is an artificially created structure that implies no history, whereas the latter 'is a code plus its history'. He distinguishes between the linguistic and the lingual, suggesting that 'lingual communication reveals itself to us as the tense intersection between adequate and inadequate lingual acts' and uses the example of an exchange of codes, e.g. 'cat' and 'gato' as a relatively easy translation between two closely related languages, whereas a translation from poetic language to that of music is presented as much more problematic, if not impossible. In these notions of adequacy and inadequacy of the translation act, and the concomitant increase in informativity in the system generated by ambiguity and the apparent impossibility of translation Lotman, here introducing the notion of extra-lingual reality, not only distances himself from common perceptions of the relationships between language and culture, but also begins to sow the seeds of the concept of 'explosion'.

In 'Gradual progress', Lotman returns to the concept of cultural development, exploring this in terms of predictability and unpredictability, continuity and discontinuity and the stability and instability of the system and how these dynamic processes contribute to the gradual or radical development of culture. To gradual processes, he assigns the metaphor of a fast flowing river in spring; to radical ones, he assigns the metaphor of 'a minefield with unexpected explosive points'. That these two are mutually co-dependent, complex and antithetical is demonstrated in the examples Lotman gives of the relationships between the dandy, his artifice and his audience. In this chapter, Lotman also elaborates his view of the positive qualities of 'explosion' as a *creative* phenomenon reflected in the epoch of the Renaissance or the Enlightenment in contrast to the common perception of 'explosion' as a *destructive* tendency linked to gunpowder and nuclear fission.

The theme of 'continuity and discontinuity' is elaborated in more detail in chapter 4. Building on the notion of gradual and radical development introduced in the previous chapter, Lotman constructs a complex picture of the unfolding of cultural development in a multilayered synchronic space. Where gradual processes ensure succession, explosive ones ensure innovation. However, the multi-discursive nature of culture ensures that its component parts develop at different rates and, in this sense explosive moments in some layers may be matched by gradual ones in others. In this way, Lotman describes culture as being immersed in a semiotic space that is greater than the sum of its parts and which forms a unified, integrated semiosic mechanism.

In chapter 5, Lotman draws an interesting limitation in relation to the use of metaphor and mathematical models to represent the intersection of semantic spaces and the explosive tension this creates. He suggests, instead, that we have in a mind a mental model which comprises a *'specific semiotic mass whose boundaries are framed by a multiplicity of individual uses'*. This notion of the indeterminate structure of the *semiosphere* and its *boundary spaces* echoes Lotman's earlier work in *Universe of the Mind* where the boundaries are described as permeable, filtering mechanisms, which intersect with the 'other' at multiple points and levels rather than boundaries in the sense of a solid line 'drawn in the sand'.

Lotman draws on the writings of Pushkin and the idea of 'inspiration' as a form of creative tension to illustrate the dynamic processes at work in the interactions of the individual in relation to the semiotic mass (that is the *semiosphere*). He frames 'inspiration' as the product of ambiguous tension in semiosic processes in which understanding is achieved and framed retrospectively as an element of 'discovery' that is simultaneously creative and logical. In a sense, Lotman, here, presents the notion of 'inspiration' as the 'moment of explosion' as an element which, as stated earlier, is 'out of time' and recognisable only in retrospect, at which stage it is no longer viewed as explosive but is framed by its participation in the gradual development of culture.

In 'Thinking reed', Lotman develops his notion of culture's opposition to non-culture which he relates to 'nature'. Lotman uses notions of harmony and disharmony in nature to frame man's disruptive presence. Whilst he acknowledges the signifying acts of animals, Lotman draws on the work of Tyutchev to distinguish these ritualised processes from those of man: 'as a "thinking reed" – he constantly finds himself at odds with the basic laws of his surroundings' whose behaviour 'gravitates towards the invention of something new and un-predicted'. Thus, we see in man's capacity to generate a mental model of reality, a unique form of semiosis linked to culture, memory and representation.

In chapter 7, Lotman takes up this notion of representation, focusing on man's use of language and the use of proper names to categorise and classify cultural artefacts. He uses this to highlight the concepts of choice, selection and the mental positioning of the individual within the dual framework of 'I' and 'Other'. Once again, the distinction between 'one's own' (*svoi*) and the 'other' (*chuzoi*) or alien is made, generating a sense of boundary in the individual's social and cultural construction of the world. At the same time, he makes much of the ludic qualities made available to humans in their use of language in the interplay between the general and the specific, the individual and the collective. In 'The fool and the madman', Lotman considers the positioning of semiotic value in terms of 'the norm', however, he introduces the notion of a ternary structure where the more traditional structure of the binary opposition is reframed as a semiotic continuum marked by the extremes of 'the fool' on the one hand and the 'madman' on the other, each of which is balanced or 'measured' against the notion of 'the wiseman' which is the norm. Focusing on the 'madman' as an unpredictable entity Lotman suggests that there are, nevertheless, moments (of explosion) in which the madman is able to present his 'madness' as a moment of genius or effective exploit, e.g. in extreme circumstances, such as war, where the unpredictable behaviour of the madman works to his advantage. He draws on examples from folklore, myth, war, chivalric literature and the theatre to demonstrate the use of 'folly' as permissible behaviour with alternating semiotic values and as a harbinger of explosive potential.

Whereas in the previous chapter, Lotman focuses on the unpredictability of the text (in the sense of a singular scenario), in chapter 9, 'The text within the text', he turns his attention to the unpredictability of the system as a whole. He argues that semiotic space is populated by multiple systems that are in con-stant and dynamic interaction not only with each other but also with fragments of those systems which have been 'destroyed' as a result of which these systems are in dialogue not only with themselves but with others with which they frequently collide, occasionally producing a third, new and unpredictable phenomenon. As an interesting example, he refers to the 'Frenchification' of the culture of the Russian nobility at the turn of the 18th century and the use of French language by Pushkin and Tolstoy as a reflection of everyday reality of the period, alongside Griboyedov's critique of the practice. In chapter 10, Lotman uses the example of the trope as a destruction or disruption of the norm to further elaborate the value of the unpredictable as a measurement of cultural development, describ-ing it as a 'complex dynamic reservoir' which constantly pushes 'the boundaries of the permissible'. He presents an interesting range of examples around fash-ion, cultural values and the 'signifying function of clothing' to demonstrate the relationship between ritualistic behaviour on the one hand and eccentricity on the other. Describing this inverted world as 'the dynamics of the non-dynamic' he makes the point that explosive moments may also arise out of unexpected shifts in fashion, ritual, and other forms of behaviour which pass beyond the bounds of the norm (e.g. tyranny, role-swapping – whether by gender, status or intellect, and homosexuality) which are subsequently 'normalised' as forms of social ritual.

In 'The logic of explosion', we are returned to the paradox of language and culture and the struggle to free ourselves from its limits. Lotman writes:

> We are immersed in the space of language. Even in the most basic abstract con-ditions, we cannot free ourselves from this space, which simply envelops us, and yet it is a space of which we are also a part and which, simultaneously, is part of us.

Here, again, Lotman draws a contrast between the seemingly stable, isolated texts of formalism and early structural studies and the heterogeneous, dynamic and (at least partially) chaotic nature of the semiosphere. Lotman presents the work of Charlie Chaplin as an example of 'a chain of sequential explosions, each of which changes the other, creating a dynamic multi-levelled unpredictability'. He points to the transfer of circus language (pantomime and gesture) to the film screen, which then developed into a completely different genre characterised by the sharp contrast between gesture and theme, e.g. the comic origins of pantomime and the depiction of life in the trenches during the First World War. The latter, in turn, paves the way for Chaplin to develop further semiotic distance between his initial forays into film and the complex melange of language and topic theme apparent in his later movies such as 'The Great Dictator'. Thus, in this final satirical frame, we find traces of the previous semiotic systems framed by circus language and early cinematic slapstick comedy.

In 'The moment of unpredictability' Lotman reiterates the view that the 'moment of explosion' is unpredictable not in the sense of randomness but in terms of 'its own collection of equally probable possibilities. . . from which only one may be realised'. At the point in which the explosive moment is realised, the 'others' are dispersed into semantic space, whereupon they become carriers of semantic difference. In chapter 13, Lotman explores culture from the point of view of its internal structures and external influences. He argues that culture is traditionally viewed as a bounded space and suggests that it is wrong to view culture this way. He posits culture as a dynamic entity which is in constant collision with the extra-cultural sphere within which it is immersed, whose development is the result of a 'constant transposition of internal and external processes'. In this sense, culture is seen to be in constant dialogue not only with itself but also with the greater *semiosphere*. What is internal is regarded as orderly, one's own (*svoi*), whereas what is outside is regarded as chaotic or alien (*chuzoi*). The perception of chaos is relative to culture itself and, Lotman suggests, the chaotic space is nevertheless organised in its own terms, albeit in a language unknown to the culture of origin. When the spaces of culture and extra-culture collide in this way, new texts are drawn into the cultural space, generating an act (or multiple acts) of explosion. In the avalanche of possibilities this presents, some elements are assimilated, whilst others are rejected and expelled. Those that are assimilated by the culture contribute, in turn, to the gradual or radical development of the cultural space.

In 'Two forms of dynamic' Lotman returns to the distinction between explosive and gradual processes. He is particularly at pains to emphasise that neither concept should be taken literally. In chapter 15, Lotman returns to the unique human trait of consciousness, contrasting this to the natural impulse of stimulus-response, which he links to the notion of memory and the development of the activity of mental representation and the translation of activity into a sign. The important element here is the notion of abstraction, the unique ability of man to generate meaning independently of the immediacy of the stimulus-response action. However, in this chapter, Lotman does not journey from symptom to language but rather, points to the threshold of meaning previously suggested in the chapter on 'inspiration' which is, here, evidenced as the dream. Interestingly, and almost in analogy to the phrase 'semiotic mass' used in chapter 5, Lotman uses the Russian word *klubok* (literally 'woollen ball') to describe the tangled web of meaning potentials and the polylingual nature of the dream space. In a beautifully expressed metaphor, he suggests that the space of the dream 'does not immerse us in visual, verbal, musical and other spaces' rather, it immerses us in their 'coalescence'. The 'coalescent' space is unpredictable, uncertain and indeterminate and, in Lotman's word equates to 'zero space' or a space absent of meaning, except in its correlation to the 'carriers of communication' which occupy it and which, in turn, are dependent on the 'interpreting culture' which generates them. To this 'zero space' Lotman assigns the value of an essential function in the development of culture, the provision of a 'reserve of semiotic uncertainty' which may act as a stimulus for creative (explosive) activity.

Following on from this Lotman, focusing on the artistic text, looks again at culture from the point of view of the move from the individual (unique) to the universal (general) and suggests that the structure "I" is one of the basic indices of culture. He points to the rationalist tendency to 'streamline contradictions' and to 'reduce diversity to singularity' but suggests that more needs to be understood about the contradictory nature of the artistic text.

In 'The phenomenon of art' Lotman outlines the transformative interaction between the 'moment of explosion', the modelling of consciousness and the act of memory, which he describes as the 'three layers of consciousness'. Turning from the realm of the dream, he focuses on the nature of art, its relation to freedom of action and, through this its ability to transform the real to the unreal, the illegitimate to the legitimate and the forbidden to the permissible. Art is construed as an experimental domain which creates its own world. As such, and like the inverted world of the trope discussed above, it generates a reservoir of dynamic processes which contribute to the explosive potential of the semiotic space of art. Here, too, Lotman provides with a much greater degree of clarity his understanding of the dynamic processes of the semiosic world.

> ... the dynamic processes of culture are constructed as a unique pendulum swing between a state of explosion and a state of organisation which is realised in gradual processes. The state of explosion is characterized by the moment of equalisation of all oppositions. That which is different appears to be the same. This renders possible unexpected leaps into completely different, unpredictable organisational structures. The impossible becomes possible. This moment is experienced out of time, even if, in reality, it stretches across a very wide temporal space. [...] This moment concludes by passing into a state of gradual movement. What was united in one integrated whole is scattered into different (opposing) elements. Although, in fact, there was no selection whatsoever (any substitution was made by chance) the past is retrospectively experienced as a choice and as a goal-oriented action. Here, the laws of the gradual processes of development enter into the fray. They aggressively seize the consciousness of culture and strive to embed the transformed picture into memory. Accordingly, the explosion loses its unpredictability and presents itself as the rapid, energetic or even catastrophic development of all the same predictable processes.

In chapter 18, the notion of the 'end' and the principles of continuity and discontinuity are reflected in the stark boundary between life and death. Death is marked out as both the beginning and the end. Lotman speaks of the 'special semantic role of death in the life of man'. It is the boundary which frames all meaningful activity and which, simultaneously, marks the contradiction between life in the general sense and the 'finite life of human existence'. And yet, what is finite, is continued in the memory of the 'son' so that even the boundary of 'death', as it were, is permeable and filtered.

In 'Perspectives', Lotman reiterates the view that explosion is part and parcel of linear dynamic processes. He distinguishes between binary and ternary structures, emphasising that explosion in the latter takes the form of a specific form of dynamic, whereas in the latter it permeates the multiple layers of semiotic space at different speeds and different intervals, such that whilst its effects are felt throughout all the layers of culture, traces of the old remain to which the ternary system strives to adapt itself, transporting them from periphery to centre. In binary structures, by contrast, the explosion penetrates life in its entirety, replacing all that previously existed in an apocalyptic manner. In these concluding remarks, Lotman expresses the hope that the events of the early 1990s in Russia reflect a shift in Russian culture from a binary structure towards a more accommodating ternary system, capable of generating renewal and innovation.

In the final chapter, Lotman offers his concluding remarks on the paradox of cultural development, returning to his initial question as to how a system (culture) can develop and at the same time, remain true to itself. He argues that the starting point of any semiotic system is not the isolated sign or model but, rather, semiotic space which itself is characterised as a 'conglomeration of elements whose relations with each other may be encountered in a variety of ways'. This interconnectivity of the system and the polylingual elements which populate it can, he argues, only be understood 'in terms of the ratio of each element to the other and all elements to the whole'. The foregrounding of the relational and interactional elements of culture in its immersion in semiotic space, and the sense that in these terms, culture is viewed as embedded in a semiotic network far greater and more inherently dynamic than itself, coupled with the heterogeneity and explosive potential of that structure, has important implications for the future study not only of culture, communication, and new trends in technology but also for the generation of new strands of interdisciplinary research into the ever expanding world of semiosis. In particular, this dynamic systemic approach to cultural analysis and semiosis offers interesting potential in the realm of new media technologies (Buckingham 2007), cultural studies (Schönle 2006), and recent streams of semiotic study such as multimodality (Kress and van Leeuwen 2001; Iedema 2003; Jewitt and Kress 2003; Thibault and Bauldry 2005), nexus analysis (Scollon 2001), semiotic remediation (Prior et al. 2006) and, of course modelling systems theory (Sebeok and Danesi 2000) itself.

In the closing chapters of the book, Lotman reflects on endings and new beginnings. It is particularly poignant in the titling of chapter 18 – '*The end! How sonorous is this word*' if we consider that at the time the book was produced, Lotman himself was sufficiently ill that this book was dictated rather than written by him and, indeed, he died less than a year after the book was published. In addition, his wife of many years had died shortly before the book was produced.

And, last but certainly not least, the former Soviet bloc was undergoing a period of immense change. The final chapter, '*In place of conclusions*' is particularly interesting as Lotman, rather than drawing conclusions, invites us, instead, to look forward . . . with an eye to the past, and our feet firmly in the present.

And to finish, a parting remark made by Professor Mikhail Lotman in the closing discussions of the 1st International Conference on Semiosphere, which may serve to illustrate Lotman's contribution to our ongoing researches:

*"For my father there were two types of scholar - the one who has the questions and the one who has the answers. He belonged to the first."*

******

## Thanks

Just as translation in the semiosphere is effected through dynamic interaction on multiple levels, so too this translation is the fruit of many voices, although responsibility for any errors, inaccuracies or omissions are, of course, solely mine. I would like to thank Professor Winfried Nöth, Professor Peeter Torop, Professor Irene Machado and Dr Martin Oliver for their support and shared belief that the translation of this book into English was an important and valuable task. I would also, and more particularly, like to thank Professor Kalevi Kull and Dr Paul Cobley, as series editors, for their enthusiasm and encouragement for this project. And a final heartfelt thank you to Associate Professor Marina Grishakova for her painstaking editorial assistance in checking, proofreading and verifying the translated manuscript.

## References

Buckingham, D.
    2007           Media education goes digital: an introduction. *Learning, Media and Technology* 32, 111–119.

Iedema, R.
    2003           Multimodality, resemiotization: extending the analysis of discourse as multi-semiotic practice. *Visual Communication,* 29–57.

Jewitt, C. and Kress, G.
    2003           *Multimodal Literacy*. New York/Oxford: Peter Lang.

Kress, G. and van Leeuwen, T.
    2001           *Multimodal Discourse: The Modes and Media of Contemporary Communication*. London: Routledge.

Lotman, Y.
  1990           *Universe of the Mind: A Semiotic Theory of Culture*. London: I. B. Tauris.
Lotman, Y. M.
  2005           [1984] On the Semiosphere. *Sign System Studies* 33, 1–15.
Lotman, Y. M., Uspenskij, B. A., Ivanov, V. V. and Toporov, A. M.
  1975           [1973] *Theses on the Semiotic Study of Culture*, vol. 2. Lisse, Netherlands: The Peter de Ridder Press.
Prior, P., Hengst, J., Roozen, K. and Shipka, J.
  2006           'I'll be the sun': From reported speech to semiotic remediation practices. *Text and Talk* 26(6), 733–766.
Schönle, A. (ed.)
  2006           *Lotman and Cultural Studies: Encounters and Extensions*. Madison, WI: The University of Wisconsin Press.
Scollon, R.
  2001           *Mediated Discourse: The Nexus of Practice*. London: Routledge.
Sebeok, T. A. and Danesi, M.
  2000           *The Forms of Meaning: Modeling Systems Theory and Semiotic Analysis*. Berlin/New York: Mouton de Gruyter.
Thibault, P. J. and Bauldry, A.
  2005           *Multimodal Transcription and Text Analysis*. London: Equinox.

# Introduction

*Edna Andrews*

In 1990 Umberto Eco wrote a brilliant introduction to Ann Shukman's remarkable translation of Lotman's book, *Universe of the Mind (Внутри мыслящих миров)*. By focusing on the emergence of the terms *semiotics* and *structuralism* in the European academic community and their interrelationship, Eco contextualizes Lotman's work historically and presents a slice of Lotman's contributions that successfully captures the essence of this powerful scholar and thinker (1990: vii–xiii). It is difficult to imagine an introductory article that can attain the profundity and scope of Eco's evaluation of Lotman's work, which makes the present task quite daunting. However, the central ideas given in what was to be Lotman's final monograph, *Culture and Explosion (Культура и взрыв)*, which he dedicated to his wife, the notable literary scholar Zara Grigorievna Mints, are sufficiently robust that they have already been the subject matter of a series of analyses attempting to further the study of the semiotics of culture, and it is to these ideas that we turn the readers' attention.

It would be impossible to discuss the ideological fundamentals of *Culture and Explosion* without evocation of Lotman's concept of the *semiosphere,* originally introduced in 1984. The *semiosphere* is the prerequisite space that guarantees the potential for semiosis, which is in essence the generation of meanings. In Lotman's own words, the semiosphere is "the semiotic space necessary for the existence and functioning of languages, not the sum total of different languages; in a sense the semiosphere has a prior existence and is in constant interaction with languages...a generator of information" (Lotman 1990: 123, 127). Semiospheric space is the precursor to and the result of cultural development (Lotman 1990: 125). Lotman outlines the fundamental organizing principles of the semiosphere in *Universe of the Mind* as *heterogeneity* of the space, *asymmetry* of internal structures, *binariness* of internal and external spaces, *boundaries* defined as bilingual filters that allow for the exchange of semiotic processes, and the "development of a metalanguage" as the final act of the system's structural organization (1990: 124–140). Of these five points, only one is discussed in *Culture and Explosion.* (In fact, the term *semiosphere* only appears in *Culture and Explosion* on two occasions.) Specifically, in the chapter entitled *The Logic of Explosion,* Lotman focuses on the notion of heterogeneity as a characteristic of not only spatial differentiation, but even different rates of change between and within individual subspaces of the semiosphere (see below and 1992a: 177):

Semiological space is filled with the freely moving fragments of a variety of structures which, however, store stably within themselves a memory of the whole which, falling into a strange environment, can suddenly and vigorously restore themselves...

Completely stable invariant semiotic structures apparently do not exist at all.

Lotman's reiteration of the importance of a complex *dynamic* within and around the semiosphere speaks to its critical role in capturing the essence of its explanatory power as a modeling system. Peeter Torop, one of the central figures of contemporary Tartu semiotics, explains the multiple perspectives from which the concept of *semiosphere* is explicated, which include a universal research level, a concept encompassing all facets of cultural semiotics, and as a functional mechanism to understand diachronic and synchronic dynamic processes. Although the term itself is hardly mentioned, it is clear that there is a profound relationship between Lotman's earlier work on the semiosphere and his work in *Culture and Explosion*. It is precisely this relationship that will be the focus of the following remarks.[1]

We are constantly reminded of the fundamental tenet of Lotman's approach to semiotics, which is the importance of semiotics as a dynamic process of *semiosis,* which is a system-level phenomenon engaging multiple sign complexes that are given simultaneously across spatio-temporal boundaries, and not merely the study of individual signs artificially frozen into one slice of the space/time continuum. As Lotman's work is contextualized into the broader fields of structuralist and non-structuralist semiotic paradigms (e.g. comparisons with the works of Saussure, Hjelmslev, Peirce, Jakobson and others) and even the cognitive sciences, it is crucial to understand Lotman's decision to target his theoretical models at the system level, and not at the individual sign level. This fact may explain, for example, why Lotman does not devote more works to explications of sign types using iconicity, indexicality and symbolic distinctions.

Lotman's work has often been read through the prism of other semiotic contributors of the twentieth century, resulting in what often appears to be an attempt to position Lotman as more of a borrower of ideas than an innovator of ideas. While it is certainly true that Lotman was deeply influenced by his own professors and some of the most outstanding intellectuals of his day, Lotman's work is unique in its achievement of a broadly-based metalanguage for the *mod-*

---

1. The term *semiotics* is also rarely used throughout the text of *Culture and Explosion.* I would suggest that Lotman wanted to present his ideas as fundamental not only to a semiotic approach to language, culture and text, but as more general concepts that are applicable within a variety of methodological approaches to the study of cultures.

*elling* of cultures, a system of systems.[2] Lotman's formulation and explication of semiospheric space is the single most powerful contributing factor to his success in presenting a usable metalanguage for cultural analysis. Vjacheslav Vsevolodovich Ivanov, Lotman's colleague and co-founder of the Tartu-Moscow School, is very emphatic in his refocusing of the semiotic agenda to contextualize itself within the defining principles and mechanisms of the semiosphere itself (1998: 792).

The discipline of cultural semiotics as viewed by Lotman has caused a significant shift away from more traditional structuralist models of semiotic space. Specifically, Lotman defines this new discipline as focused on analyzing the interaction and mutual influence of diversely-structured semiotic spaces, the ever-present irregularities and unevenness (неравномерность) contained in the structures of semiotic space, and an obligatory shift to cultural and semiotic *polyglotism* (1992b: I. 129). It is precisely the last point that is featured early on in *Culture and Explosion* and emerges many times throughout the book. In the opening chapter, Lotman outlines the importance of a minimum of two languages in order for semiotic space to realize its meaning-generation potential, and it is precisely these languages ("a minimum of two, but in all actuality the list is open-ended" [see below and 1992a: 9–10]) that, by definition, mutually require each other in order to provide the inevitability of the *other*. Furthermore, he notes that those spaces beyond the boundaries of a given semiotic space (which he calls "reality" or the "external world") also can never be captured by a single language; rather, only an aggregate of languages can meet this requirement (see below and 1992a: 9). The idea of a single, ideal language is, at best an illusion and must be abandoned (ibid.). Ironically, the desire to achieve a single, universal language is one of the trends that helps create cultural space (see below and 1992a: 10).

Lotman's requirement of multiple languages as "the minimal meaning-generating unit" may be interpreted in a variety of ways and on a variety of levels (see below and 1992a: 16). For instance, these different languages could be the languages of the internal spaces of the semiosphere and the surrounding spaces in which the semiosphere is situated or could include Lotman's fundamental distinction between I–I (also called *autocommunication*) and I-s/he models of communication as presented in *Universe of the Mind* (1990: 21–33). Although not mentioned in *Culture and Explosion,* the concept of *autocommunication* is

---

2. Lotman's interest in modelling systems involves two major trajectories: (1) the creation of metasemiotics, which focuses more on modelling the text than the text itself, and (2) the specific semiotic functioning of actual texts (see below and 1992a: I. 129). It is the second trajectory that gives rise to a developed discipline of cultural semiotics.

one of the most powerful concepts given by Lotman for defining mechanisms for the generation of meaning within the semiosphere. The primary function of autocommunication is to create new information at both the cultural and individual levels. This new information displays an important series of characteristics, including (1) its qualitative reconstruction, (2) not being self-contained or redundant, and (3) the doubling and redefinition of both the *message* and the *code* (1990: 21–22).[3]

This is an appropriate point to mention Lotman's baseline requirement, which is actually a corollary of the requirement of a minimum of two languages: all phenomena must be translated in order to be perceived in semiospheric space. Such a formulation brings Lotman close to the non-structuralist semiotic theory of C. S. Peirce. Furthermore, all translations necessarily change meaning, and the act of non-comprehension is as salient as the act of comprehension. The importance of non-comprehension deserves further explication.

The relationship between translatability and nontranslatability in Lotmanian theory is an important source of *tension,* which is a basic structural principle of all semiotic space that plays an integral part in the realization of discontinuities in the dynamic form of *explosions.* In the introductory chapter of *Culture and Explosion,* Lotman describes the interrelationship of the multiple languages that lie at the heart of semiotic space and their mutual untranslatability (or limited translatability) as the "source of adjustment of the extra-lingual object to its reflection in the world of languages" (see below and 1992a: 10). Lotman expands this description in his definition of semiotic space (see below and 1992a: 42)

> Semiotic space appears before us as the multi-layered intersection of various texts, which are woven together in a specific layer characterized by complex internal relationships and variable degrees of translatability and spaces of untranslatability.

While it is generally true that the internally distinct and bilingual filter-like boundaries within semiotic space provide a baseline for potential translatability, it is also the case that cultural spaces and texts in a diachronic perspective may contain pockets of information that are not accessible to particular synchronic spaces because of the different languages and codes used, or even due to a breakdown in the cultural knowledge of the codes defining the internal spaces. In each of these cases, the heterogeneous structure of semiotic space gives rise to different types of *tension,* including the tension that gives value to the "translation of the untranslatable" (see below and 1992a: 15). In short, there are two types of contradictory *tension* that are at work simultaneously in

---

3. The terms *code* and *message* are borrowed by Lotman from Roman Jakobson's communication act model (Jakobson 1987 [1960]: 62–94).

all communication acts: (1) the attempt to make comprehension easier by expanding the intersecting spaces of the addresser and addressee, accompanied by (2) an attempt to increase the value of the communication by maximizing the non-intersecting spaces of the addresser and addressee (see below and 1992a: 14). Extracting knowledge and new meanings from these less accessible textual spaces increases the value of the content of the utterance.

One of the most significant outcomes of the interplay of *tension* in the semiotic act is reiteration of the fact that the semiotic process does not guarantee a veridical outcome. It is on this point that Lotman and Peirce are in profound agreement. Lotman notes that misunderstanding and breakdown in communication are as significant as successful transmissions (1992b: I. 18), while Peirce talks about the role of *false signs* and *underdeveloped signs* (Peirce 8.315; Savan 1980: 257–260; Short 1981: 200; Andrews 2003: 147). And thus, "misunderstanding (conversation in non-identical languages) is as valuable a meaning-generating mechanism as understanding" (Lotman see below and 1992a: 16).

Lotman's definition of *tension* and *explosion* are at the heart of his final monograph. Tension, as we have shown above, is manifested in a variety of guises, some of which are contradictory in nature. It serves as a structural principle for endless dynamic change in semiotic space that leads to different levels of information growth. Tension is at the basis of the primary mechanisms of *gradual* and *explosive* cultural change (Lotman see below and 1992a: 17–43). These two mechanisms are inextricably linked, both coexisting and alternating in space-time, and illustrate and explain cultural evolution. One of the ways to contextualize the importance of these two types of mechanisms is to look more closely at the connection between discontinuity and explosion conceptually. As we noted earlier, the notion of *boundedness* is one of the central defining characteristics of the semiosphere. With boundedness comes the implication of discontinuity and discreteness of structures. In any given cut of semiospheric space, Lotman guarantees that both continuous and discrete (explosive) processes occur in an feedback configuration, such that continuity guarantees discontinuity, and discontinuity guarantees future continuity (1992a: 26–27). I have argued elsewhere (2003: 35–39, 167) that the "moment of explosion" clarifies Lotman's understanding of gradual and explosive processes. Specifically, the inception of the explosion (discontinuity) is the beginning of a new stage of development for the semiotic system that is a focal point for extraordinary expansion of information on the one hand, and a signal of the beginning of a new era on the other; however, this new stage is of a cyclic, not linear, nature, and the force of change in one area evokes an equally powerful change in the other (see Lotman see below and 1992a: 26). Furthermore, Lotman is careful to distinguish between *actual discontinuity* and the *perception of discontinuity*. Periods of cultural self-awareness are "usually recorded as intermissions" (1990: 144), resulting in an asymmetrically-defined culture text. This asymmetry is clearly seen in the relationship constructed between the past and the future (1992a: 27):

> The spectator, having mentally placed himself in that "present moment" in which the text was realised ..., seems then to turn his attention to the past which converges in a cone, whose apex touches the present moment. Facing the future, the audience is immersed in an array of possibilities which have not yet met with potential selection. The uncertainty of the future allows significance to be assigned to everything.

Lotman's definition of *explosion* is differentiated into distinct segments and incorporates the viewer/participant's perspective by establishing specific relationships of present to future or present to past. In the first case (present to future), one has "a flash of a space of meaning not yet unfolded" (see below and 1992a: 28), where potentially everything is meaningful, whereas in the second case (present to past), the situation becomes regularized, law-based, the result being interpreted as inevitable and other possibilities becoming unthinkable (see below and 1992a: 32–3).

One of the distinct segments of the moment of explosion identified by Lotman is the *moment of exhaustion of the explosion (момент исчерпания взрыва)*, a turning point in the process that is realized as both the "moment of future development" and the "place of self-realization" (see below and 1992a: 30). Self-realization leads to a qualitative re-evaluation of the process that has just occurred, and facilitates the interpretation of what was, in fact, a purely random event as the only possible outcome.

I have often been struck by an important philosophical overlap between Lotman's characterizations of *tension* and *explosion* and manifestations of these notions in the fiction and philosophical writings of E. I. Zamiatin and have found that many of Lotman's central theoretical principles seem to speak directly to Zamiatin's work (Andrews 2003: 49, 112–114). I have imagined what insightful analyses Lotman could have provided on Zamiatin, especially given Lotman's rich body of literary, historical and semiotic analyses of Russian texts and Russian culture. However, Zamiatin's works were forbidden and removed from the Russian canon in the early 1920s and his works only reappeared in print in the Soviet Union in 1988. Zamiatin's works provide a wonderful set of case studies that reinforce Lotmanian principles on the creation of culture texts and characterizations of cultural space. I would like to mention here that there are two passages in *Culture and Explosion* that could be substituted into the narrative of Zamiatin's novel *We,* and no one would notice them as "foreign" (инород-ные) texts; namely Lotman's discussion of individual and collective behavior

in chapter one (see below and 1992a: 11), and his statements on removing ambiguity and "straightening all contradictions" (выпрямлять противоречия)
in chapter 16 (entitled "Я и Я") ( see below and 1992a: 230).[4]

While much of *Culture and Explosion* remains unexplored in this essay, I
would like to make one more observation that speaks to the richness of the analyses presented in Lotman's last work – his contributions to the study of Russian
culture and Russian culture texts. Lotman himself serves as a profound model
of his conceptualizations of semiospheric principles as universal mechanisms
of cultural spaces and individualized strategies for understanding culture texts.
Lotman gently inundates his entire work with wonderful examples and studies
taken from Russian cultural space. His references to masterpieces of Russian
literature and important critical contributions to the study of Russian literature,
history and culture are vibrant examples of the unprecedented depth and breadth
of his knowledge and profound critical understanding of Russian culture texts.
Ivanov notes that Lotman had no equals in his knowledge of Russian culture in
general, and specific subcultural phenomena. Ivanov mentions Lotman's knowledge of the specific rules of Russian duels and the special features of Russian
dueling weapons as one example of his "bottomless" knowledge (1998: 705).
*Culture and Explosion* is an invaluable source of information about Russian
culture and is an important link that synthesizes a large cross-section of Lotman's contribution to a theory of semiotics with individual representations of
cultural meanings. This synthesis includes important moments of intersection
with Lotman's unforgettable series of lectures entitled "Dialogues on Russian
Culture" (Беседы о русской культуре), which were first televised in 1986.

*Culture and Explosion* is a remarkable contribution to the study of cultures
and cultural spaces, semiospheres and the mechanisms of meaning-generation
that define these spaces. It is a brilliant conclusion to the body of invaluable
contributions made by Juri Mikhailovich Lotman, a scholar whose lifetime of
work is characterized not only by extraordinary and original research, but also
by unlimited generosity to his students and colleagues.

---

4. Beyond the obvious connection of *We* to Lotman's "I and I," Zamiatin opens the novel
   *We* with an interesting use of the verb выпрямлять: ". . . проинтегрировать гран-
   диозное вселенское уравнение . . . разогнуть дикую кривую, выпрямить ее
   по касательной – асимптоте – по прямой" (1988: 10). In personal conversation,
   Mikhail Lotman noted his father's admiration of Zamiatin, and confirmed that he
   knew Zamiatin's works well.

# References

Andrews, Edna
2003            *Conversations with Lotman: Cultural Semiotics in Language, Litera-
                ture, and Cognition*. Toronto: University of Toronto Press.
Ivanov, V. V.
1998            *Izbrannye trudy po semiotike i istorii kul'tury*, vol. I. Moscow: Shkola.
Jakobson, Roman
1987 [1960]     Linguistics and poetics. In Pomorska, Krystyna; Rudy, Stephen (eds.),
                *Language in Literature*. Cambridge: Belknap Press of Harvard Uni-
                versity Press, 62–94.
Lotman, Juri M.
1990            *Universe of the Mind: A Semiotic Theory of Culture*. [Trans. by
                A. Shukman, introduction by U. Eco.] Bloomington, IN: Indiana Uni-
                versity Press.
1992a           *Kul'tura i vzryv*. Moscow: Gnozis.
1992b           *Izbrannye statji v trex tomax*, vol. 1. Tallinn: Aleksandra.
2005            *Vospitanie duši*. St. Petersburg: Iskusstvo-SPB.
Zamiatin, Evgeny I.
1988            *My*. In *Sochinenija*. Moscow: Kniga.

# Foreword
# Lotmanian explosion

*Peeter Torop*

*Theses on the Semiotic Study of Cultures* (1973), the programmatic work of the Tartu-Moscow School, defines the semiotics of culture as a science investigating the functional correlation of different sign systems. This approach entails also the recognition of the hierarchy of sign systems:

> In defining culture as a certain secondary language, we introduce the concept of a 'culture text', a text in this secondary language. So long as some natural language is a part of the language of culture, there arises the question of the relationship between the text in the natural language and the verbal text of culture. (*Theses* 1973: 43)

We could add here another aspect related to the logic of possible worlds: "The place of the text in the textual space is defined as the sum total of potential texts" (*Theses* 1973: 45).

In 1992 Lotman wrote in the foreword of *Sign Systems Studies* vol. 25 (the last volume to appear during his lifetime) that:

> During the past decades semiotics has changed. One achievement on its hard path was unification with history. The cognition of history became semiotic, but semiotic thinking obtained historic traits. [...] Semiotic approach tries to avoid the conditional stopping of the historical process. (Lotman 1992: 3)

Lotman also concluded that "each generation has a language for describing yesterday and principally lacks a language for tomorrow" (Lotman 1992: 4).

Space and time became the terms through which Lotman put an individual text into contact with the general cultural processes of creation and reception in which any description process taking place in one part of culture became this culture's self-description on the level of culture as a whole. When description on one level can be regarded as self-description on another level, then it is possible to see an auto-communication process in communication processes. One aspect is culture's actual functioning and diversity in the reception processes. Another aspect encompasses the analyst's interest in the fate of a text as an artistic whole and in the comparison of the immanent peculiarity of a text with the text as a cultural text or the peculiarity of a text accepted by culture. Text reception and text creation are both autocommunicative processes. The auto-communicativeness of culture is not much different from the auto-communicativeness of an individual creator. In neither case do we know with certainty whether the case is about mnemonic auto-communication (i.e., about reporting on the already known in another form or other sign systems) or about discovering auto-communication (i.e., with the creation of novel correlations with what exists in memory).

When Lotman's approach to text became parametric, combining different possibilities of analysis, there emerged a need for a unity of a higher order that would join together the individual and the general, the part and the whole, description and self-description. The juxtaposition, in textual analysis, of a delimited whole and a communicating whole created the need to keep system and process apart, as exemplified in the approach of Hjelmslev. In 1978, Lotman wrote an article, "The phenomenon of culture", where he created a typology distinguishing between statics and dynamics. The basis for the typology is the distinction between the static and dynamic aspects of cultural languages. From the *static* perspective, cultural languages divide into the discrete and the continual (iconic-spatial), and for Lotman this forms the semiotic primordial dualism. In discrete languages signs come first and meanings are created through the meanings of signs. In continual languages text comes first and meaning emerges through a holistic text that integrates even the most heterogeneous elements. These are the two languages between which it is difficult to create translatability.

In *dynamism* the simultaneity of the two processes in culture is important. On the one hand, in different fields of culture, specialisation of cultural languages takes place as a result of autocommunication and identity searches. On the other hand, on the level of culture as a whole, the integration of cultural languages emerges as a possibility of self-communication and self-understanding. Yet the dynamism of integration is revealed in the simultaneity of the two processes: self-descriptions and alongside them, meta-descriptions or descriptions from the position of culture as a whole. These processes are being created in different parts of the culture, resulting in integration through autonomies. But cultural languages also diffuse and become creolised due to the communication between different parts of culture. Creolisation is a feature of dynamism and an intermediary stage at reaching a new autonomy, or pure (self)description (Lotman 1978: 9–11).

As a result of the descriptive processes, one can talk about cultural self-models. Cultural self-description as a process can be viewed as proceeding in three directions. Culture's self-model is the result of the first direction, whose goal is maximum similarity to the actually existing culture. Secondly, cultural self-models may emerge that differ from ordinary cultural practice and may even have been designed for changing that practice. Thirdly, there are self-models that exist as an ideal cultural self-consciousness, separately from culture and not oriented toward it. By this formulation Lotman does not exclude conflict between culture and its self-models. But the creation of self-models reflects the creativity of culture. In the 1980s Juri Lotman described creativity, relying on Ilya Prigogine. In the article "Culture as a subject and object for itself," Lotman maintains that:

> The main question of semiotics of culture is the problem of meaning generation. What we shall call meaning generation is the ability both of culture as a whole and of its parts to put out, in the 'output', nontrivial new texts. New texts are the texts that emerge as results of irreversible processes (in Ilya Prigogine's sense), i.e. texts that are unpredictable to a certain degree. (Lotman 2000: 640)

Lotman's perspective enables one to combine the treatment of text as culture and the treatment of culture as text, which at the same time means a possibility to consider these simultaneously as wholes at different levels of the same system. This hierarchy and the dynamics of the relations between part and whole form the basis for the semiospheric approach to culture. This again means that culture can be described as textual identities defined on different levels. For Lotman the significance of history means understanding the importance of seeing statics and dynamics together. From the complementarity of statics and dynamics a new understanding of unpredictability is born, which relates non-trivially not only with the innovative generation of texts but also with the semiotic structure of the cultural environment.

Disciplinary logic demands that culture be declared the research object of the semiotics of culture. But only a few years ago, in the epilogue to his study "The outlines of the prehistory and history of semiotics", Vyacheslav Vs. Ivanov, one of the founders of the semiotics of culture and of the Tartu-Moscow School of Semiotics, wrote:

> The task of semiotics is to describe the semiosphere without which the noosphere is inconceivable. Semiotics has to help us in orienting in history. The joint effort of all those who have been active in this science or the whole cycle of sciences must contribute to the ultimate future establishment of semiotics. (Ivanov 1998: 792)

Ivanov's statement clearly relies already on interdisciplinary logic as the term "semiosphere" is here placed between biosphere and noosphere. It follows from this logic that the description of the semiosphere by semiotics helps us to orient in history. But "history" is a complicated concept, according to the scholars of the Tartu-Moscow School.

In the context of semiosphere, the interest of Juri Lotman as a literary and cultural historian in unmaterialized possibilities of historical choices is important. He had an extraordinary interest in imagining the consequences to which a different choice of development strategies could have led, during pivotal moments, in the situation of cultural explosion. He speaks about this here in his last book *Culture and Explosion* published in 1992. At the request of Spanish colleagues, I had a discussion with Juri Lotman in the same year as this book was published. I will quote a passage from Lotman's part in this talk:

> A chance, an accident is not really so accidental, I would say. A chance is so diffused, leaves such a wide range of choices that many things can find their place in there. But chance is not predictable. I think that if, among new ideas, there is something that we have now in reality, one of them – and I think the most important of them – is the idea of historical, scientific, and of yet some other kind of unpredictability. Unpredictability as the object of science. By the way, unpredictability [...] whose mechanism is one of the most important objects of science, introduces into science in a totally new manner the component of art. [...] Art has always been oriented towards unpredictability. To my mind, at the moment something most interesting is happening: it is as if science is becoming aestheticized. [...] Art is a totally different way of thinking, a different system of modelling the world. Essentially it is the creation of a different world, a parallel world to our world. It is thought that we can live in a world that is based on the model of science, or that we can live in a world that is based on the model of art. In fact, however, we live in a world that is based on the conflictual unity of these two models. From here follow also the different levels of predictability and different meanings of unpredictability. (cf.: Torop 2000: 13–14)

The logic of this argument is close to our contemporary transdisciplinary thinking. But at the end of discussion Lotman presented a rhetorical question:

> What in fact is this enormous amount of people who now live on this planet and will maybe live here also in the future? Is it a conglomeration of individuals who live only in order to take over from each other territory and the right to live? Or is this conglomeration of individuals one method of description and each individual by himself or herself another method of description? Thus no method of description rules out another method of description. It is as if in their reciprocal tension they create a third viewpoint. (Torop 2000: 14–15)

The formulation of this third viewpoint would in fact mean that semiotics is given the status of metadiscipline.

Since the year 1984 when Lotman's article "On semiosphere" was published, this concept has been moving from one terminological field to another. In the disciplinary terminological field of the Tartu-Moscow School semiotics of culture, "semiosphere" is connected with the terms "language – secondary modelling system – text – culture". From interdisciplinary terminological fields, the association, on the one hand, with biosphere and noosphere, and on the other hand, with logosphere, is perhaps more important. As a metadisciplinary concept, semiosphere belongs to the methodology of culture studies and is associated with the concepts of holism and the part and the whole. And as a transdisciplinary concept, "semiosphere" is very close to the concept of symbol in symbolism: symbol as an indefinable term is suitable for conveying the cognition of the incognizable, and at the same time symbol can have an enormous semantic volume as a reduced myth. In this context, semiosphere marks the complementarity of disciplines studying culture, the movement towards the creation of general culture studies and "understanding methodology".

For example, when we observe the scholarly reception of the concept of semiosphere, we can notice the emergence of some dominants. The first dominant is related to semiosphere as a universal research level. For instance, Irene Portis-Winner in her recent book remarks that Lotman's concept of semiosphere creates a perspective of holistic analysis: "Lotman's concept of the semiosphere subsumes all aspects of the semiotics of culture, all the heterogeneous semiotic systems or 'languages' that are constantly changing and that in an abstract sense, have some unifying qualities" (Portis-Winner 2002: 63; cf. also Portis-Winner 1999). Edna Andrews, again, argues that the concept of semiosphere is helpful in better understanding of semiosis: "Lotman's extensive work on the semiosphere and the semiotics of communication provide some invaluable concepts and categories that offer insights into the structural principles of semiosis" (Andrews 1999: 8; see, also, Andrews' introduction to this volume, above).

The next dominant is dynamism. Bogusław Żyłko stresses, from the perspective of Lotman's evolution, that the concept of semiosphere signifies transfer from static to dynamic analysis, and the basis of this transfer is understanding the relationship between holism and heterogeneity: "The shift, from the conception of culture as a bundle of primary and secondary modelling systems to the notion of semiosphere, is also a shift from static to dynamic thinking. If we took the former approach, culture would resemble a motionless unit made up of semiotic systems; whereas if we follow the semiospheric approach, culture takes the shape of a heterogeneous whole bustling with multiple rhythms of development and transient dominants" (Żyłko 2001: 400). Dynamism is stressed also by Floyd Merrell in his comparison of Peirce and Lotman and his treatment of biosemiosphere: "Cultures are processes, never products ..." (Merrell 2001: 400).

I brought out these two dominants in the reception of semiosphere in order to emphasize one of Lotman's methodological principles, on which also his own treatment of semiosphere is based. This is the principle of dialogism. Usually the term "dialogue" is associated with the name of Mihhail Bakhtin, and Lotman's treatment certainly has its connections to Bakhtin's approach. The treatise published under the name of Valentin Vološinov, *Marxism and the Philosophy of Language*, suggests that

> any element of an utterance that forwards a thought and is being foregrounded, or even a full utterance is translated by us into corresponding context that is different and active. Any understanding is dialogic. Understanding is contrasted to utterance as a speaker's words are contrasted to those of another speaker in a dialogue. Understanding is looking for a counterword to the word of a speaker. Only understanding of a foreign word seeks for 'a similar' word in the native language. (Bakhtin 2000: 436)

Several scholarly works have been dedicated to the comparison of Bakhtin's and Lotman's dialogisms (Shukman, Lachmann, Danow, Bonafin), but the simultaneity of the dual understanding has not been stressed much. In essence, this is a situation in which understanding is a process that on the one hand creates differences (word and the counterword), and, on the other hand, similarities (word and its translation). And if the dialogism of understanding is borne in mind, we can in principle talk about two types of dialogue (cf. Torop 2002: 599–602).

Furthermore, in Lotman's opinion, in order to understand dialogue, it is not enough to understand the language that is used in the dialogue. In his article "On semiosphere" he wrote:

> Consciousness is impossible without communication. In this sense it can be said that dialogue precedes language and generates the language. The idea of semiosphere is based exactly on this: the ensemble of semiotic formations precedes (not heuristically, but functionally) a single isolated language and is a precondition for its existence. Without semiosphere a language not only does not work, but does not even exist. (Lotman 1984: 16)

In the next stage of discussion on semiosphere, in his book *Universe of the Mind* published in 1990, Lotman emphasized that the dialogic situation has to be understood before dialogue: ". . . the need for dialogue, the dialogic situation, precedes both real dialogue and even the existence of a language in which to conduct it: the semiotic situation precedes the instruments of semiosis" (Lotman 1990: 143–144). Thus dialogue becomes not only a term closely related to semiosphere, but it becomes one of its ontological characteristics. The concept of a dialogical model of culture appeared in Lotman's works in 1983 and the discussion on semiosphere develops this model first of all on the level of dynamics between the part and the whole:

> Since all the levels of the semiosphere – ranging from a human individual or an individual text to global semiotic unities – are all like semiospheres inserted into

each other, then each and one of them is both a participant in the dialogue (a part of the semiosphere) as well as the space of the dialogue (an entire semiosphere). (Lotman 1984: 22)

The understanding of dialogue as an ontological characteristic of semiosphere in turn means that the outer and inner borders of semiosphere are seen as bilingual. Borders separate and thus create identities, but borders also connect and construe these identities by juxtaposing the familiar and the alien. Therefore for Lotman the most important feature of the borders of semiosphere is their role as translation mechanisms. But, also, human consciousness is related to the same mechanisms since in determining one's identity, a person needs first to describe it to himself or herself. Translation mechanisms form the basis also for this thinking activity. And thus Lotman reaches the conclusion "that the elementary act of thinking is translation" and "the elementary mechanism of translation is dialogue" (Lotman 1990: 143).

Speaking about semiosphere in the context of contemporary trends in science it has to be remembered that semiosphere is simultaneously an object- and a meta-concept. Semiosphere is what is being studied in or as culture, and semiosphere is the means that is used in studying culture. A phrase *semiosphere is studied by means of semiosphere* is not a paradox but points at the dialogue between the research object and its description language. The dynamism of culture as a research object forces science to search for new description languages but the new description languages in turn influence the cultural dynamics as they offer new possibilities for self-description. Often, however, from a historical perspective, a new description language is nothing but a methodological translation. Thus, also, the term semiosphere joins together several concepts that are related to semiotics of culture and that have gained new relevance in light of culture's developmental dynamics.

The first who deserves rereading is one of the leading figures of Russian Formalism Juri Tynyanov. In his article "Literary fact" of 1924 he wrote: "Literary fact is heterogeneous, and in this sense literature is an incessantly evolutioning order" (Tynyanov 1977: 270). The question of literary order or system is for Tynyanov inseparable from the question of function:

A literary system is first of all a *system of the functions of the literary order which are in continual interrelationship with other orders*. Systems change in their composition, but the differentiation of human activities remains. The evolution of literature, as of any other cultural system, does not coincide either in tempo or in character with the systems with which it is interrelated. This is owing to the specificity of the material with which it is concerned. The evolution of the structural function occurs rapidly; the evolution of the literary function occurs over epochs; and the evolution of the functions of a whole literary system in relation to neighbouring systems occurs over centuries. (Tynyanov 1977: 277)

In Tynyanov's system, we can observe the relatedness of the literary order to other orders – with the order of everyday life, the order of culture, social order. Everyday life is correlated with literary order in its verbal aspect, and thus, literature has a *verbal function* in relation to everyday life. An author's attitude towards the elements of his text expresses *structural function*, and the same text as a literary work has a *literary function* in its relations to the literary order. The reciprocal influence of literature on everyday life, again, expresses *social function*. The study of literary evolution presupposes the investigation of connections first of all between the closest neighbouring orders or systems, and the logical path leads from the structural to the literary function, from the literary to the verbal function. This follows from the position that "evolution is the change in interrelationships between the elements of a system – between functions and formal elements" (Tynyanov 1977: 281; cf. Torop 1995–96; 2003: 328–330).

The next author belonging to the history of semiosphere is Roman Jakobson who in his article "Metalanguage as a linguistic problem" published in 1956 wrote: "Language must be investigated in all the variety of its functions" (Jakobson 1985: 113). With regard to the six factors of his communication model and their functions he wrote: "The diversity lies not in a monopoly of some one of these several functions but in their different hierarchical order" (Jakobson 1985: 113). With regard to the rapid development of the culture's technological environment, I suggest that the hierarchical principle is the basis for Jakobson's approach both to translation as well as the perception processes. His interlinguistic, intralinguistic and intersemiotic types of translation can be regarded individually but also as an inner dynamic hierarchy of a single translation process and, partly, of any communication process. The situation is the same when he stresses the semiotic value of the five senses: "All five external senses carry semiotic functions in human society" (Jakobson 1971: 701). Foreseeing the increase in the varieties of textual ontologies and problems of understanding, Jakobson stresses the importance of distinguishing between homogeneous messages, i.e. those based on a single sign system, and syncretic messages, i.e. those based on the combination of several sign systems: "The study of communication must distinguish between homogeneous messages which use a single semiotic system and syncretic messages based on a combination or merger of different sign patterns" (Jakobson 1971: 705).

Another semiospheric scholar is Mikhail Bakhtin, of whose works I would like to mention in the present context the theory of chronotope even though this work was left unfinished. Nevertheless, it is still possible to reconstruct

Bakhtin's general understanding of a literary work as a chronotopical hierarchy (Bakhtin 1979: 338). On the horizontal plane this refers to the levels of to-pographic chronotope or homophony, psychological chronotope or polyphony, and metaphysical chronotope or heterophony. But on all these levels we can also speak of the binarity of the familiar and the alien (cf. Torop 1997), which is the basis for the so-called small chronotopes, such as road, bridge, stairs, and so forth. In Bakhtin's view, without understanding chronotopicality, it is impossible to understand artistic worlds (Bakhtin 1975: 406).

Thus there are three research strategies in front of us, which prepare the ground for the emergence of the concept of semiosphere: Tynyanov and the hierarchical treatment of the evolutionary process, Jakobson and the hierarchical treatment of communication process, and Bakhtin and the treatment of text as a chronotopical hierarchy.

Until then, when speaking of text, Lotman had emphasized the importance of the beginning and the end, or the frame. Therefore for him, text was a de-limited whole and the possibility of delimiting, either natural or artificial, made it possible to speak about levels of material, the coherence and hierarchy of levels. When the material was not natural language but film language, he tried to describe the system of distinctive features and to analyse the text on the basis of markedness-unmarkedness. A fundamental turn took place in 1981. In his ar-ticle "Cultural Semiotics and the Notion of Text" Lotman replaces the notion of deciphering or decoding the text with the term of 'communication' and creates, by describing the circulation of texts in culture and relations between the text and the reader, a typology of different, although complementary, processes:

1. communication of the addresser and the addressee,
2. communication between the audience and cultural tradition,
3. communication of the reader with him/herself,
4. communication of the reader with the text,
5. communication between the text and cultural tradition.

(Lotman 2002: 88)

The usage of the term communication in textual analysis meant, in fact, a semio-spherical turn already before the concept was born. The same way as it is possible to understand texts in various ways, it is also possible to analyse this understand-ing in several ways.

Semiosphere is a concept that allows semiotics of culture to reach a new un-derstanding of holism, a holistic analysis of dynamic processes. In semiotics of culture, the term semiosphere converges all that which recently in the sciences studying culture converges into semiotics – a wish for finding a description lan-guage that could be translated into and that could unify different disciplinary and interdisciplinary languages. In elaborating the general principles of cultural analysis in the interests of understanding comprehensive methodology, science needs to search for possibilities to interpret as many diverse and nontrivial cultural phenomena and texts as possible and to promote cultural self-descriptions. At the same time, from the historical perspective, the metalinguistic and conceptual heterogeneity of our contemporary science is much more homogeneous.

Therefore, in conclusion it has to be said that the concept of semiosphere brings semiotics of culture again into contact with its history, as it also brings applicable cultural analysis into contact with the history of culture and with the newest phenomena in culture. The science of signs comes into contact with the art of signs. These contacts determine the place of the semiotics of culture among the sciences studying culture. And it is not paradoxical that semiosphere studies semiosphere and culture studies culture. This is so because all this takes place within one single semiosphere of human culture and each attempt to describe culture from any scientific position proves, on a different level, to be a self-description of culture. By creating treatments of culture, we also can be part of culture's creativity.

The concept of explosion is closely related to that of semiosphere. In the concept of explosion, critics too have perceived the desire to synthesise cultural processes, but unlike with semiosphere, the end of a politically turbulent era and the appearance of a new, politically oriented discourse may be detected in the concept of explosion (Deltcheva 1996: 148). Such a politics is, of course, mostly historiosophical, as Lotman calls Russia to follow the Western models of development, that is, to move from a binary model of evolution to a ternary one. Social explosions do not have to inevitably destroy everything, as happened during the revolution of 1917, but should rather preserve that particular layer of culture that guarantees consistency. The historic-philosophical aspect of explosion and the dream of the democratization of Russia is nevertheless but one aspect of Lotman's treatment of explosion.

Lotman's *Culture and Explosion* has also received general theoretical attention, such as from Andrews, who has emphasized the need to make Lotman's views topical for contemporary theoretical discussions (Andrews 1999, cf. Andrews 2000). Explosion is but one part of the communicative processes in culture and associated not merely with social disasters, but also with all kinds of innovation. Everything novel in society and culture has an explosive impact. And the fact that Lotman distinguishes between the moment of explosion and the moment following it raises the complementarity between communication and autocommunication to an entirely new level. Because if there were nothing but moments of explosion, culture would be nothing but a dissipative chaos; innovation would remain unnoticed, lessons from the explosion unlearned. The moment of explosion as the moment of the unpredictable, the moment of open possibilities and of the weight of decision making presumes a temporal relationship with the explosion. Those caught inside the processes are unable to escape from the space of the explosion, and as insiders are unable to notice all of the possible choices, all possibilities for the future. With the passage of time, these choices will have been made, or then again left unmade through the suppression of the explosion, after which the post-explosive moment, that is the moment for describing the explosion, will be actualized. The chaos and diversity of communicative processes will become ordered in autocommunicative self-description.

Lotman emphasizes the ethical position of cultural semioticians, together with every other social scientist and humanities researcher. In order to assure the continuity of development, every culture requires constant feedback, an endless engagement with itself. Communicative processes are, on a higher level, parts of autocommunicative processes, and it is vitally important to take notice of this autocommunication. It is here that the diagnostic power of cultural analysis lies, and with it we can increase the coherence between different parts of culture and different levels and groups of culture-bearers. On the other hand, Lotman transfers the logic of explosion to a new field of cultural analysis. With his *Culture and Explosion*, he invites people to study unrealized paths of development, unborn texts and cultural phenomena. To study what might have happened, but nevertheless failed to, amounts to the identification of what did happen, or of paths of development that were in fact realized. Thus, with this book, Lotman has entered a new field of complex cultural analysis, in which the actual and the possible are equally relevant and where the analysis of the unrealized and thus the nonexistent opens up new possibilities for the analysis of the realized and the existent.

*Culture and Explosion* is thus not just the last book of a scientist, but its author's glimpse of the future, which might have been his present. And in this present, although he has physically left us, Lotman continues his intellectual dialogue and keeps worrying that the part of culture which has perhaps the greatest responsibility for safeguarding continuity, capacity for development, and intellectual welfare, that is, science – would better be able to describe and thereby value the development of culture and society. *Culture and Explosion* is a book that turned out to be an explosion itself, and it is pleasing that it finally reaches English-speaking readers and renders this post-explosive moment as fruitful and diverse as possible. Simultaneously, however, this book is a phenomenon deriving from after the explosion, as it summarizes the explosion called 'the works of Lotman', and will provide the avid reader with both an understanding of his movement towards this book as well as of the direction in which Lotman did not have the time to move. And it is here that we, the readers, await. To enjoy the moment that casts light to the past and shines towards the future.

# References

Andrews, Edna
    1999            Lotman's communication act and semiosis. *Semiotica* 126(1/4), 1–15.
    2000            The Tartu school at the end of the twentieth century. *Semiotica* 131 (3/4), 267–271.

Bakhtin, Mikhail
    1975            Бахтин, Михаил. *Вопросы литературы и эстетики.* Москва: Художественная литература.
    1979            Бахтин, Михаил. *Эстетика словесного творчества.* Москва: Искусство.
    2000            Бахтин, Михаил М. *Фрейдизм. Формальный метод в литературоведении. Марксизм и философия языка.* Статьи. Москва: Лабиринт.

Bonafin, Massimo
    1997            Typology of culture and carnival: Note on the models of Bachtin and Lotman. *Russian Literature* XLI(III), 255–268.

Danow, David K.
    1991            *The Thought of Mikhail Bakhtin. From Word to Culture.* Houndmills/London: MacMillan.

Deltcheva, Vlasov
    1996            Deltcheva, Roumiana, Vlasov, Eduard, "Lotman's *Culture and Explosion*: a shift in the paradigm of the semiotics of culture". *Slavic and East European Journal* 40(1), 148–152.

Ivanov, V. V.
    1998            Izbrannye trudy po semiotike i istorii kul'tury. T. I. Moskva: Jazyki russkoj kul'tury.

Jakobson, Roman
    1971            Language in relation to other communication systems. *Roman Jakobson. Selected Writings*, vol. II. The Hague/Paris: Mouton, 697–708.
    1985            Metalanguage as a linguistic problem. *Roman Jakobson. Selected Writings*, vol. VII. The Hague/Paris: Mouton, 113–121.

Lachmann, Renate
    198             Value aspects in Jurij Lotman's Semiotics of Culture/Semiotics of Text. *Dispositio* 12(30–32), 13–33.

Lotman, Y. M.
    1984            Лотман, Юрий М. О семиосфере. *Труды по знаковым системам* 17, 5–23.
    1990            *Universe of the Mind: A Semiotic Theory of Culture.* London/New York: I. B. Tauris.

1992    Лотман, Юрий М. От редколлегии. *Труды по знаковым системам* 25, 3–4. Ot redkollegii (Editorial note). *Sign Systems Studies* 25, 3–4. (in russian).

2000    Лотман, Юрий. *О семиосфере. Культура и взрыв. Внутри мыслящих миров. Статьи. Исследования. Заметки.* Санкт-Петербург: Искусство-СПБ.

2002    Лотман, Юрий. *Статьи по семиотике культуры и искусства.* Санкт-Петербург: Академический проект.

Merrell, Floyd
2001    Lotman's semiosphere, Peirce's categories, and cultural forms of life. *Sign Systems Studies* 29(2), 385–415.

Portis-Winner, Irene
1999    The dynamics of semiotics of culture; its pertinence to anthropology. *Sign Systems Studies* 27, 24–45.

2002    *Semiotics of Peasants in Transition. Slovene Villagers and Their Ethnic Relatives in America.* Durham/London: Duke University Press.

Shukman, Ann
1989    Semiotics of Culture and the influence of M. M. Bakhtin. In *Issues in Slavic Literary and Cultural Theory.* K. Eimermacher, P. Grzybek, G. Witte (eds.). Bochum: Universitätsverlag Dr. Norbert Brockmeyer, 193–207.

Theses
1973    *Theses on the Semiotic Study of Cultures.* Tartu Semiotics Library 1. Tartu: Tartu University Press, 1998.

Torop, Peeter
1995–96    Тороп, Пеэтер. Статус Тынянова. In *Седьмые тыняновские чтения. Материалы для обсуждения.* Рига, Москва, 49–58.

1997    Тороп, Пеэтер. *Достоевский: история и идеология.* Tartu: Tartu University Press.

2000    New Tartu Semiotics. *S-European Journal for Semiotic Studies* 2(1), 5–22.

2002    Translation as translating as culture. *Sign Systems Studies* 30(2), 593–605.

2003    Semiospherical understanding: Textuality. *Sign Systems Studies* 31(2), 323–329.

Tynyanov, Juri
1977    Тынянов, Юрий. *Поэтика. История литературы. Кино.* Москва: Наука.

Ýyùko, Bogusùaw
2001    Culture and semiotics: Notes on Lotman's conception of culture. *New Literary History* 32(2), 391–408.

# Chapter 1
# Statement of the problem

*To the unforgettable memory*
*of Zara Grigorievna Mints*

The fundamental questions relating to the description of any semiotic system are, firstly, its relation to the extra-system, to the world which lies beyond its borders and, secondly, its static and dynamic relations. The latter question could be formulated thus: how can a system develop and yet remain true to itself? Well, both these questions are of the most radical and the most complex type.

The relationship of the system to external reality and their mutual impenetrability has, since Kant, been examined many times. From the semiotic point of view, they represent the antinomy between language and the world beyond the borders of language. That space, lying outside of language, enters the sphere of language and is transformed into "content" only as a constituent element of the dichotomy content/expression. To speak of unexpressed content is non-sensical.[1] Thus, we must not speak of the relationship between content and expression, but rather of the opposition of the sphere of language and its content and expression to the world external to it. In fact, this question is linked to the second problem: the nature of the dynamics of language.

The plane of content, as conceived by F. de Saussure, is a conventional reality. Language creates its own world. At the same time, the question arises as to the level of adaptability of a world created by language towards a world existing outside of language, i.e. beyond its borders. This is the age-old Kantian problem of the noumenal world. In Kantian terminology, the plane of content

> "... it is that self-consciousness which, because it produces the representation *I think,* which must be able to accompany all others, and which in all consciousness is one and the same, cannot be accompanied by any further representation. I also call its *unity* the *transcendental* unity of self-consciousness, in order to designate the possibility of a priori cognition which can be obtained from it. For the manifold representations that are given in a certain intuition would not all together be my representations, if they did not all together belong to a self-consciousness, i.e., as my representations (even if I am not conscious of them as such), they must yet

---

1. The statement does not exclude the possibility that expression may be realised by a *semiotic null (empty signifier), presented* as an absence: "... And only silence speaks clearly ..." (Zhukovsky, V. A. *Sobranie sochinenii v 4 t.* Moscow/Leningrad, 1959, vol. 1, p. 337).

necessarily accord with the condition under which alone they can stand together in a universal self-consciousness, because otherwise they would not throughout belong to me ... "[2]

In this way, initially, the existence of two levels of objectivity may be surmised: one relates to the world of languages (this is objective from its point of view) and one relates to the world outside the borders of language.[3] One of the key problems is that of the translation of the world of the content of the system (its internal reality) to the reality that lies outside, beyond the borders of language. Out of this, two specific issues arise:

1. The necessity that more than one language (a minimum of two) is required in order to reflect a given reality
2. The inevitable fact that the space of reality cannot be represented by a single language but only by an aggregate of languages.

The idea of the possibility for a single ideal language to serve as an optimal mechanism for the representation of reality is an illusion. A minimally functional structure requires the presence of at least two languages and their incapacity, each independently of the other, to embrace the world external to each of them. This incapacity is not a deficiency, but rather a condition of existence, as it dictates the necessity of *the other* (another person, another language, another culture). The idea of an optimal model, consisting of a single perfect universal language, is replaced by the image of a structure equipped with a minimum of two or, rather, by an open number of diverse languages, each of which is reciprocally dependent on the other, due to the incapacity of each to express the world independently. These languages superimpose themselves on each other in such a way as to reflect one and the same thing in diverse ways, so that they appear to be situated on a "single plane" and form its internal borders. Their mutual untranslatability (or limited translatability) represents a source of adjustment of the extra-lingual object to its reflection in the world of languages. The situation of a multiplicity of languages is original and primary, but later aspiration towards a single universal language (towards a single, final truth)

2. Kant, I. *Critique of Pure Reason*. (Trans. Paul Guyer and Allen W. Wood). Cambridge: Cambridge University Press, 1998 (Translator's note: This quotation is taken from the standard English translation and it should be noted that, whilst Lotman emphasises and makes specific reference to 'primary apperception' this is omitted in the standard text, the designation having appeared earlier in the original translation, in the section as... "I call this *pure apperception*, in order to distinguish it from the empirical one, or also the *original apperception,* since it is self-consciousness ... ")
3. We are deliberately introducing a particular transformation in the ideas of Kant, identifying his "I" with the subject of language.

stems from this. This aspiration becomes the kind of secondary reality created by culture.

The relationship between multiplicity and unity is a fundamental characteristic of culture. It is here that logical and historical reality diverges: logical reality constructs a conventional model of an abstraction, introducing a unique situation, which must reproduce an ideal unit.

Thus, in order to understand the essence of humanity, Enlightenment philosophy created the model of Man. Real development, however, came by other means. We may take as a conventional starting-point gregarious behaviour and/or that kind of genetically inherited behaviour which was considered as neither individual nor collective, insofar as this opposition was not known. Anything that did not fall within these habitual types of behaviour was semiotically non-existent. The only opposition to this category of "normal" behaviour, itself devoid of characteristics, was that exhibited by the sick or the wounded, those who were perceived as "non-existent". Thus, for example, Tolstoy, in *War and Peace,* revealed, in a very deep way, the essence of this ancient gregarious psychology when describing how Platon Karataev died during the retreat of Russian prisoners alongside the defeated French army. Pierre Bezukhov, who is making this hard march with him, stops noticing his friend. Even in that very moment when a French soldier kills Platon Karataev, Pierre sees it and does not see it: physical and psychological vision are divided.

Subsequently, atypical behaviour is introduced into consciousness as a possible destructor of norms: abnormality, crime, heroism. At this stage, a division between individual (abnormal) and collective ("normal") behaviour occurs. It is only in the subsequent stage that the possibility of individual behaviour becoming an example and norm for collective behaviour, and for collective behaviour to act as an evaluative parameter for the individual, occurs: in this way, a unique system arises, in which these two possibilities are rendered as indivisible aspects of a unitary whole.

Thus, individual and collective behaviour arise simultaneously as mutually interdependent contrasting alternatives. A state of ignorance and, consequently, of their "social non-existence" precedes their manifestation. The first stage of the fall from this state of ignorance relates to the sick, the wounded, the abnormal, or to periodic physiological disturbances. Through such processes, individuality is first revealed, and is lost again, in the absence of individuality. Pre-determined and stable differences of behaviour (gender, age) are transformed from the physiological to the psychological only with the introduction of personality, that is, when there is freedom to choose. In this way, psychology and culture are gradually conquering the space of unconscious physiology.

# Chapter 2
# A monolingual system

The long-established communication model, of the type:

addresser                                                                                          addressee

text

LANGUAGE

perfected by R. O. Jakobson, has become the basis for all models of communication. According to this schema, the aim of communication (as is suggested by the very word *communitas* – community, communication) is adequate intercourse. Interference caused by inevitable technical imperfections is regarded as a hindrance. In an ideal model, as in the theoretical domain, it appears that these may be disregarded.

Such arguments are based on an abstraction, which implies that the addresser and addressee are fully identical, being translated into lingual reality. However, the abstract model of communication not only implies the use of one and the same code, but also the identical memory capacity of both addresser and addressee. In fact, the substitution of the term "language" by the term "code" is not as harmless as it seems. The term "code" carries with it the idea of an artificial, newly created structure, introduced by instantaneous agreement. A code does not imply history, that is, psychologically it orients us towards artificial language, which is also, in general, assumed to be an ideal model of language. "Language", albeit unconsciously, awakes in us an image of the historical reach of existence. Language – is a code plus its history. Such an understanding of communication includes within itself some fundamental principles.

The transfer of information within a "structure without memory" actively guarantees a high level of identity. If we assume an addresser and an addressee possessing identical codes and fully devoid of memory, then the understanding between them will be ideal, but the value of the transferred information will be minimal and the information itself – severely limited. Such a system cannot fulfil all the multivariate functions that are historically attributed to language. You could say that, ideally, an identical addresser and addressee would understand each other very well, but they would not be able to talk about anything. The ideal of information of this type is found in the transfer of commands. The model of ideal understanding does not even apply to man's internal communication with himself since the latter situation implies the transfer of an intense dialogue within a single personality. In the words of Goethe's Faust:

*Zwei Seelen wohnen, ach, in meinen Brust!*
*Die eine will sich von der andern trennen.*[1]

In normal human communication and, most of all, in the normal functioning of language, a pre-supposition is made as to the initial non-identity of speaker and hearer.

In these circumstances, an area of intersection in the lingual space between speaker and hearer is normally established:

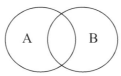

In a situation where there is no intersection, communication appears to be impossible, whilst a full intersection (where A and B are deemed identical) renders communication insipid. Thus, whilst a specific intersection between these spaces is admitted, at the same time an intersection between two contradictory tendencies appears: the struggle to facilitate understanding, which will always attempt to extend the area of the intersection, and the struggle to amplify the value of the communication, which is linked to the tendency of maximally amplifying the difference between A and B. Thus, in normal lingual communication it is necessary to introduce the concept of tension, some form of resistance, which the spaces A and B use to oppose one another.

The space of intersection between A and B becomes the natural basis of communication. Meanwhile, or so it seems, the non-intersecting parts of these spaces are excluded from the dialogue. However, here we find ourselves faced by yet another contradiction: the exchange of information within the intersecting parts of the semantic space suffers from the self-same flaw of triviality. It appears that the value of dialogue is linked not to the intersecting part, but to the transfer of information between non-intersecting parts. This places us face-to-face with an insoluble contradiction: we are interested in communication in the very sphere which complicates communication and, in actual fact, renders it impossible. Moreover, the more difficult and inadequate the translation of one non-intersecting part of the space into the language of the other, the more valuable, in informative and social terms, the fact of this paradoxical communication

1. Two souls, alas! reside within my breast,
   And each withdraws from, and repels, its brother.
   (Goethe, J. W. *Faust*. [trans. A. V. Beresford], Cassel 1862. p. 55)

becomes. You could say that the translation of the untranslatable may in turn become the carrier of information of the highest value.

Let us consider some examples: on the one hand, the translation of two closely related languages and, on the other – one where the two are, in principle, different. The translation, in the first instance will be relatively easy. In the second instance, it will inevitably meet with difficulties and will result in a vagueness of meaning. Thus, for example, if we take as the first case – the translation of a non-literary text from one natural language to another, then a reverse translation will, to a certain extent, bring us to the root meaning. If, however, we consider the case of a translation from the language of poetry to that of music, then the achievement of a singularly exact meaning is, in principle, impossible. This is also reflected in the enormous number of potential variants that occur in cases of reverse translation.[2]

Lingual communication reveals itself to us as the tense intersection between adequate and inadequate lingual acts. Most of all, non-comprehension (conversation in languages which are not fully identical) reveals itself to be just as valuable a meaning-making mechanism as comprehension. The exclusive victory of either of these poles lies in the destruction of information created in the area of mutual tension. Different forms of contact – where normal lingual communication is situated in one of the poles and artistic language in the other – represent displacements from a neutral central point both towards the facilitation of understanding and towards its opposite. But the absolute victory of any of these poles is theoretically impossible and, in practical terms, fatal. A situation in which the minimal meaning-generating unit is not one language, but two, creates a whole chain of consequences. First of all, even the nature of the intellectual act could be described in terms of being a translation, a definition of meaning as a translation from one language to another, whereas extra-lingual reality may be regarded as yet another type of language. It is endowed with a structural organisation and the potential to function as the content of a heterogeneous set of expressions.

---

2. The case of translation from the language of artistic prose to the language of cinematography is one of the most complex realisations of the second type, for the commonality between the language of literature and that of the cinema is illusory. The difficulties here are not reduced; on the contrary they are augmented. Ignorance of this is the source of many unsuccessful screen-adaptations.

# Chapter 3
# Gradual progress

Forward movement arises in two ways. Our sense organs react to minor stimuli, which, at the conscious level, are perceived as continuous movement. In this sense, continuity represents a perceived predictability, the antithesis of which is unpredictability, a change occurring in the form of explosion. Against this background, predictable development is regarded as a significantly less important form of movement.

The unpredictability of explosive processes by no means represents the only path to novelty. On the contrary, whole spheres of culture may achieve movement only in the form of gradual processes. Gradual and explosive processes, although antithetical, exist only in terms of their mutual reciprocity. The destruction of one pole would cause the disappearance of the other.

All explosive dynamic processes occur via a dynamically complex dialogue with stabilising mechanisms. We must not be deceived by the fact that in historical reality they appear to be enemies striving for the full destruction of the other pole. Any such destruction would be fatal to culture but, luckily, it is not feasible. Even when people are strongly convinced that they are putting into practice some kind of ideal theory the practical sphere also includes within itself opposing tendencies: they may adopt abnormal forms but they cannot be destroyed.

Gradual processes represent a powerful force of progress. In this sense, the correlation between scientific discoveries and their technical realisation is interesting. The greatest scientific ideas have, in a certain sense, an affinity with art: insofar as their origins are like an explosion. However, the technical realisation of new ideas develops according to the laws of gradual dynamics. Therefore, scientific ideas may be ill-timed.

Technology, of course, also knows occasions where its possibilities have remained unnoticed (for example, the use of powder in ancient China only for fireworks). However, on the whole, it is in the nature of technology that practical necessities act as powerful stimuli in its progress. Therefore realisation of technological novelty is predictable, whereas the occurrence of novelty in science and art is unpredictable. Out of this also arises the peculiar situation that in the conventional phrase "science and technology" the conjunction *and* in no way signifies an ideal harmony. Rather, it rests on the edge of a deep conflict.

In this sense, the position of the historians of "L'école de la longue durée"[1] is very significant. Thanks to their efforts, slow and gradual processes were introduced into history as being equivalent to its already established parts. The development of technology, of material goods, of commerce pushed into the background not only the trials of political struggle but also the phenomena of art. Also of interest is the innovative work of Jean Delumeau in *La civilisation de la Renaissance*[2] in which he gives a carefully considered analysis of those spheres of historical reality organised by gradual dynamic processes. The author examines geographical discoveries, the role of technological progress, of commerce, changes in the forms of production and the development of finance. Technological inventions and even historical discoveries are described in this monumental picture of general movement as drawn by the hand of Delumeau, which movement appears before us like the flow of a wide and powerful river. The individual with his discoveries and inventions finds his existence only insofar as he gives himself up to the strength of this flowing river.

A minefield with unexpected explosive points and a river in spring with its powerful but directed stream – these are the two images visualised by the historian studying dynamic (explosive) and gradual processes. The mutual dependency of these two structural tendencies does not change and on the contrary sharply emphasises their mutual stipulation. Neither can exist without the other. However, from the viewpoint of each, the other represents an obstacle which must be overcome or an enemy which should be destroyed.

Thus, from the point of view of the "explosive" position, the opposing position takes the form of an incarnation of a whole range of negative qualities. A limited example might be the treatment of the gradualists (*postepenovcy*, a term used by I. S. Turgenev) by nihilists or liberals, by revolutionaries. But this very same opposition may be translated in the language of the romantic antithesis of "the genius and crowd". Bulwer-Lytton renders a dialogue between an authentic dandy and a vulgar imitator of dandyism – a dialogue between a fashion genius and his pathetic imitator.

> "True", said Russelton, with a very faint smile at a pun, somewhat in his own way, and levelled at a tradesman, of whom he was, perhaps, a little jealous – "True, Stultz aims at making *gentlemen,* not *coats*; there is a degree of aristocratic pretension in his stitches, which is vulgar to a common degree. You can tell a Stultz coat anywhere, which is quite enough to damn it: the moment a man's known by

---

1. "The long duration" (Fr.) or *La nouvelle histoire* (The new history).
2. It is significant that the author deliberately dedicated his book to civilisation rather than to culture. We could interpret this contradiction as an antithesis between gradual and explosive processes.

an invariable cut, and that not original, it ought to be all over with him. Give me the man who makes the tailor, not the tailor who makes the man."

"Right, by jove!" cried Sir Willoughby, who was as badly dressed as one of Sir E's dinners. "Right; just my opinion. I have always told my Schneiders to make my clothes neither in the fashion nor out of it; to copy no other man's coat, and to cut their cloth according to my natural body, not according to an isosceles triangle. Look at this coat, for instance," and Sir Willoughby Townshend made a dead halt, that we might admire his garment the more accurately.

"Coat!" said Russelton, with an appearance of the most *naïve* surprise, and taking hold of the collar, suspiciously, by the finger and thumb; "coat, Sir Willoughby! do you call *this thing a coat*?"[3]

There are two possible perspectives on Sir Willoughby: from the point of view of authentic dandyism, he is an imitator and a mimic, and from the point of view of his surrounding audience, he is a dandy, destroying accepted norms and creating new ones.

Thus arises the problem of the authentic explosion and imitative explosions as a form of anti-explosive structure. Such are the relationships between Pechorin and Grushnitsky, and between Lermontov and Martynov. In the same way, so also arises the criticism of Belinsky towards Marlinsky. The mutual accusations brought by the adepts of explosion and the gradualists each against the other are those of affectation and banality. The stagnation, which occurred in Russian society after the defeat of the Decembrists in conditions of repressive censorship, the death of Pushkin and the voluntary suicide of Baratynsky, generated a wave of imagined innovation. And it was those very authors who were most closely aligned to the banal tastes of the average reader whose actions imitated impetuous innovation. Banality stylised itself under the guise of originality. The mark of such self-disguise lies in the later films of Einsenstein. However, in complex secondary models the accusers switch swords, like Hamlet and Laertes, and then the refinement appears:

It is not seemly to be famous.[4]

Pasternak, in point of fact, develops the Pushkinian representation on the poetics of the everyday and, in the highest sense, the immutable.

If we abstain from evaluative statements, then what we have before us are two sides of one process, mutually dependent and constantly replacing each other in the unity of dynamic development. The contradictory complexity of the historic

---

3. Bulwer-Lytton, E. *Pelham; Or Adventures of a Gentleman*. London: Routledge, 1855, p. 84.
4. Boris Pasternak. *Poems*. Trans. Lydia Pasternak Slater. London: Unwin Paperbacks, 1984, p. 80.

process subsequently activates first one, then the other form. At the present moment, European civilisation (including America and Russia) is experiencing a period of general discreditation of the very idea of explosion. Humanity lived through a period between the 18th and 20th centuries which may be described as the realisation of the explosive metaphor wherein the image of explosion in popular consciousness came to be associated with gunpowder, dynamite and the nucleus of the atom rather than its potential as a philosophical construct. To the contemporary man, explosion as a phenomenon of physics, transferable to other processes only in the metaphorical sense has come to be associated with ideas of devastation and has turned into a symbol of destruction. But if, at the core of our contemporary representations, there lay the kind of associations that existed during periods of great openness such as the Renaissance or in art in general then our understanding of the concept of explosion would evoke in us such phenomena as the birth of a new living creature or any other creative transformation of the structure of life.

The literary-critical heritage of Belinsky contains some unexpected ideas, first raised to attention by N. I. Mordovchenko in his historical analysis.[5] They relate to the opposition between geniuses and men of talent and between, respectively, literature and publicity. Geniuses – the creators of art – are unpredictable in their oeuvre and do not allow themselves to be directly influenced by the critic. At the same time, between the genius and the reader there is always some kind of "inaccessible line" (according to Pushkin). The reader's lack of understanding of the creative act is the rule rather than the exception. From this, Belinsky reached the audacious conclusion that the genius working towards eternity and posterity may not only be misunderstood by his peers but may even be considered useless to them. His usefulness is concealed by the historical perspective. But the contemporary man needs art and although not as deep nor as long-lived he may nevertheless be taken as the reader of today.

This idea of Belinsky lends itself well to an interpretation of the antithesis of "explosive" and "gradual" processes. From it there flows yet another particularity. In order that the process may be assimilated by its contemporaries, it must take on a gradual character, but at the same time, the contemporary man is drawn to explosive moments that remain inaccessible to him, at least in art. The reader would like his author to be a genius, but in so doing he would also like the work of his author to be understandable. This is the way that writers like Kukolnik or Benediktov came to the fore – writers who occupied the vacant

5. Mordovchenko, N. I. 1950. Belinskii – teoretik i organizator natural'noi shkoly. In Mordovchenko, N. I. *Belinskii i russkaya literatura ego vremeni.* Moskva/Leningrad, p. 213.

seat of genius – imitators. Such an "accessible genius" pleased the reader via his comprehensible art and the critic via his predictability. Any critic, indicating the indubitable future path of such a writer is inclined to see in such a prognostication a result of his own critical acumen. Thus, the prose of Marlinsky, in its antithesis to the prose of Mérimée or Lermontov, may be analysed in terms of its particular orientation towards the reader. This is all the more interesting for the fact that Marlinsky's romantic position raised him "above vulgarity" and demanded the unification of romanticism and the Sternian derision of the reader.

The question cannot here be reduced to the opposition of one artistic movement to another given that the two-step gradual explosion appears at various stages of art and is a property that does not belong only to art. Even Belinsky, when he founded the natural school, in principle, treated the adepts of this movement as fiction writers, creators of art necessary to the reader and corresponding to his level of understanding. In this way, between literature and fiction there also exists the very same interval as exists between the moment of explosion and the new foundational stage of gradual development which appears on this basis. In actual fact, analogous processes occur in the field of cognition. Conventionally, these may be defined as the opposition of theoretical science and technology.

# Chapter 4
# Continuity and discontinuity

So far, we have focussed our attention on the correlation of explosive moments and gradual development as two phases, each of which alternately supersedes the other. However, the relation between them also develops in synchronic space. In the dynamics of cultural development they relate not only in sequential terms but also in terms of their existence as part of a unified, simultaneously operating mechanism. Culture, whilst it is a complex whole, is created from elements which develop at different rates, so that any one of its synchronic sections reveals the simultaneous presence of these different stages. Explosions in some layers may be combined with gradual development in others. This, however, does not preclude the interdependence of these layers.

Thus, for example, dynamic processes in the sphere of language and politics or of morals and fashion demonstrate the different rates at which these processes move. And although more rapid processes may exert an accelerating influence on those that move more slowly, and whilst the latter may appropriate for themselves the self-description of those that move more quickly and thus accelerate their own development their dynamics are not synchronic.

The simultaneous combination of explosive and gradual processes in the various spheres of culture is even more important. This question is made more complex by the inadequate self-description which these processes appropriate for themselves. This usually confuses researchers. The latter, characteristically, reduce the synchronic to a structural unity, interpreting the aggression of any self-description as the establishment of a structural unity. First there is the wave of self-descriptions, then the second wave – of research terminology – both artificially unifying the image of the process, smoothing out contradictory structures. Meanwhile, it is precisely in these contradictions that the foundational structures of the dynamic mechanisms are located.

Both gradual and explosive processes play equally important roles in a structure which operates synchronically: some ensure innovation, others succession. In the self-appraisal of contemporaries, these tendencies are regarded as hostile and the battle between them is construed as a battle to the death. In reality, these represent two parts of a unified, integrated mechanism and its synchronic structure, and the aggression of one does not subdue but, rather, stimulates the development of the opposite tendency.

As, for instance, the aggression of the Karamzin-Zhukovsky school of thought at the beginning of the XIX century stimulated the aggression and development of the Shishkov-Katenin-Griboyedov school of thought.[1] The victorious march of Balzac and Flaubert's "anti-romanticism" was synchronically linked to the rise of Hugo's romanticism.

The intersection of a variety of structural organisations forms the source of dynamics. Until such time as the artistic text is active for its public audience it represents a dynamic system.

Traditional structuralism was based on a principle previously espoused by the Russian formalists: the text was considered to be a closed, self-sufficient, synchronically organised system; isolated not only in time, between past and future, but also in space – from the audience and to everything located outside of the text.

The contemporary phase of structural-semiotic analysis has rendered these principles more complex. In time, the text is perceived as a kind of freeze-frame, artificially "capturing" the moment between past and future. The relationship between past and future is not symmetrical. The past is outlined in two ways: internally – in the direct memory of the text, personified in its structure, its inevitable contradictions, and the immanent battle with its internal synchronicity; and externally – in its correlation to extra-textual memory.

The spectator, having mentally placed himself in that "present moment" in which the text was realised (for example, in *a given* frame, at the moment when I am looking at it), seems then to turn his attention to the past which converges in a cone, whose apex touches the present moment. Facing the future, the audience is immersed in an array of possibilities, which have not yet met with potential selection. The uncertainty of the future allows significance to be assigned to everything. The famous Chekhovian gun which on the instructions of the writer himself, having appeared at the beginning of the play must be discharged at the end, is by no means always discharged. The Chekhovian rule only made sense within the framework of a specific genre and, furthermore, the genre stabilised in established forms. In actual fact, it is precisely this ignorance of whether the gun will be discharged or not that determines whether or not the wound will be fatal, or whether we only imitate this by the drop of the tin, which lends the moment subjective significance.

However, future uncertainty has its albeit eroded limits. Those elements which, in a given system, cannot deliberately enter into it are excluded from it. The future appears as the space of possible states. The relationship between present and future may be outlined as follows. The present – this is the outbreak

---

1. Editor's note: Lotman refers to the polemics of the so-called "innovators" of the Karamzin-Zhukovsky school and "archaists" of the Shishkov school in the early 19th century Russian literature. – M.G.

of the as yet space of meaning generation. It includes within itself the potential of all possible future paths of development. It is important to emphasise that the selection of any one of these is determined by neither the laws of causality nor those of probability: at the moment of explosion these mechanisms are wholly inactive. Future choice comes about by chance. Consequently, it possesses a very high level of informativity. The moment of choice and the cut-off point for potential paths of possibility and the moment whereby the laws of cause-effect once again come into play exist simultaneously.

The moment of explosion is also the place where a sharp increase in the informativity of the entire system takes place. The developmental curve jumps, here, to a completely new, unpredictable and much more complex path. The dominant element, which appears as a result of the explosion and which de-termines future movement, can come from any element of the system or may even be an element of another system, randomly pulled by the explosion into the web of possibilities of future movement. However, in the following stage, this element will already have created a predictable chain of events.

The death of a soldier from a randomly directed piece of shrapnel breaks a whole chain of potentially possible future events. The eldest of the Turgenev brothers died of a sudden illness at the very start of his work. According to Küchelbecker, this genial young man, whose talent could truly have been com-pared to that of Pushkin, could have had a profound effect on Russian literature. Here we may recall the words of Pushkin on Lensky:

> ... his silenced lyre
> Might well have raised, before it ceased,
> A call to ring throughout the ages.[2]

By removing the moment of unpredictability from the historical process, we make it totally redundant. From the position of a bearer of Reason who holds to the process of the internal point of view (such as may be God, Hegel or any other philosopher, who has mastered the "singular scientific method"), this movement is deprived of informativity. Meanwhile, all attempts to predict the future in its cardinal-explosive moments demonstrate the impossibility of the unequivocal prevision of the sharp turns of history. The historical process can be compared to an experiment. However, this is not the kind of experiment that the physics teacher demonstrates to his audience, where he knows the exact results in ad-vance. This is the kind of experiment where the scientist puts himself to the test so as to discover those laws which are, as yet, completely unknown to him. From our point of view, the Supreme Experimenter is not a teacher demonstrat-

---

2. Alexander Pushkin. *Eugene Onegin*. Trans. by James E. Falen. Carbondale and Ed-wardsville: Southern Illinois University Press, 1990, p.160.

ing his knowledge but the researcher who reveals spontaneous information by experimentation.

The moment in which the explosion is exhausted represents the turning point of the process. In the sphere of history this is not only the originating moment of future development but also the place of self-knowledge: the inclusion of those mechanisms of history which must themselves explain what has occurred.

Further development seems to take us back to the original point of explosion, which already exists in our consciousness. What has occurred takes on a new form of existence, and is reflected in the ideas of the observer. In this way a radically transformative event occurs: that which occurred, as we have seen, by chance, now appears to be the only possibility. The element of unpredictability is substituted in the mind of the observer by an element of regularity. From this point of view, the choice was fictitious; in "objective" terms it was predetermined by the entire cause-effect motion of the preceding events.

Specifically, such a process occurs when the complex interweaving of causal and random events, which we call "history", becomes the object of description first by contemporaries, then by historians. This dual layer of description is intended to remove the element of chance from these events. This kind of substitution is easily achieved in those spheres of history in which gradual and explosive processes play a minimal role. These are those layers of history where, firstly, activity has developed most slowly and, secondly, where individual personality plays a lesser role.

Thus, the description of history given by researchers of the French school of *La nouvelle histoire* provides a most convincing study of the results of slow and gradual processes. Just as notable is the fact that the history of technology, as a rule, has for epochs been considered to be anonymous. Paintings are remembered by the name of their artists but brands of automobile are recalled by the name of a company or model.

In Chekhov's tale "The First Class Passenger" the protagonist, an important engineer, who in his lifetime has built many bridges and is the author of a range of technical discoveries, is agitated because his name is not known to the public: "In the course of my life I have built in Russia some two dozen magnificent bridges, I have laid aqueducts for three towns; I have worked in Russia, in England, in Belgium. . . . Secondly, I am the author of several special treatises in my own line. [ . . . ] I discovered methods of obtaining certain organic acids, so that you will find my name in all the foreign manuals of chemistry [ . . . ] I will not fatigue your attention by enumerating my works and my merits, I will only say that I have done far more than some celebrities. And yet here I am in my old age, I am getting ready for my coffin, so to say, and I am as celebrated as that black dog yonder running on the embankment." The protagonist of the story is further agitated by the fact that his mistress, a talented provincial singer, enjoys a wide reputation, and her name is always appearing in the newspapers: "The hussy was empty-headed, ill-tempered, greedy, and what's more, she was a fool." The protagonist agitatedly describes the following episode: "As I remember now, a public ceremony took place to celebrate the opening of the newly constructed bridge. [...] 'Oh,' I thought, 'now the eyes of all the public will be on me! Where shall I hide myself?' Well, I need not have worried myself, sir – alas!" The protagonist did not draw the attention of the public. "All at once the public became agitated; a whisper ran through the crowd ... a smile came on their faces, their shoulders began to move. 'They must have seen me,' I thought. A likely idea!"[3] The animation of the public was due to the very same singer about whom he had spoken so ironically.

The protagonist blames this ignorance and lack of culture on the public. It's true that, here, he has fallen into a comic position, insofar as he has never heard of the interlocutor, who turns out to be an important scientist. The narrator complains about the injustice. However, the roots of the matter, recognised by Chekhov, go much deeper. It is not only the superficiality and lack of culture prevalent in society that is noted by Chekhov. The fact is that the artistic work of even a poor singer is individual by nature, whereas the creation of even a good engineer is somehow dissolved in the general anonymity of technological progress. If the bridge fell down, the name of the engineer would, most probably, be remembered, because this would be an unusual event. The merits of a good bridge, if they are not extraordinary, are not noticed by anyone. Technological development is in general terms predictable, as proved for example by the most successful works from the realms of science fiction. Until such time as one or another discovery is included in the regular process of sequential development it is not assimilated by technology.

Thus, the moment of explosion is marked by the beginning of another stage. In processes, which are accomplished through active participation of the mechanisms of self-consciousness, this is the critical moment. Consciousness appears to be carried backwards, to the moment which preceded the moment of explosion, retrospectively interpreting all that has occurred. The real process in the past is substituted by a model generated by the consciousness of the participant to the act. A retrospective transformation occurs. That which has occurred is declared to be uniquely possible – "its foundations being historically predetermined". The fact that it did not occur is interpreted as being impossible. The weighting of that which is regular and inevitable is attributed to the random act.

---

3. Chekhov, A. *The Schoolmistress and Other Stories: The First Class Passenger* (Trans. Constance Garnett). London: Chatto and Windus, 1920, p. 183.

In this way, events are transferred to the memory of the historian. He receives them already transformed by the influence of the primary selection mechanisms of memory. It is thus especially important that all elements of chance are isolated from this material and that the explosion is transformed into a regular line of development. If discussion of the explosion is permitted, then the concept itself would suffer a decisive loss of content: in it are included representations relating to the energy and rate of the event and the means used to overcome opposing forces; but it deliberately excludes the idea of the unpredictable resulting from the choosing of one over many possibilities. Thus, the concept of "explosion" excludes the moment of informativity and replaces it with fatalism.

The historian's view relies on the secondary process of retrospective transformation. The historian regards an event from a point of view which is oriented from present to past. This view, by its very nature, transforms the object of description. The picture of events, which appears chaotic to the casual observer, leaves the hands of the historian in the form of a secondary organisation. It is natural for the historian to proceed from the inevitability of what has occurred. However, his creative activity is manifested in other ways: from the abundance of facts stored in memory, he constructs a sequential line, leading with the utmost reliability towards this conclusive point. This point, whose foundations lie in the element of chance, covered over by a whole layer of arbitrary assumptions and quasi-convincing elements of cause-effect acquires under the light touch of the historian an almost mystical character. In this we see the celebration of divine or historic predestination, carrying with it the concept espoused by all preceding processes. The concept of an objective which is wholly alien to it is introduced to history.

In his time, Ignatius Loyola had the courage to say that the end justifies the means; however, this principle was widely known before the appearance of the Jesuits and guided people who had never heard, nor thought of the Jesuits. This forms the basis for the justification of history and the introduction to it of the Higher Order. However, this is a fact of history and not a tool for understanding it. And it is not an accident that each similar event – "the salt of the salt of history" is cancelled out by the subsequent explosion and consigned to oblivion. Reality consists of something other than this.

At the moment of explosion, eschatological ideas, such as the affirmation of the proximity of Doomsday, of world revolution, regardless of whether it begins in Paris or St Petersburg, and other analogous historical facts are significant not for the fact that they generate the "last and decisive battle" beyond which must come the reign of God on earth but rather for the fact that they induce an unprecedented tension in popular forces and introduce dynamic elements to the apparently static layers of history. Humanity characteristically evaluates these moments in categories which are either positive or negative. For the historian, it is sufficient to acknowledge them and to make them an object of study insofar as this is objectively possible.

# Chapter 5
# Semantic intersection as the explosion of meanings. Inspiration

The problem of the intersection of semantic spaces is complicated by the fact that the circles we draw on paper represent a particular visual metaphor rather than a precise model of the object. Metaphorism, when it surfaces under the mask of models and scientific definitions, is especially insidious. Any semantic space may only be represented in a metaphorical sense in a two-dimensional manner with clear and definite boundaries. More realistic is its representation as a specific semantic mass whose boundaries are framed by a multiplicity of individual uses. Metaphorically, this can be compared to the boundaries on a map and its locations: during real movement through the geographical locality a clear line on the map blurs into a spot.

The intersections of semantic spaces which generate new meanings are linked to individual consciousness. In the distribution of these intersections across the entire space of a language, so-called linguistic metaphors are generated. The latter appear as a fact of the common language of the community. Artistic metaphors are located on another pole. Here, semantic space is also ambiguous: metaphor-clichés, common to a variety of literary schools and periods, or metaphors which pass gradually from triviality to individual creativity illustrate various levels of semantic intersection. The most extreme case is represented by the metaphor which is principally innovative and which is treated by the carriers of traditional meaning as arbitrary and offensive to their feelings; this scandalizing metaphor is always the result of a creative act, a factor which does not preclude its future transformation into a current or even trivial metaphor.

This continually active process of the "aging" of the various means of meaning-generation is compensated on the one hand by the introduction and use of new, previously forbidden, meaning-generating structures and, on the other, by the rejuvenation of old, already forgotten ones. The process of individual meaning-generation is one which in the slightly imprecise quoting of Lomonosov by Tynyanov is defined as "the rapprochement of distant ideas", or, according to Zhukovsky:

A vision for an instant fleeting
Of what the gulf of time concealed.[1]

This conjunction of the incompatible under the influence of a certain creative tension is defined as inspiration. Pushkin, with characteristic clarity, shrewdly rejected the romantic formula of Küchelbecker which identified *inspiration* with *enthusiasm:*

> "*Inspiration?* That is the submission of the soul to the most lively reception of impressions and consequently to the quick grasp of concepts, thus facilitating their explanation. Inspiration is as needed in poetry as in geometry."[2]

As such, for Pushkin poetic tension is not opposed to logical, scientific discovery and presents itself not as the refusal of Knowledge but rather as its highest state, in the light of which what was incomprehensible becomes obvious.

However, it is also possible to take the antithetical point of view: creative inspiration is thought of as the supreme element of tension pulling humanity out of the sphere of logic into the arena of unpredictable creativity. This process was expressed with documentary precision by Blok:

THE ARTIST

I, on your wedding days, funerals, holidays,
Listen and wait under heatwave and blizzard
Stifled with boredom I long to have swept away,
Chased by a gentle note never yet heard.

There, it begins! And with cold concentration
I wait to capture it, leave it for dead,
While in advance of my keen expectation
Stretches its barely discernible thread.

Is it a wind from the ocean, a heavenly
Choir in the leaves? Has time stopped? Is it spring –
Snow from the apple-trees scattering evenly?
Is it the pulse of an angel's wing?

Sound gathers, motion and daylight increase, as my
Hours stretch out, carrying all that I know.
Yesterday wildly stares into tomorrow's eye.

---

1. Zhukovsky, V. Song (1818). In *An Age Ago. A Selection of 19th-Century Russian Poetry*. Selected and translated by Alan Myers. New York: Farrar, Straus & Giroux, 1988, p. 6.
2. A. Pushkin. On Küchelbecker's articles published in *Mnemozina*. In *Critical and Autobiographical Prose* in *The Complete Works of Alexander Pushkin*, vol. 13, p. 65, Milner and Company Limited, 1999 (Trans. Tatiana Wolff).

There is no present, no pitiful "now".

And when at last conception is imminent –
New soul, new forces about to draw breath –
Meteor-like a curse strikes. In a moment
Artifice chokes inspiration to death.

Then in a glacial cage I incarcerate
This gentle bird, this wind-following featherweight,
Bird that intended to break death's control,
Bird that descended to rescue my soul.

Here is my cage, an immovable metal one,
Now with the sunset's brush gilding its grill.
Here is my bird, my once jubilant little one,
Perched in a ring singing over my sill.

Those wings are clipped, all those songs learnt by heart. Are you
Happy to stand sometimes under my sill?
So the songs please you. But waiting for something new,
Stifled with boredom, I'm listening still.[3]

The poem, dedicated to the role of the unconscious, is nevertheless sustained albeit in a stringent almost precise terminology. In this sense, the poem reproduces a radical contradiction in the moment of inspiration as described above. The unfolding textual meaning passes through several stages. The first is the external world, "your world", the world on that side of poetry, the world of "weddings, funerals, holidays". The next level is the world of the poetic "I". However, it is not isolated: it is through the outer layer of logic that this world is understood. The third, poetic, world is submerged in the depths and its usual state is sleep. In certain moments of unpredictability it awakens as a "gentle note never yet heard". Here a passage from the verbally expressed world to that world, which lies beyond the boundaries of language, takes place. For Blok the latter is, more likely than not, the world of sound – "note". The following stage is that of introspection; the logical verbal world of the artist who "with cold concentration" struggles to "capture it, leave it for dead" – to render the inexpressible in words and to express the world, which lies beyond the limits of logic, in logical terms.

The stanza which follows is dedicated precisely to this futile attempt: Blok as the poet whose material is the word is constrained to try to express that which, within the limits of this material cannot in principle be expressed. In the third stanza a series of fragmentary sentences follow. Their interrogative intonation expresses doubt as to the adequacy of the word to provide the desired meaning.

3.  Blok, A. A. The Artist. In *Selected Poems*. Manchester: Carcanet, 2000 (Trans. Jon Stallworthy and Peter France), p. 87.

This is combined with a fundamental semantic incompatibility: they do not form a unified logical frame. It is as if the syntactic construction of the stanza was a continuation of the well-known question posed by Zhukovsky:

Is the inexpressible subject to expression...?[4]

The stanza, which demonstrates the absence of adequate language and the need to replace it with a multiplicity of mutually conflicting languages, is superseded by the compositional centre of the poem in the fourth stanza – which describes the moment of supreme tension that is poetic inspiration. The world of signs and materialisations gives way to a world of supreme clarity, which cancels out the contradictions in their particular deep-level unity.

"Hours stretch out" – the possibility of prolonging the hour and the fact that the brief minute of inspiration is described in terms of hours attests to the fact that the discussion is not about the singular measurement of time but rather the breakthrough of non-time. Polarities are considered identical: "sound, motion and daylight" appear as synonyms.

Of particular interest is the disappearance of the present time. It appears only as a deprived reality in the form of a geometric line; the space between past and future. And the phrase "Yesterday wildly stares into tomorrow's eye" sounds like the prophetic prediction of contemporary ideas concerning the transference of our consciousness of the past into the future.

The moment of supreme tension removes all boundaries of untranslatability and unites the incompatible. Before us now lies the poetic description of new meaning. Blok wanted to go beyond the limits of meaning, but the same thing happened to him as happened to the prophet Balaam who, meaning to curse, blessed. Blok, with exceptional precision, wrote about that which he considered indescribable.

There then follows a descent along the same lines – the "inexpressible" inspiration pours into the words:

Then in a glacial cage I incarcerate
This gentle bird, this wind-following featherweight,
Bird that intended to break death's control,
Bird that descended to rescue my soul.

The transfixed and trivialized poetry is displaced further into the external sphere, towards the reader.

---

4. Zhukovsky, V. A. *Sobr. soch. T. 1*, p. 336. (Translator's note: English translation my own.)

The inexpressible reproduced by Blok actually results in a translation and the whole process of creation is reproduced as a sort of tension which renders the untranslatable translatable.

The polarity of Pushkin's and Blok's messages serves only to highlight their deep unity: in both cases the moment of unpredictable explosion renders the incompatible adequate and the untranslatable translatable.

Blok's text is particularly interesting in the sense that it reveals the metaphoric nature of the word "moment"[5] described earlier: in actual fact it refers not to a contraction of time but rather to a moment 'out of time'; a leap in the passage of time from the "past" to the "future". The entire content of the poem represents a description of semantic explosion, the passage through the boundary of unpredictability.

It is interesting that Pushkin, from completely different positions and persistently deviating from the stamp of romanticism, also describes inspiration as the passage from untranslatability to translatability. Thus, whilst working on *Boris Godunov*, he reports in a letter that the tragedy is easily written. This is so, even when he reaches the "scene which demands inspiration",[6] and he skips it and carries on writing. As with Blok, two creative possibilities are isolated: one within the limits of a pre-given language and another beyond the limits of an unpredictable explosion.

In the unfinished novel *Egyptian Nights* we come across a significant description of the moment of creation. It is characteristic of Pushkin that he taboos the word itself, while describing inspiration: "He was a poet nevertheless, and his passion for poetry was indomitable; when he felt this nonsense approach (that was what he called inspiration), he locked himself in his study and wrote from morning till late night. He confessed to his genuine friends that he knew true happiness only at such times. The rest of the time he led his dissipated life, put on airs, dissembled, and perpetually heard the famous question, "Have you written a new little something?"[7]

Semiotic space appears before us as the multi-layered intersection of various texts, which are woven together in a specific layer characterised by complex internal relationships and variable degrees of translatability and spaces of untranslatability. The layer of "reality" is located underneath this textual layer –

5.  Translator's note: in the selected translation by Stallworthy and France, the word 'moment' is translated as 'the conception is imminent'.

6.  A. Pushkin. The Letters of Alexander Pushkin 1815–1826. In *The Complete Works of Alexander Pushkin*, vol. 11, p. 238, Milner and Company Limited, 1999 (Trans. J. Thomas Shaw).

7.  A. Pushkin. Egyptian Nights. In *The Complete Works of Alexander Pushkin*, vol. 10, pp. 254–255, Milner and Company Limited, 1999 (Trans. John Bayley).

the kind of reality that is organised by a multiplicity of languages and has a hierarchical relationship with them. Together, both these layers constitute the semiotics of culture. That reality which is external to the boundaries of language lies beyond the limits of the semiotics of culture.

The word "reality" denotes two different phenomena. On the one hand, this reality is phenomenal, in the Kantian sense, i.e. it is that reality which correlates to culture, either resisting it, or merging with it. On the other, there is the noumenal sense (in Kantian terminology) in which we may refer to reality as a space which is forever beyond the limits of culture. However, the whole structure of these definitions and terms changes, if at the centre of our world we place not one isolate "I" but a more complex organised space of the many mutually dependent correlative "I"s.

In this way, according to the ideas of Kant, external reality would be transcendental only if the layer of culture possessed just one single language. But the relationships between the translatable and the untranslatable are so complex that possibilities for a breakthrough into the space beyond the limits are created. This function is also fulfilled by moments of explosion, which can create a kind of window in the semiotic layer. Thus, the world of semiosis is not fatally locked in on itself: it forms a complex structure, which always "plays" with the space external to it, first drawing it into itself, then throwing into it those elements of its own which have already been used and which have lost their semiotic activity.

From the aforesaid we may draw two conclusions: firstly, the abstraction of a single language of communication as a basis for semiosis is an erroneous abstraction as this distorts, in an imperceptible way, the whole essence of the mechanism. Of course, we can examine cases, where the transmitting and receiving mechanisms are relatively identical and can, therefore, communicate via a single channel. However, this is not a general model but a particular space isolated from the "normal" polylingual model.

The second aspect concerns the dynamic nature of lingual space. The idea that we can give a static representation and then add motion to it is also an erroneous abstraction. The static state is a particular model (ideally existing only in abstraction) that reveals itself as a speculative generalisation of the dynamic structure which represents the sole reality.

# Chapter 6
# Thinking reed

The problem of culture cannot be resolved without a determination of its place in extra-cultural space.

The question may be formulated as follows: the unique quality of man as a cultural 'artefact' requires the opposition of his world to nature; which is understood as extra-cultural space. The boundary between these two worlds will not only separate man from other extra-cultural artefacts but will also pass into the realm of the human psyche and human activity. Some of these boundaries place man in the realm of culture; others are linked to the extra-cultural world. Similarly, it would be careless to categorically exclude the animal world from the sphere of culture.

In this way the boundary is eroded and the definition of any concrete fact as belonging to a cultural or extra-cultural sphere necessarily includes a high degree of relativity. However, the 'relativity' of a specific case is sufficiently obvious when we are talking about categories of abstract classification. With this reservation we can elaborate the world of culture as an object that requires further elucidation.

Tyutchev, in the poetic epigraph:

*Est in arundineis modulatio musica ripis*[1]

with philosophical precision noted this, for him, eternally agonising question concerning the dual nature of man as 'artefact', inscribed in nature but not limited by it:

A song is born with billows' speed,
And harmony in nature's rages;
The rustling music of the ages
Streams through the straight but supple reed.

The world is like a perfect score,
With not a single note discordant;
Man, free to mock and self-important,
Alone is with this world at war.

Whence is the flaw in the design?
Is there a force that will restore us
To nature's undivided chorus?
Why does the thinking rush repine?

---

1. There is a musical order in coastal reeds (Lat.)

[As in the wilderness, the cry
Is never answered, never noticed,
So is the soul's despairing protest
Lost on the earth and in the sky.][2]

The Tyutchevian theme of the "dual abyss", which has had a major impact on the philosophical-poetic tradition,[3] is here attributed a specific interpretation: nature, according to Tyutchev, is endowed with harmony. And it is opposed to the disharmony of the human soul. The philosophical concept of harmony implies "... unity in variety; in music, it signifies the accord of many tones in

2. *On the Heights of Creation. The Lyrics of Fedor Tyutchev.* Trans. Anatoly Liberman. London-Greenwich: JAI Press, 1993, pp. 124–125.
3. A contradiction is expressed here – one of the agonising themes for Tyutchev generally

And things will grow that grow today,
The rose will seek the morning ray,
　　　And so will weeds ...
But you, my listless, lifeless flower [the poet's beloved],
You will not see a better hour:
　　　Nor will you seeds!
(*On the Heights of Creation. The Lyrics of Fedor Tyutchev.* Trans. Anatoly Liberman. London-Greenwich: JAI Press, 1993, p. 73)

See also, in Derzhavin:

My body sinks to endless slumber,
And yet my mind commands the thunder ...
(Derzhavin, G. R. God. In: *Poetic Works. A Bilingual Album.* Ed. A. Levitsky. Trans. Alexander Levitsky and Martha T. Kitchen. Brown Slavic Contributions, vol. 12. Providence: Brown University Press, 2001, p. 20)

See also, in Baratynsky:

So winter comes, and all the starveling plain,
The spreading bald-patches of weakness,
The glowing squares of gladsome fields of grain,
The cornstalks ripening to sleekness,
Both life and death, both beggary and wealth –
Each picture of the year that's over
At one under the snow's all-shrouding stealth
'Neath one monotonous white cover –
Such is the world that henceforth you will see;
For you, alas, no harvest shall there be!
(Baratynsky, E. Autumn. In: *An Age Ago. A Selection of 19th-Century Russian Poetry.* Selected and translated by Alan Myers. New York: Farrar, Straus & Giroux, 1988, p. 70).

a single whole and, from there, it was taken up by the Pythagoreans in their study of the harmony of the spheres, i.e. on the regular rotation of the celestial bodies, which form the hexachord, around a central flame." After citing this definition E. L. Radlov adds: "Svedenborg speaks of an "established" harmony, which brings order to the organic world."[4] The Tyutchevian gap between man and the world represents the contradiction between harmony and disharmony. But at the same time, Tyutchev considers harmony to be an eternally constant or eternally immutable being, whereas man is involved in a disharmonious, i.e. an asymmetrically, unfolding motion.

We now approach a core issue: the conflict between 'closed' motion, i.e. regenerative, and linear motion.

In the animal world, we encounter motion in a closed circle: both seasonal and developmental; these and other changes in this world are subordinated to the law of repetition. In this sense, the characteristic difference between animal learning (here and henceforth, when speaking of animals, we have in mind mainly higher order mammals) and that of humans in whom scientists frequently note a parallel of such processes.

In animals significant forms of behaviour – the purpose and object of learning – oppose insignificant ones. Significant behaviour possesses a ritualised character: hunting, the competitivity of the male, the identification of a leader and other significant behavioural moments are formulated in a complex system of "correctness", i.e. poses and gestures which are considered to have equal value and meaning both for the actor and for his partner. All significant forms of behaviour have the character of dialogue. An encounter between two competing predators (such an encounter is possible, as a rule, if one of them, due to extraordinary circumstances, most frequently the interference of man but occasionally due to hunger or spontaneous catastrophe, is forced out of "its" space and turned into a "vagrant") despite man-made legends about the "disorganisation" and "disorderly" behaviour of animals generates a complex system of animal rituals which facilitate the exchange of information.

Using a system of gestures, animals inform each other of their "rights" to this space; force, hunger, intention to do battle and so forth. With regular frequency this dialogue will often conclude with one of the participants, without entering the battle, recognising itself as defeated and reporting this fact to its enemy by means of a specific gesture, for example, by lowering its tail. Conrad Lawrence noted that when, at the end of a duel between crows, one crow exposes its eyes to the other, or the predator presents its throat to the other, this is a sign of its subjugation, the battle is over and the victor, as a rule, does not take the

---

4.  Radlov, E. L. *Filosofskii slovar*. Moskva 1913, p. 112.

opportunity to physically destroy the vanquished. The difference between the combative behaviour of animals and man expressed here is at the root of the Russian saying: the crow does not peck out the eyes of the crow.

Motion in a closed circle also determines (predominant in the archaic world) aspects of human behaviour. Plato based his ideal construction of the social world on this model:

> **Athenian.** So, in a society where the laws relating to culture, education and recreation are, or will be in the future, properly established, do we imagine that authors will be given a free hand? The choruses will be composed of the young children of law-abiding citizens: will the composer be free to teach them *anything* by way of rhythm, tune and words that amuse him when he composes, without bothering what effect he may have on them as regards virtue and vice?
>
> **Cleinias.** That's certainly not sensible; how could it be?
>
> **Athenian.** But it is precisely this that they are allowed to do in virtually all stages – except in Egypt.
>
> **Cleinias.** Egypt! Well then, you'd better tell us what laws have been enacted there.
>
> **Athenian.** Merely to hear about it is startling enough. Long ago, apparently, they realised the truth of the principle we are putting forward only now, that the movements and tunes which the children of the state are to practise in their rehearsals must be good ones. They compiled a list of them according to style, and displayed it in their temples. Painters and everyone else who represent movements of the body of any kind were restricted to these forms; modification and innovation outside this traditional framework were prohibited, and are prohibited even today, both in this field and in the arts in general. If you examine their art on the spot, you will find that ten thousand years ago (and I'm not speaking loosely: I mean literally ten thousand), paintings and reliefs were produced that were no better and no worse than those of today, because the same artistic rules were applied in making them.[5]

It is not accidental that the ideal embodiment of art, for Plato, should appear in the "ancient sacred round dances". The closed round dance – a symbol of cyclical reiteration in nature – becomes, for Plato, an ideal embodiment of art.

Cyclical reiteration is a law of biological existence; the animal world (and the world of man as part of this world) is subordinate to it. However, man is not fully submerged in this world: as a "thinking reed" – he constantly finds himself at odds with the basic laws of his surroundings.

This is manifested in the differences which are characteristic of the means of instruction. The animal learns, as we noted earlier, through the system of ritual behaviour. Superiority is achieved by strength or the rapidity of gesture

---

5.  Plato. *The Laws*. London: Penguin Books, (trans. Trevor J. Saunders), 1970, p. 91.

but never by means of a gesture which is unexpected and new to the opponent. The animal may be compared to a dancer, who, although he has the capacity to improve the dance, nevertheless may not sharply and unexpectedly change the dance itself for something other than the dance. The behaviour of animals is ritualistic; the behaviour of man gravitates towards the invention of something new and unpredicted by his enemies. From man's point of view, animals are stupid; from the animal's point of view, man is dishonest (he doesn't play by the rules). Man constructs his view of the animal as a foolish person. The animal constructs his view of man as a dishonourable animal.

It is an enigmatic fact of human history that our predecessors survived despite the fact that they were surrounded by predators infinitely superior to them in terms of tooth and claw. It is not possible to attribute the survival of man to his ability to use tools. Primitive tools could not assure a decisive superiority over the teeth and claws of predators; furthermore, men had children who were not armed with axes or spears.

Of course, we have all heard of cases where, famished by winter, wolves have attacked people or similar cases where people have fallen prey to other predators. However, these are the exception rather than the rule. It cannot be said that wolves eat people; wolves eat mice, small rodents, hares and on certain occasions – young cattle. Hunger also causes cases of cannibalism amongst people, however it is not possible to conclude from this that people eat people (here we are excluding from examination cases of ritual cannibalism, which assume the character of a 'magic act' for some people, or cases where people have been eaten, for example, by tigers, which are clearly distinguished by their individual character).

In "normal" situations animals strive to avoid contact with humans, and even from the goal of eating them: they distance themselves from man and at the same time man as hunter and trapper has from the very beginning sought to make contact with them. The relationship of animals to man could be called one of elimination; a tendency to avoid contact. If we were to assign human psychology to animals, we might call this fastidiousness. More realistically, this tendency to instinctively avoid unpredictable situations is similar to that experienced by the man who encounters a madman.

# Chapter 7
# The world of proper names

The identification of heuristic convenience and empirical reality gave birth to many scientific myths. To them may be attributed the idea that the natural path of knowledge leads from the concrete and the individual to the abstract and the general.

First of all, let us turn to zoosemiotic data. The cat, like many other animals, can identify the total number of its young but cannot distinguish them individually by appearance. If one of its kittens is substituted by another, if there is no noticeable change in the total quantity, the cat is not alarmed. Let us focus our attention, then, on the fact that the child, looking at recently born kittens, immediately distinguishes them by specific features of colouring, stripes and spots, even by individual behavioural tendencies. The sight of the mother-cat is oriented to the perception of the collective as a unified whole. The combat of two stags for supremacy of the herd is carried out above the herd and the herd follows the winner, collectively erasing the defeated stag from its memory. To conceive of a scene where one of the female deer from the herd, not sharing the general sentiment, stays with the defeated stag is just not possible.

Of course, the true picture is considerably more complex: it would be possible to identify cases of sharp, individual markings, especially in pairs of animals during the mating period. But still there remains one indisputable fact: the language of animals does not 'know' proper names. The latter appear only in relation to domestic animals, and always as a result of the interference of man. In the language of even the most complex animals the appearance of proper names has, thus far, proved impossible to elucidate. When the hero of Chekhov's tale trains his young wife to kiss his hand, because all "...women who loved him kissed his hand and he had gotten used to this..."[1] he is actualising male behaviour (in the exact, and not in the pejorative sense), creating for himself a generalised image of "his woman".

The aforesaid is in striking contradiction to the behaviour of a child – the human young. Despite the trivialisation of the concept, it is possible to say that nowhere is the difference between man and animal so striking as in the child. The "animalistic tendency" of the child, which at this stage is sharply apparent in the physiological domain, hides the marked originality of the child's cultural-psychological behaviour from the observer. Those cases where the child does

---

1. Chekhov, A. *Sobr. soch.,* T 8, p. 222. (Translator's note: English translation my own.)

not behave like an animal (i.e. where the child behaves like a human) appear trivial and are not noticed.

Perhaps the sharpest manifestation of human nature is in the use of proper names and, linked to this, the isolation of individuality, the uniqueness of the individual personality as foundational values for "other" and "others"; "I" and "other" represent two sides of the unified act of self-consciousness and one is impossible without the other.

Similarly, it is only the possibility of a lie that converts truth into a conscious, freely-selected behaviour and the possibility of anomalous, criminal, immoral behaviour that converts the conscious selection of a moral standard into a behavioural act. The human young is a much less pleasant entity than its counterpart in the animal world: it is capricious, it lies; it knowingly causes damage and breaks the rules. This occurs because the human child has the ability to accomplish, or not to accomplish, these or other forms of behaviour and to determine the boundaries of its possibilities by experimentation. The possibility of doing wrong is the first step towards the ability to consciously choose not to do so. Childish whims do not have an equivalent in the world of the young of animals, although negative experience also plays an important role in their learning process.

A sharp difference in the young of animals and of humans is manifested in the actualisation of talent. If we define 'talent' as a special ability to undertake any form of activity, then a "talented" animal with special success accomplishes pre-existent actions (we are not considering here the kind of training introduced by man); the behaviour of a child whether "good" or "poor" is, by its very nature, experimental. In this lies the same fundamental difference between learning and training (although, in practice, any learning includes within it an element of training). Conscious behaviour is impossible without selection, i.e. the moment of individuality[2] and thus implies the existence of a space filled with proper names.

The language of animals, insofar as it is possible to judge, without the interference of man, does not possess proper names. Meanwhile, it is precisely these that create that tension between the individual and the general which is fundamental to human consciousness. By mastering the tension between the individual word, created in such an *ad hoc* fashion and the general word "for all", the child

---

2. When we speak of individuality, we are not identifying this concept with the idea of the individual man in the biological sense. The category of individuality may apply to any social group. The only requirement is that it fulfils not only the unitary state (this includes the herd), but that it also includes a state where there is freedom of choice, without which the category of personality cannot exist.

includes itself in a fundamentally new mechanism of consciousness. Most frequently, this is manifested in the aggressive nature of the sphere of proper names, in which a tendency towards limitless expansion appears, although the opposite is also possible. What is important is the very fact of semantic tension and not the victory, which is always short-term, of one tendency over the other. This is the period of the turbulent creation of words, as only the new and unique word which has only just been created is absolutely inseparable from its signification.

This tendency aggressively penetrates the language of the parents via the language of the child. Thus one may hear from the parents: "She's called Tanya, but we call her Tyulya, because that was one of her first words and she called herself that."

The distinction between "one's own" and "other" divides the world of the child into my own and the alien world, embedding that boundary in the consciousness which remains the most important dominant feature of culture. And so the semantic boundary appears, which will subsequently play a fundamental role in the social, cultural, cosmogonical[3] and ethical construction of the world.

This feature of children's consciousness is a fundamental moment in the construction of specifically human traits. It is manifested especially in a number of personalities. Thus, Vladimir Solovyev, in his childhood, had special names for each of his pencils. Also linked to this is the tendency to view as 'taboo' the use by others of "childhood" names. At first this may manifest in the psychological defence of the secrets of "one's own" world. Later it may manifest in adolescent embarrassment of a childhood only recently left behind, which may motivate an element of taboo around his early use of language. Motives may change, but the taboo remains.

The tendency of the child to enlarge the sphere of proper names, introducing therein a whole circle of nouns denoting his "domestic" world, has been noticed repeatedly and this has been seen as a manifestation of the special concreteness of children's consciousness. However, the opposite tendency is also active: running from tree to tree in the park, a three year old child excitedly and enthusiastically strikes birches, firs, poplars and shouts: "A tree!" Then he, with the same cry, strikes the electricity pole and bursts out laughing: this was a joke – he didn't think the post was a tree. Thus we have the ability not only to generalise but also the ability to play with this ability, an activity linked to those processes which exist only in *human* consciousness.

---

3.  Translator's note: the study of the origin and development of the universe or of a particular system within the universe, from the Greek: -*cosmos* (universe) and -*gonos* (creation).

The separation of the word from the thing – here is that cliff-face, which creates the precipice between man and the rest of the animal world, and the child, the border guard on the edge of this precipice might, perhaps, be brighter than the "adult", revealing features of that consciousness by the neophyte that he is.

Rousseau, in *On the Origin of Inequality*, expressed himself brilliantly in relation to the psychology of the discrimination between things and phenomena:

> One must infer that since the first words which men made use of had in their minds a much more extensive meaning than those which we use in languages already formed and that, since men knew nothing about the division of discourse into its constitutive parts, at first they gave to each word the sense of an entire proposition. [...] Every object at first received a particular name, without regard to genus and species, something which those first founders were not in a position to distinguish, and all the individuals presented themselves to their minds as isolated instances, as they are in the spectacle of nature. If one oak tree was called A, another oak tree was called B. For the first idea one derives from two objects is that they are not the same, and often a good deal of time is necessary to observe what they have in common. Hence, the more limited their knowledge, the more extensive their dictionary. The inconvenience of all this nomenclature could not have been easily removed, for to arrange beings under common and generic denominations, they had to know their properties and their differences; they required observations and definitions, that is, natural history and metaphysics, a great deal more than the men of those times could have had ... "[4]

Further, Rousseau with characteristic boldness, declared that the monkey "jumping from one nut to another" does not consider these items as something united (such a monkey, in defiance of the philosopher's opinion would, of course, die of hunger). It is specifically this feature, separating the monkey from the child, which is the source of the specific character of man. Here begins the game between proper names and common names, between "this" and "every". And precisely because the concept "this and only it" is a new concept, it first of all attracts the attention of the neophyte. There is no "I" without "others". But only in human consciousness do "I" and "all others, except me" hide within themselves something that is both unified and conflicting at one and the same time.

One of the fundamental semiotic mechanisms inherent in humanity begins with the possibility of being "only itself"; to be a thing (proper name) and to simultaneously appear as the "representative" of a group, as one of many

---

4. Rousseau, J. J. *Discourse on the Origin and the Foundations of Inequality Among Men* (1754). Trans. Ian Johnston of Malaspina University-College, Nanaimo, British Columbia. Prideaux Street Publications, Canada, 2004.

(common noun). This possibility of stepping into the role of another, of acting as a substitute for someone or something, indicates that you "are not what you are".

Thus, for example, when in a fight between male baboons, the defeated baboon assumes a position of sexual subordination; we come across a very interesting example of the starting point of semiosis. Despite potential Freudian interpretations, what we have before us is not a case of the celebration of sexual aspirations but a sharp manifestation of the possibility of a release from their authority in their own domain, transformed into language, i.e. into something formal, isolated from its usual meaning. The male baboon uses the sexual gesture of the female as a sign of non-sexual relations – in terms of a readiness to take up a subordinate position of authority. Natural biological poses, genetically derived from nature, are repeated in the forms of signs to which it is possible to assign an arbitrary value.

M. Bulgakov in his *Theatrical Novel* describes the following accidental event, caused by the imperative prohibition by the director of the use of bloody scenes. As a result, the action, in which the author depicted a quarrel between heroes and the death of one of them, underwent a transformation on stage: "During ordinary rehearsals the stage manager simulated the shot by clapping his hands, but at the dress rehearsal it was done by letting off a blank cartridge in the wings. Well, Nastasya Ivanovna fainted – she had never heard a shot fired in her life – and Ludmilla Silvestrovna had hysterics. Since then there have been no more shots. The play was changed, the hero didn't shoot but instead he waved a watering-can and shouted: "I'll kill you, you scoundrel!" and stamped his foot – all of which, according to Ivan Vasilievich, was the solitary cause of the play's success".[5]

There is a comic sense of episode in the comparison of the author's text and the editorial processing of this text in the censorship of Ivan Vasilievich. This makes it possible to consider the given texts as antonyms from the point of view of the author, and as improved synonyms – in the opinion of the director. The possibility of two texts simultaneously appearing, each with respect to the other acting as both synonyms and antonyms brings us to a new question.

A similar semantic game is not necessarily linked to the artistic function – its sphere is much wider.[6] This is one of the mechanisms of meaning-generation. Its special feature, in particular, lies in the fact that the very nature of meaning

5. Bulgakov, M. A. *Black Snow: A Theatrical Novel*. Trans. Michael Glenny. London: Hodder and Stoughton, 1967, p. 180.
6. On irony as trope, see Tomashevsky, B. V. *Teoriya literatury. Poetika*. Leningrad, 1925, p. 39.

can only be determined by virtue of its context, i.e. as a result of turning to that wider space that lies outside of meaning.

"Good day, my learned friend, and where may you have been?"[7]

Only knowledge of the fact that these words are addressed to the ass (and this knowledge required a considerably wider context) makes it possible to identify the fact that we are dealing with irony. So that here, in essence, it is necessary to speak not of the structure of the text but about its function. In actual fact, irony implies a personal knowledge of the addressee. Mockery always, directly or indirectly, has in mind concrete *unity*, i.e. it is linked to a proper name. The problem becomes even more complicated when we enter the domain of the artistic text.

In principle, the artistic text proceeds from the possibility of complicated relations between the first and third person, i.e between the gravitation towards the space of proper names and the objective narrative of the third person. In this respect, the very possibility of the artistic text recalls the psychological experience of dreams. It is specifically here that man encounters the experience of "flickering" between the first and third person, between real and conventional spheres of activity. Thus, in sleep, the grammatical possibilities of language operate "as though in reality". The perceptive domain, previously and simply identified with reality, appears as a space in which all permissible transformations of language are possible: conventional and unreal narration, a selection of actions in space and in time, a changing point of view. One of the special features of sleep lies in the fact that the categories of speech are transferred into visual space. Without this experience, such spheres as art and religion, i.e. the highest manifestations of consciousness, would not be possible.

The transfer of the sphere of dreams into an area of consciousness itself entails a fundamental realignment of its nature. Only these changes provide the possibility of building a bridge between sleep and artistic activity. The experience, extracted from dreams, undergoes the same transformation which is accomplished when we recount our dreams. The brilliant hypothesis of P. Florensky, according to which at the moment of recounting a dream, the beginning, end and direction of the dream change places, has not, even now, been proven by experiment and so we will not dwell on it any longer. For us, it is more important to note that in the recounting of a dream, an obvious increase in the degree of organisation occurs: a narrative structure is imposed on our speech.

---

7. Krylov, I. A. Fox and Ass. In *Krylov's Fables*. Trans. Bernard Pares. Westport, Connecticut: Hyperion Press, 1977, p. 210. We are using the example of B. V. Tomashevsky (see ibid).

Thus, the transformation of the visual into narrative leads to an unavoidable increase in the degree of organisation. This is how text is created. The process of narrating displaces in memory the real traces of the dream, and man is convinced that he actually saw precisely that which he described. Subsequently, in our memory, this verbally narrated text is laid aside. However, this is only part of the process of memorization: the verbally organised text reverts back to the images preserved in the memory and are memorized in its visual form. In this way, a visibly narrated structure is created, connecting the sense of reality, inherent in all that has been seen, to all the grammatical possibilities of unreality. This represents potential material for artistic creation.

The ability of the highest animals to dream allows us to assume that the boundary of art[8] is not so far from their consciousness. However, our information in this area is so problematic that it deprives us of any possibilities for the drawing of conclusions.

Art is the most developed space of conventional reality. In more specific terms, this makes it the "testing ground" for the sphere of mental experiment and, taking this further still, for investigating the processes of intellectual dynamics. The ability of art to unify the domains of proper and common names interests us in this regard.

The whole extensive spheres of art, originating in the most archaic layers of culture, are linked to the first person and establish itself as *ich-Erzählung* – narration in the first person. However, this "I" simultaneously carries the meaning of "all the others in the position I". This, in fact, is the same contradiction which Pushkin outlined in the words:

My fancy draw sweet tears from me...[9]

Radishchev in his *Diary of a Week* having led his hero to the theatre showing Saurin's play *Béverlei*, asks himself the question: "He's drinking poison – why do you care?"[10] There was a natural answer to the question until, according to the laws of folklore, the performer was simultaneously a spectator of himself: "I" and "He" merged into one action. The separation of the performer and the spectator, singing and listening created a completely new and internally contradictory situation: the performer for me is "He", but I transfer all his speech and feelings to my "I". "I" see, through my own feelings.

In this sense the special role of the ballet in the moment when relations between first and third person become complicated is characteristic. "I" transfer

8. Translators note: in the sense of 'art'.
9. A. Pushkin. Elegy. In *Lyric Poems: 1826-1836* in *The Complete Works of Alexander Pushkin*, vol. 2, p. 133, Milner and Company Limited, 1999 (Trans. Alan Myers).
10. Radishchev, A. N. *Poln. sobr. soch.* Moskva/Leningrad, 1938, T. 1, p. 140.

the function of the third person to the scene: everything that it is possible to see, I transfer to another person (him), and everything that remains in the sphere of internal experiences, I appropriate to myself, assuming the role of the first person. However, the relation between "scene – spectator" is indicative of only one aspect of the question, another is realised on the axis "I – another spectator". Gogol in his "After the Play" wrote: "Stories! . . . Look how the balconies and the balustrades of the theatres groan: everything from top to bottom is shaken and transformed into one motion, into one instant, *into one man* (italics mine, J. L) all the people have met like brothers in one upsurge of emotion and thunderous applause rises in a hymn to him who has been dead for five hundred years."[11]

It is necessary, however, to emphasise that the value of this unity lies precisely in the fact that it is based on the individual differences of the spectators and does not abolish this difference. It is a psychological violence, which is only possible in the situation of emotional tension created in the theatre.

---

11. Gogol, N. V. After the Play. An appendix to *"The Inspector General"* (1836). In *The Tulane Drama Review*, vol. 4, no. 2, Dec 1959, p. 144 (Trans. David Magarshack).

# Chapter 8
# The fool and the madman

The binary opposition fool/madman may be analysed in terms of a generalisation of two contrasting positions: the fool and the wiseman – the wiseman and the madman. Together they form a single ternary structure: fool – wiseman – madman. In this construction, the fool and the madman are not synonyms; but antonyms, polar extremes.

The fool is deprived of the ability to react flexibly to surrounding circumstances. His behaviour is entirely predictable. The only form of activity accessible to him is the violation of proper relations between situation and action. His actions are stereotypical, but enacted out of place; he cries at weddings and dances at funerals. He is incapable of novel thought. As a result, his behaviour appears absurd but is nevertheless wholly predictable.

The "fool" is contrasted to the "wiseman", whose behaviour is defined as normal. The wiseman thinks according to custom, reason and experience. Thus, his behaviour is also predictable, is described as normative and corresponds to customary rules and regulations.

The third element of the system is the insane behaviour of the madman. The latter is characterised by the fact that its carrier benefits from additional freedom in his violation of the rules and is therefore able to achieve forms of behaviour forbidden to 'normal' people. This lends an unpredictable character to his actions. This latter quality, destructive insofar as it represents a continuously operating system of behaviour, may prove unexpectedly effective in moments of extreme conflict.

We reported that moments of extreme conflict in the behaviour of animals are tied to ritual and instinctive action. A unique characteristic of man is his ability to use his individual initiative, i.e. man has the ability to switch from those actions, gestures, and predictable behaviours deemed to be most effective into a completely new sphere of *unpredictable* activity. A participant in a battle, a competition or any conflicting situation, can abide 'by the rules' following traditional norms. In such a case victory will be achieved by the skilful application of the rules. A hero of this type, in order to remain always victorious, must be skilful in the most common type of activity but in hypertrophied form. This, then, requires a hero of tremendous stature and strength. The fantasy directs us towards the world of giants. Thus, the victory of a hero of this type, and more especially, his triumph over others is determined by his physical superiority.

However, the world of folklore knows of yet another situation: the victory of the weak (in the ideal – the child) over the strong.[1] This situation generates an entire cycle of histories of the triumph of the clever but weak hero over the strong but foolish giant.[2] The wiseman conquers by means of his resourcefulness, astuteness, craftiness and wiliness, in short, through his amorality.

Ulysses escapes from the hands of the Cyclops by means of an ingenious play on words and sheer wiliness. As the Cyclops is a giant, Ulysses, in his battle with him, is represented not as a hero with superhuman powers but rather as a weak, short, crafty fellow. The 'dwarf-like' stature of Ulysses and his warriors in this situation is foregrounded by the gigantic stature of, not only Cyclops, but also his sheep which allows the Greeks to flee from the cave attached to the underbellies of the animals (the blind and stupid giant counts the sheep by tapping their backs but it does not occur to him to feel their bellies). The wiseman is he who accomplishes unexpected, unpredictable actions in the face of the enemy. Intelligence is actualised as astuteness. The clever Puss in Boots in Perrault's tale deceives the foolish cannibal-magician by first suggesting he become a lion, and then a mouse, which he quickly and victoriously eats.

Unpredictable actions are effective because they dislodge the enemy from his usual situations. In the conflict with the stupid giant, who is capable only of stereotypical actions, the sly weakling resorts to the unexpected, creating a situation in which stereotypical behaviour is rendered senseless and ineffective. The same kind of situation is repeated in the collision between the 'normal person' and the madman. Whereas the 'fool' has less freedom than the normal person, the 'madman' has more. The madman's actions are unpredictable, a factor which places his normal opponent in a defenceless situation. This, in particular, in many cultures led to the use of madmen in conditions of war. The use of folly as an effective type of combat behaviour is well-known to a wide circle of peoples and is based on the general psychological rule of creating a situation in which the enemy loses its orientation.

Thus, for example, Scandinavian epics describe the *berserkers*. The *berserker* is a soldier who is constantly or at the moment of battle in a state of 'combat folly'. He participates in the battle either completely naked or dressed in animal skins – in any event, he feels no pain from his wounds. In the act of combat

---

1. The image of the child is dual. Folklore allows for situations where childhood is used as a means of representing a non-infantile strength or gigantic size. Such is the youth Heracles, such are the giant children of Rabelais.
2. This is also referred to in the ancient Russian saying of Daniil Zatotchnik, on the situation of the strong army, led by a fool: "a big beast, but no brain". *Pamyatniki literatury Drevnei Rusi: XII vek.* (Red.) Dmitrieva, L. A. and Likhacheva, M. 1980, p. 392).

he behaves like an animal discarding all limitations of human behaviour: he gnaws his own shield and throws himself at the enemy, violating all the rules of combat. The inclusion of such a soldier in the combat group sharply increases the combat efficiency of the entire force because it dislodges the enemy from its usual position. It is interesting to note that in such a case the comparison of man to animal is seen as a release from all prohibitions although, as we saw, the true conduct of the animal is governed by much greater prohibitions than those of man.

In the *Saga of Grettir* we come across a mélange characteristic of the epoch of the destruction of these ideas: faith in the fantastic folly of the *berserkers* has already broken down and the name now simply defines seafaring bandits. The following fable is rather characteristic: the astute and clever Grettir by wiliness conquers the foolish but strong *berserkers*, whose leaders are described thus: "They came from Halogaland and were *bigger and stronger than other people*. When angry they used to fall into the *berserk's fury*, and *nothing escaped that was before them*".[3] However, these so-called *berserkers (berserks)* traditionally presented as fantastical personages are here presented in the role of "stupid strongmen". This could be compared with the medieval German practice (one such example was set in Estland in the XVIII century) whereby man is 'transformed' into a wolf. This man-wolf, combining the behaviour of a predatory beast and robber-thief can become invincible, from the point of view of its enemies. Significantly, sources describe such behaviour as nocturne, sharply contrasting it with diurnal behaviour.

The hero of the Irish *Saga of Cú Chulainn* may also be compared to the *berserkers*. His appearance represents a complex contamination of the earliest archaic elements combined with traits generated by the concept of everyday folly. Cú Chulainn is endowed with mythological features but, characteristically, victory in the battle falls to a weaker hero, who is capable of utilising 'combat folly': "There were seven pupils in the royal eyes, four in one eye and three in the other. On each hand he had seven fingers and seven toes on each foot. He had many gifts: first of all – the gift of wisdom (until he fell into the fury of combat), further – the gift of gaming at table, the gift of counting, the gift of prophecy and prediction."[4]

---

3.  *The Saga of Grettir the Strong.* Trans. George Ainslie Hight. London/New York: Dent & Sons, Dutton & Co, 1929, p. 46. Chapter XIX. Berserks at Haramarsey (*italics* by J. Lotman).

4.  Author Unknown. *Táin Bó Cúalnge* from the *Book of Leinster* (Translator's note: the English translation here is my own). The cited text reads: "He had seven toes on each of his feet and seven fingers on each of his hands. He had seven pupils in each of his royal eyes and seven gems sparkling in each pupil (p. 171)", and "Now Cú Chulainn

The widespread use of alcohol during combat, in actual fact, creates the same effect of combat folly. It is significant that whilst alcoholic intoxication is not the norm for field troops it is, as a general rule, rife in the special forces. The author of these lines recalls the enormous psychological impact, at the beginning of World War II of a spectacle to which he was a witness. A division of German motorcyclists, heading directly for the dugout trenches of the enemy reproduced, perhaps unconsciously, the behaviour of the *berserkers*: the motorcycles were laden with passengers (four to each one), armed with sub-machine guns, completely naked, but wearing leather boots, their wide tops crammed with automatic magazines. The gunners were drunk and rushing directly at the enemy, shouting loudly and continuously shooting long bursts into the air. To complete the impression, it must be added that, for both the author of this memoir and his fellow soldiers, this was the first time any of them had seen a sub-machine gun.

Episodes of lunacy, of mad, insane behaviour – specifically mad, rather than foolish, i.e. possessing a particular superhuman intelligence and simultaneously requiring superhuman action – are widely encountered in the literature. So far as daily life is concerned, however, they appear as a kind of unattainable ideal. This unique fury is, in many cultures, linked to the ideal behaviour of the lover or the artist.

In chapter XXV of Part 1 of Cervantes' *Don Quixote*, there is a uniquely interesting episode: the imitation by Don Quixote of the amorous folly of the heroes of the chivalric novel. We refer to the words of Don Quixote: "... the famous Amadis de Gaul was one of the most complete knights-errant: I should not have said one of – he was the sole, the principal, the only one, in short the prince of all that were in his time in the world. [...] In this very manner was Amadis the polar, the morning star, and the sun of all valiant and enamoured knights, and he whom all we, who militate under the banners of love and chivalry, ought to follow. This being so, friend Sancho, the knight-errant who imitates him the most nearly, will, I take it, stand the fairest to arrive at the *perfection of chivalry* (italics mine – J. L). And one circumstance in which this knight most eminently discovered his prudence, worth, courage, patience, constancy, and love, was his retiring, when disdained by the lady Oriana, to do penance on Peña Pobre, changing his name to that of Beltenebros; a name most certainly significant, and proper for the life he had voluntarily chosen."

Sancho replies to Don Quixote's monologue to the effect that from a common sense point of view the behaviour of his hero is unjustified, since the knights were

---

possessed many and various gifts: the gift of beauty, the gift of form ... the gift of battle, the gift of fighting, the gift of conflict, the gift of sight, the gift of speech, the gift of counsel..." etc. (p. 152).

induced to folly by the trickery or the severity of their beloveds: "... but, pray, what cause has your worship to run mad? What lady has disdained you?" Don Quixote's answer transfers us from the domain of everyday logic into the sphere of the supra logic of amorous chivalric folly: "There lies the point," answered Don Quixote, "and in this consists the finesse of my affair: a knight-errant who runs mad upon a just occasion deserves no thanks; but to do so without reason is business, giving my lady to understand what I should perform in the wet, if I do this in the dry." These theoretical reasonings of Don Quixote are accompanied by foolish behaviour: "Then stripping off his breeches in all haste he remained naked from the waist downwards and covered only with the tail of his shirt: and presently, without more ado, he cut a couple of capers in the air, and a brace of tumbles, head down and heels up, exposing things that made Sancho turn Rosinante about, that he might not see them a second time; and fully satisfied him that he might safely swear his master was stark mad."[5]

The concept of folly, not in the medical sense but as a form of permissible, albeit strange behaviour, may be encountered in two opposing values. It is also connected with another concept – that of theatricality. Dividing the surrounding world into the natural (normal) and the madman, Leo Tolstoy saw a clear example of the latter in the theatre. The possibility of a theatrical space, in which people on stage do not see the people in the auditorium and artificially imitate everyday life, was, for Tolstoy, the visible embodiment of madness. In fact, the problem of the stage occupies a central position in the differentiation between "normal" and "folly".

The antithesis of theatrical and non-theatrical behaviour emerges as one of the possible interpretations of the contrast between "folly" and "normal". In this sense, it is essential to envision the possible use of the terms "theatrical" and "theatrical behaviour" in two opposite senses. What Michelle Perrot and Anne Martin-Fugier in the chapter "The Artists" (Les acteurs), which appeared in the IV volume of the *History of a Private Life* present to the reader, however, is not entirely a description of theatre. The discussion deals with the everyday behaviour of a normal family in French society. The cult of familiar things, the quotidian nature of family life, are described as a form of theatre. Particularly characteristic is M. Perrot's chapter entitled "Actors and Roles" (*Figures et roles*) which reproduces the ritual of familial performance.

In this way, the norms of life are lived out as theatre. This implies that the narrator himself must live the usual as strange, in order to establish his point of view as being somewhere beyond the limits of the normative forms of life, a

---

5. Miguel de Cervantes Saavedra. *Don Quixote de la Mancha*. Trans. Charles Jarvis. Oxford: Oxford University Press, 1999, pp. 231–233, 245.

situation similar to that of the description of native language which, naturally, demands the alienated position as already outlined by the formalists. The natural must be represented as strange, the known as unknown. Only in this sense can it be considered as theatre.[6]

The cases, which we will now consider, have quite another character. Here, the sphere of art – and, more generally, any semiotically significant sphere – will be experienced as something opposed to nature. Life and theatre, from this point of view, are presented as antipodes and it is precisely this opposition that gives meaning and semiotic value to their combination.[7]

An interesting example is the theatrical life of Nero. Considering himself as a genial, professional actor and stepping out onto the stage the emperor simultaneously theatralises life beyond the limits of the stage precisely because it is life and not theatre and because it is this theatrical transformation that gives it meaning.

Suetonius writes thus on the operatic appearances of Nero: "And he did actually appear in operatic tragedies taking the parts of heroes and gods, sometimes even of heroines and goddesses, wearing masks either modelled on his own face or the face of whatever woman happened to be his current mistress".[8] Here, interestingly, two opposing tendencies are combined in a unity which reveals the essence of theatre. The actor of antiquity, in order to separate himself from his natural, extra-theatrical appearance uses a mask. Nero, however, has given to the mask features which portray similarities to himself. Thus, if the mask of the actor appears to erase his extra-theatrical personality then, here, to the contrary

---

6. Parallel processes are characteristic of the aesthetics of the theatre: the strange life is a worthy object for art, precisely because it is strange; in order to become an objet d'art its familiar life must become unknown. In other words, what is near must become distant.

7. The behaviour of the amorous knight represents a special case in the relationship between the theatrical and non-theatrical. Here, the relationship of rule and excess acquires a specific nature. The rules of chivalric love are formulated in special treatises, such as that by canon André, and also in the lyric poetry of the troubadours (see: Moshu Lazar. *Amour courtois et jeux amors dans la littérature du XII siècle*. Paris, 1964). However, these rules are not calculated to produce the possibility of practical behaviour and in and of themselves represent heroic excess. It is possible to pursue these rules but it is not possible to achieve them, and their realisation is always a kind of miracle. Thus, the chivalric exploit can be described both as a realisation of the rules (from the point of view of the researcher), as a heroic miracle from the point of view of the external observer and as the unique combination of merit and its highest reward by the knight himself.

8. Gaius Suetonius Tranquillus. *The Twelve Caesars*. Trans. Robert Graves. London: The Folio Society, 1991, p. 221.

it stands out. But in order for the face of Nero to become a part of the play it must first be destroyed and then restored, i.e. it must be substituted by its own mask.

A more refined artistry is apparent in the changing of the sexes. Of course, in the action of Nero, the latter acquires a perverse character, delineating as it were the unlimited nature of his destructive sensuality and overturning all natural limits to which the sexes are subordinated. At the same time, however, the power of the theatre to reduce sexual difference to a matter of makeup cannot be ignored. We recall, for example, that in Shakespearean theatre all female roles were played by men and that the transfiguration of the sexes is one of the most ancient and universal theatrical procedures.

The episode related by Suetonius is no more than anecdote and is interesting purely in its repetition. It originates in an anecdote of antiquity which tells of a competition between painters in which Apelles took part and runs all the way through to the anecdotal reaction of an American soldier to *Othello*. The anecdote of antiquity recounts the tale of how the fruits on one canvas were so realistically painted that birds dropped by to eat them. However, a second canvas surpassed the first: the artist painted a cloth covering a painting, fooling even his competitors who demanded that he remove the cloth and show them the painting. At the other extreme is the story of an American guard who was on duty at the theatre close to the seat of the governor. The soldier shot Othello, shouting: "No one will say that a black man killed a white woman in my presence!"

The anecdote related by Suetonius is built on the same principles: the mélange of theatre and life. The constant switching between the role of emperor to the role of actor and vice versa becomes normal behaviour for Nero: "No one was allowed to leave the theatre during his recitals, however pressing the reason, and the gates were kept barred. We read of women in the audience giving birth, and of men being so bored with the music and the applause that they furtively dropped down from the wall at the rear or shammed dead and were carried away." There is a significant mixing here of semantic modes: the emperor on the stage adopts the role of an actor; the actor adopts the dramatic role of the emperor and the spectators wishing to leave the auditorium adopt the role of corpses. The dual role of the emperor and the actor reveals itself in the fact that in the theatrical production "Nero insisted on announcing his own victories" and, redoubling the effect, "set up several statues of himself playing the lyre". This is a significant transformation: if the theatrical appearance is considered as human weakness, then the statue is meant to reaffirm his position as emperor. Nero, however, uses the transformation: the statue recalls his position as an actor and that he is deified as a man of art, not as the head of Rome.

Nero's passion for masquerade manifests itself also off-stage. By night and in disguise he frequented places of ill repute and, preparing for battle, arranged for his concubines "to have male haircuts and be issued with Amazonian shields and axes." The constant blending of theatre and the reality of daily life, the consideration of life off-stage as a spectacle became the basis for the famous episode of the burning of Rome: "Nero watched the conflagration from the Tower of Maecenas, enraptured by what he called 'the beauty of the flames'; then put on his tragedian's costume and sang *The Fall of Ilium* from beginning to end."

This entire theatre of life is consummated in his last words: "Dead! And so great an artist!"[9]

For Suetonius, the constant blending of theatre and life was a perverse situation, which turned the whole of life into a spectacle. This, in turn, is only one part of the abolition of all oppositions: the actor and the spectator, the emperor and the comedian, the Roman and the Greek and, even, between man and woman; i.e. that it is possible to fulfil any role whilst simultaneously assuming the power function which these roles are designed to generate. Nero's goal is, on the one hand, to exhaust all possible variants, and on the other, to go beyond the limits of the possible, to realise the impossible. We find a similar complex later in Ivan the Terrible.

In beginning our discussion on "the theatre of everyday behaviour", we have set the French concept of the theatricality of the highly formalised and repetitive everyday gesture and act against the unpredictable excesses of behaviour which interest us. Despite the apparent opposition between these two poles, they are not lacking in reciprocity. A unique and extravagant act, through repetition, may pass from the sphere of "explosion" into the sphere of the habitual. No sooner is the action accomplished than it may become the object of imitation.

Thus, Brummell's innovative concepts in the field of male fashion were rapidly accepted by those who favoured dandyism and thus became a fact of mass culture. In the above-mentioned extract, Cervantes showed how folly passes into the sphere of imitation and is thus converted into an element of mass culture.

The norm has no distinctive features. It is a singular space located between the fool and the madman. Explosion, too, has no distinctive features, or to be more exact, possesses a whole range of possible features. In the case of individual behaviour, it distances itself from the norm and in such a case represents itself as folly; translated into mass culture, it becomes a form of stupidity.

From the aforesaid, it becomes clear that any form of folly must inevitably result in an excess in individual behaviour and place itself beyond the limits of the predictable.

---

9. Gaius Suetonius Tranquillus. *The Twelve Caesars*. Trans. Robert Graves. London: The Folio Society, 1991, pp. 222–223, 232, 236, 239.

Thus, for example, the hero of the Byzantine epic Digenis (in Russian – *Devgeny*) completes a series of acts, which from an everyday point of view (from the position of conventional behaviour) may be regarded as strange or foolish, but which from an internalised position appear as the realisation of the chivalric pursuit of perfection. The folkloric theme of the "dangerous" bride-to-be whose hand has already cost the lives of many suitors is here reinterpreted in the spirit of chivalry. The hero, Devgeny, having learned of the existence of an inaccessible beauty whose many suitors had been killed by her bloodthirsty father and brothers, immediately falls in love with the maiden. Then, as common sense dictates, luck smiles upon him: he arrives at the palace, around which lie the cadavers of his predecessors, and in the absence of the maiden's dangerous relatives, he succeeds in seducing her and marries her unhindered. Everything that follows is "logical" from the point of view of Don Quixote and "absurd" in the opinion of Sancho Panza: the success so easily won by Devgeny doesn't please him but, instead and in a manner inexplicable to the contemporary reader, plunges him into despair. He strives to enter into the already futile battle with the father and brothers of Stratigovna. And so we find ourselves confronted with a significant transformation of the theme: "battle/victory/conquest of the bride" is substituted by "conquest of the bride/battle/victory". All logical reasons for the battle have been eliminated, but from the chivalric point of view, logical reasons are not necessary in order to do battle. The battle is a self-sufficient act: it does not influence the fate of the hero but rather demonstrates that the hero is worthy of his fate. Devgeny "... began to shout in a loud, clear voice, calling upon Stratig and his strong sons to come out and see the seizure of their sister. The servants began to call Stratig, recounting to him the insolence of Devgeny, standing without fear in the courtyard and calling upon Stratig" But Stratig refused to take up the call, "not believing" that an intrepid suitor had won his daughter's hand. The refusal of Stratig's relatives to do battle plunges Devgeny into a level of desperation incomprehensible to us: "It is the greatest of shames that cover me if I am not pursued; I want to return and dishonour them".[10] There then follows a complex system of rituals, senseless from the point of view of common sense, but full of deep significance in the chivalric value system. Here, the excess lies not in the actions of the Stratig, but in the superhuman application of the chivalric ritual actualised by Devgeny.

The sense of such texts differs in principle from the customary ideas of the contemporary reader. They do not represent events as such, but rather an

---

10. Kuz'mina, V. D. *Devgenievo Deyanie (Deyanie prezhnikh vremen khrabrykh che-lovek)* [The Exploit of Devgeny]. Moscow, 1962, p. 149. (Translator's note: English translation my own.)

ideal behaviour towards which a real person may only strive. This is why the same thorough and meticulous application of the ritual of the heroic deed and the match-making ritual as is made by Devgeny appears as parody when Don Quixote, in Cervantes, attempts to carry this out in everyday life. Having conquered the father-in-law and the brothers-in-law who wanted to take his wife away, Devgeny does not solve a difficult task, but rather places himself in an even more complex situation: without a victory, he risked losing his wife, but achieving the victory, his wife, now the daughter and sister of prisoners, is dishonoured in defeat and ceases to be socially equal to her husband. Thus the marriage is yet again impossible for yet another reason. Devgeny liberates the captive relatives and once again assumes the ideal chivalric behaviour: returning to them, he declares himself their vassal and once more asks for the hand of his wife, solemnly obtaining the agreement of her relatives and is finally able to celebrate a fully validated feudal wedding.

Here we encounter a characteristic situation: the inimitable heroic act is realised not through romantic lawlessness, but through the fulfilment of the most refined and impracticably ideal standards, impossible for the ordinary man. This determines, in particular, the absolutely specific relations between literature (the heroic epic, ballad, chivalric novel) and reality. Literature assigns the unprecedented and fantastical standards of heroic behaviour and heroes attempt to realise them in real life. Literature does not reproduce life, but rather it is life that attempts to recreate literature.

From this point of view, the hero of *The Song of Igor's Campaign* typifies the chivalric genre. After the futile attempt of the coalition army of the Russian princes to conquer the Polovtsians on the Dnieper and so achieve the difficult but very real task of restoring links to the sea, Igor plunged into a battle with an unrealistic but immensely heroic goal: to open a route through the Polovtsian steppe and to restore the ancient but long since lost links with T'mutarakan. The grand plan, conceived in Kiev under the direction of the Grand Prince of Kiev, rested on the collective action of the Kievan princes. As is well-known, Igor didn't participate in this campaign and, insofar as the inhabitants of Rus were well-acquainted with his longstanding relationships – first warlike, then friendly – with the Polovtsians, his participation in the coalition army could have been interpreted as being an offence to his honour. The personal motivations of the chivalric knight – the desire to retain his honour at all costs – led Igor to attempt to realise his fantastical and heroic plan.

The author's duplicity with respect to the behaviour of Prince Igor is characteristic. As a man who remains immersed in the code of chivalric honour, he admires the fact that the heroic plan is a hopeless one – the fact that realistic and practical considerations are rejected in the face of chivalric impulse – but at the same time, he is also a man who remains outside of the stringent ethics of chivalry. The chronicler, describing the same events, contrasts the heroic individualism of the chivalric knight with the religious collectivism of Christianity. Christianity, for him, signals the beginning of a public voice above and beyond that of chivalry. The *Song of Igor's Campaign* is devoid of Christian motivations and is completely immersed in the ethics of chivalry. Igor is here condemned as a rebellious vassal whose heroic egotism violated the will of his sovereign prince, the Grand Prince of Kiev. The sovereign prince is by divine decree the highest authority and the head of the Russian lands. Thus, Igor reflects a double system of ethics: as feudal lord, he is imbued with bravery which leads him to folly whilst, as vassal, his actions represent heroic insubordination. The incompatibility of these two ethical principles only serves to accentuate their value.[11]

Medieval ethics are simultaneously dogmatic and individualistic – the latter insofar as any man must seek the unattainable ideal in all spheres of his activity. That specific feature of medieval behaviour – maximalism – is linked to this notion. That which is the norm has no value. Value may be assigned to the same action, but only where it is perfected on an unprecedented scale or produced under incredibly difficult conditions, such that its accomplishment is practically impossible.

Medieval cultural texts possess a high level of semiotic saturation. However, in this case, the relationship between the text which establishes the norm and the text that violates it (the "folly") is constructed in a manner quite different to that of the romantic structure familiar to the contemporary reader. In the latter, "the rule" and "the folly" are polar opposites and the journey into the space of folly automatically signifies the violation of all rules.

With medieval consciousness, we become witnesses to a completely different structure: the ideal, the highest degree of value (holiness, heroism, criminality, love) can only be achieved whilst in a state of folly. In this way, only those who are mad can implement the highest rules. Rules appear not as a phenomenon of mass behaviour, but only as the inherent nature of the exceptional hero in an exceptional situation. Thus, if, in the romantic consciousness, rules are represented as banal and easily accessible, then in the medieval consciousness they are the unattainable goals of an exceptional personality. In the same way, so the creator of the rules changes. For the romantic, this is the crowd. The transformation of

---

11. See the indepth analysis of chivalric tradition in *Slovo o polku Igoreve* (*The Song of Igor's Campaign*) by I. P. Eremin (Eremin, I. P. *Povest' vremennykh let*. Leningrad, 1944).

the word "banal" to its age-old meaning "customary" is notable here.[12] For the medieval consciousness, the norm, i.e. that which is inaccessible, is the only ideal point towards which motivation may be directed. This, in particular, determines the ambiguity of medieval texts, which set down the norms of behaviour, and, consequently, the possibility for their dual interpretation.

The researcher who constructs his work around a variety of normative texts (especially if he seeks to find forms of real behaviour in works of art, even if he then makes corresponding corrections based on juridical documents) is inclined to believe that the real behaviour of everyday life was fulfilled precisely according to similar rules.

However, these same texts should be considered from another point of view – it is possible to see in them the ideal, which may be approached but which can never be reached. On this, amongst other things, rests the enigma of all the agonising failures of Don Quixote. He takes the ideal as the norm. That which must be admired is that which, in the best of cases, must be aspired to (or to which one pretends to aspire), and he uses this as the norm for everyday behaviour. Therein lies the source of his tragicomical failure.[13]

Thus, from one and the same text, we may ascertain the boundaries between everyday reality and the ideal reality of the population of the epoch. The picture is further complicated by the fact that medieval life is a ladder of many rungs and, between the ideal realisation of the rules (the lot of the hero) and the equally ideal total destruction of them (the role of the devil), an extended ladder exists which, more than anything else, approaches the reality that is real life.

Real texts rarely manifest theoretical models in pure form: as a rule, we are presented with dynamic, transitional, fluid forms, which do not fully realise

---

12. "Banal" in Fasmer's dictionary – ancient, age-old, previous, usual (see Fasmer, M. *Etimologicheskii slovar' russkogo yazyka v 4 t.*, Moscow, 1987, T. 3, s. 349). According to Sreznevsky – ancient, age-old, belonging to antiquity, previous, usual (see Sreznevskii, I. I. *Materialy dlya slovarya drevnerusskogo yazyka po pis'mennym pamyatnikam* v 3 t. Saint Petersburg, 1895, T 2. Stb. 1335–1336). The definition of "banal" (poshlyi) as "usual, accepted" was maintained in the word "(monetary) duty" (poshlina). From the same point of view, Ivan the Terrible referred to the English queen as a "banal girl", i.e. in the sense that she was a usual, simple woman (see *Poslaniya Ivana Groznogo* / red. D. S. Likhachev and Y. S. Lurye. Moskva/Leningrad, 1951, p. 216).

13. An interesting parallel may be drawn here with the path of Soviet literature which later became known as "varnishing reality". Authors such as Babaevsky or Pyryev in "Kubansky Cossacks" did not, in principle, check their art against reality, and the Soviet critique of this type argued, in the vein of medieval theses, that authentic 'reality' is not that which exists, but rather that which should exist.

these ideal constructions, but rather are in some way or another organised by them. Similar models relative to these texts are dispersed on another level (they are realised either as a tendency, such as a cultural code which is visible but not yet formulated, or as a metatext: rules, instructions, legalised or theoretical treaties, of which there was an abundance in the Middle Ages).

The analysis of these materials is enough to convince us of the fact that, in terms of that aspect which interests us, Russian texts of the early Middle Ages followed a strict system and that this system, in its basic features, is the same as those of analogous social structures in other cultural cycles.

First of all, it should be noted that the early Middle Ages knew not one, but two models of the *glory*: that of the Christian-ecclesiastic and that of the feudal-chivalric. The former rested on a strict distinction between terrestrial and celestial glory. Here, relevance was not attached to the opposition: "glory/ignominy" ("notoriety/obscurity", "praise/denigration"), but "eternity/ perishability". Terrestrial glory – is instantaneous. Thomas Aquinas stated that: "he is not truly virtuous who does virtuous deeds for the sake of human glory,"[14] whilst Saint Isidor asserted that: "no one can simultaneously fulfil the glory of god and the glory of his century."[15] Raymond Lully also considered that true honour belongs singularly to God.[16] We find analogous assertions in Russian texts. Such, for example, is the assertion of Vladimir Monomakh: "Who are we, sinful and foul people? Living today and dead in the morning, today bathed in honour and glory, tomorrow buried and forgotten; and others will reap what we have sown."[17] This point of view is interesting not only in and of itself, but because it exerted a strong influence, especially in Russia, on those strictly chivalric texts, creating such creolised, internally contradictory works as *The Life of Alexander Nevsky*, and strongly influencing the monk-chronicler conception of honour and glory.

In the secular literature, e.g. the chivalresque and those texts circulating in the princely troops (*druzhina*[18]), the semiotic nature of honour and glory is developed in considerably greater detail. Western material on this question has been assembled in the monograph of the Argentinian researcher, Maria Rosa Lida de Malkiel *The Notion of Glory in the Western Tradition. Antiquity, the*

---

14. *Summa Theologica. Secunda secundae, quaestio.* CXXXII, art. 1.
15. Migne, J. P. *Patrologia Latina.* LXXX: Livre II, §42.
16. Lull, R. Oeuvres: T I – IV. Ed. J. Rosselo. Palma de Majorque, 1903, vol. 4, p. 3.
17. *Pamyatniki literatury Drevnei Rusi. Nachalo russkoi literatury: XI – nachalo XII veka*, p. 410. (Translators' note: English translation my own.)
18. *Druzhina* – the Prince's armed force in medieval Russia.

*Western Middle Ages, Castille.*[19] From the data she supplies, it is obvious that in the classical model of western chivalry a strict distinction is made between the sign of knightly merit, which was connected to its material expression, i.e. by a material reward, and that of the verbal sign, i.e. by praise. The first, invariably, is constructed so as to reflect a correlation between the size of reward and the value of the merit. This is also emphasized in the dictionary of A. Greimas.[20] The concept of the reward as a signifying material, whose significance is the merit of the knight, penetrates numerous texts. Although *honneur* and *gloire* are constantly used as a pair as a dyadic formula,[21] their meanings are deeply variable. These differences, in the final analysis, may be reduced to the opposition of the thing in its signifying function and the word, which also performs the role of the social sign. The closest system to that used in the early Russian Middle Ages may be found in *The Poem of the Cid.* "Honour" here is invariably taken to mean: booty, a reward, a sign, whose value is determined by the value of its plan of expression, as the latter is captured by its non-signifying function. For this very reason Cid can exclaim:

> Let them know
> in what richness I send off my sons-in-law, let them
> know in Galicia, in Castille, and in Leon
> (The Third Cantar, 124).[22]

---

19. The book was published in Spanish in Mexico in 1952. Here we have used the French translation. (see: Malkiel, M. R. L. de. *L'idée de la gloire dans la tradition occidentale. Antiquité, moyen âge occidental, Castille.* Paris: Libr. C. Klincksieck. 1958).
20. The words: onor, enor, anor are given the following values: "I. Honneur dans lequel quelqu'un est tenu; (the esteem with which someone is held) 2. Avantages matériels qui en résultent ... (material benefits which result from it) 4. Fief, bénéfice féodal ... (fiefdom or feudal benefit) 5. Bien, richesse en général ... (Wealth, riches in general) 8. Marques, attributs de la dignite (signs, attributed to dignity)" (*Dictionnaire de l'ancien français jusqu'au milieu du XIVe siècle*, par A. Greimas. Paris: Larousse, 1969, p. 454).
21. The troubadour, Giraut de Bornelh, mourning the death of Richard the Lionheart speaks of his "glory and honour" (see: Bornelh, G de. *Somtliche Lieder des trobadors Giraut de Bornelh*, mit Ubersetzung. Komentar und Glossar/Ed. Kolsen. Halle. Bd. 1. 1910. p. 466). The same formula is taken up by the medieval poet Gonzalo de Berceo: "That his honour and glory may grow" (cited in: Malkiel, M. R. L. De. Op. Cit. p. 128). In the medieval Spanish epic text: "*Libro de Alexandre*" we read:
    There is neither honour nor glory for a worthy man
    Who seeks adventure in impious places. (ibid., p. 179)
    The examples are many.
22. *Poem of the Cid.* Trans. Paul Blackburn. University of Oklahoma Press, 1998, p. 123.

However "honour" is not only a sign of merit: it is a sign and a specific social relation:

> Honour is, essentially, linked to social relations (*données sociales*) and is, there-
> fore, subordinate to an entire juridical system, whose rules are thoroughly fixed
> and for a judgment about the finesse of their functioning, few documents are as
> meaningful as the Song [of El Cid]. Specifically, the king as the source of honour
> takes this gift away from the hero. And then the hero himself, thanks only to his
> loyalty, his exploits and his strong will, is able to restore his lost honour.[23]

The researcher emphasises the specific combination of the poetry of faithfulness and service on the one part, and notions of extreme individualism, wilfulness and independent nature, on the other, which makes the chivalric concept of honour so difficult to translate into the language of subsequent political terminologies.

The link between honour and vassal relations is also outlined distinctly in Russian sources. Significantly, *honour* always *gives*, *takes*, *renders*, *lends*. This micro-context is never applied to *glory*. Honour is invariably connected to the act of exchange, which requires a material sign, and some kind of reciprocity in social relations, which afford the right of respect and social value.

However, the analysis of the concept of honour and its verbal derivatives in the texts of Kievan times require that we keep in mind one special feature: *honour is always included in the contexts of exchange*. It is possible to give, to render and to accept. The accepted synonymy of the seemingly oppositional verbs "to give" and "to take" is explained by the ambivalence of the action itself in the system of early feudal-vassal relations. The act of giving was simultaneously a sign of entry into the vassal system and of adoption by it. In this way, the future vassal, entering into what was, for him, a new dependency, had to bring himself, and his land as a gift to the feudal patron, in order to immediately receive them back (frequently with additions), but now in the form of a feudal reward. Thus, the gift is converted into a sign, which is exchanged, and thus strengthened by specific social agreements. With this ambivalence of giving-receiving, when each recipient is at one and the same time also the donor, the link is made between honour which is given from low to high and is simultaneously made from high to low. In this way, the notion that the source of honour, just as with wealth, comes to the subordinates from the feudal lord is invariably emphasised.[24]

---

23. Malkiel, M. R. L. de. *Op. cit.* pp. 121–122. (Translator's note: English translation my own.)
24. And in the second case this concept has a specifically feudal-vassal conventional character: the prince is the source of wealth, insofar as he delivers to each of his guards their allotted portion. But the guard seizes booty in combat. He returns this to the prince and receives it back already as favour and reward. It is significant, that the

Further, we may also meet with cases, where *honour* is rendered by equal to equal. However, in such a case, we are already confronted with the rite of courtesy, the formal ritual, indicating a conditional entry into service, which, however, has no more real meaning than was usual at the end of 19th century letters, which concluded with the formula: "I remain, Your Excellency, your most obedient servant".

"Glory" – is also a sign, but it is a verbal sign and therefore functions by fundamentally different means. It is neither transferred nor received but rather "reaches to the remotest languages" and to the furthest posterity. Aural signs are always attributed to 'glory': glory is "announced", "heard". False glory perishes "with noise". Furthermore, glory shows signs of collective *memory*. Hierarchically, glory occupies a higher place when compared to honour.

Honour is accompanied by established precepts, which correspond to the place of the man endowed with honour in the hierarchical spectrum. In the medieval Castilian epic *The Book of Apollonius*, the king turns to an unknown knight who arrives during the feast:

*Friend, choose your place,*
*You know, which place is yours,*
*And which, according to courtesy, belongs to you,*
*Lest we, without knowing, who you are, may be mistaken.*[25]

The measure of honour exerted is, here, more important than the personal name. The latter may be hidden but the former must be known otherwise social contact is rendered quite impossible (religious texts are a different matter, see, for example, *The Life of Aleksei, A Man of God*, which is constructed around the fact that the hero consciously lowers his social status). Glory is measured not by value but by longevity. Glory in its most basic sense means praise. In contrast to honour, glory does not entertain a direct correlation between expression and content. If honour is linked to the notion that a larger expression denotes larger content, then glory as a verbal sign sees this connection as conventional: the *instantaneous* human word denotes *immortal* glory. Insofar as medieval man was inclined to consider *all* signs as iconic, he attempts to remove this contradiction, linking glory not to the usual word, but to a singularly authoritative word. In this way, the Godly word, the word as it is recorded "in the charters" enshrined

---

rupture of vassal relations takes shape in the form of the return honour. A. Greimas gives the following text: "Rendre son hommage et son fief, Se dégager des obligations de vassalité" (ibid., p. 453; to return its honour and its fief – to be freed from the responsibilities of the vassal).

25. *Libro de Apolonio* / Ed. Ñ. Caroll Marden. Paris, 1917, p. 158. (Translator's note: English translation my own.)

in the "Psalms" or the word of "remote languages" is able to emerge. And in this way we find an absolute parallelism between the terminology of both the Russian and the western early Middle Ages.[26]

In principle, glory is attached to the highest rungs of the feudal hierarchy. However, an exception is also possible: the soldier, who conquers glory at the cost of his life, seemingly equates himself with the highest rung. He becomes the *equal of all*. And, as we recall from *The Anthology of 1076*, glory is given to *the equals*.[27]

This system, distinguishing between honour and glory, is consecutively maintained in the oldest texts of the Kievan period: the *Anthology of 1076* (*Izbornik 1076 g.*), *The Acts of Devgeni* (*Devgenievy Deyaniya*), *Judaic War* (*Iudeiskaya Voina*), and, in part, in the *The Tale of By-Gone Years* or Nestor's Chronicle (*Povest' vremmenykh let*) (in combination with the ecclesiastical treatment of the term) and an array of other texts. The *Judaic War* is especially significant in this respect, an observation made, even long ago, by Barsov. N. K. Gudzii wrote: "... the terminology and phraseology, which characterize the ideological and everyday way of life in princely (*druzhinnaya*) Russia ..." are reflected in the Russian translation of Flavius's books, as used "in the contemporary translation of original Russian works, especially chronicles. Such understandings of honour, of glory, are substituted for other concepts in the Greek text – happiness, abundant hospitality, reward".[28] A detailed analysis of the translation of concepts from the original Greek into a different system, specifically a feudal system, is given by N. A. Meshchersky. Let us only take note of the fact that when the translator of *Judaic War* translates the Greek word εὐφημια (happiness) as "honour" ("And we met the Sepphorians with honour and praise"[29]), he is not simply reinterpreting Greek terminology, but also does so whilst exhibiting a striking knowledge of the fundamental concepts of Romanic chivalry. Let us recall that such an interpretation of εὐφημια corresponds completely, for example, with the synonym of "honour" *joi* from the *The Song of El Cid*. The dictionary of medieval French also fixes *joieler* as meaning "to bring gifts".[30] If we recall that "praise" here is the indisputable synonym of "glory" (old French. *laude*) then we also see here as essential for Russian feudalism and, generally,

26. See: Malkiel, M. R. L. de. Op. cit., p. 121–128.

27. See: *Izbornik 1076 g.* edited by V. S. Golyshenko, V. F. Dubrovina, V. G. Demyanova, G. F. Nefedova. Moscow, 1965, p. 243.

28. *Istoriya russkoi literatury*: v 10 T. Moskva/Leningrad, 1941. T. 1: Literatura XI veka – nachala XIII veka. p. 148.

29. Meshcherskii, N. A. *Istoriya "Iudeiskoi voiny"*. Moskva/Leningrad 1958. c. 80.

30. See: *Dictionnaire de l'ancien français jusqu'au milieu du XIV siècle*, par A. Greimas, p. 347.

for a number of countries in the early Middle Ages the formula for "honour and glory". It would seem simultaneously appropriate to focus attention on the specificity of term "veseliye" (merry, jolly, gaiety) in the *The Song of Igor's Campaign*: "and already we, [your] Guards, hanker after mirth".[31] In this case the term is, most probably, used as a synonym for "honour-reward" (let us recall that in Greimas' dictionary the term *joiete* in the French chivalric texts of the XIII century is defined as *usufruit*, a juridical term, designating the transfer of the use of another's property, which for the knight was always reward-honour). It is not by chance, apparently, that such expressions as "merriment has drooped", or "a cheerless tide has set in" in the *Song* are invariably accompanied by indications of the material nature of the loss "as to gold and silver, none at all shall we touch!" the pagans "took tribute of one vair from every homestead".[32] Then the formula: "despondent are the voices", "merriment has drooped"[33] can be considered as a negative transformation of the combination "glory and honour": the "voice" is a synonym of "praise", and of "song" (singing as glorification figures in the *Tale*, and in the translator's note in the *Judaic War* and in a number of other texts) as a *reverberating* (aural) sign of merit, whilst *"veseliye"* (joy) is a material sign, an honour.

Thus, the dyadic nature of the formula "honour and glory" does not remove the sharply specific terminology of each of its components, especially those relating to the chivalric context and *druzhina*. In the ecclesiastical texts, where the author assigns to the character, deity or saint the full possible weight of merit and value "glory and honour" are used as indissoluble elements of the same formula. It is particularly in these texts that their specific meanings related to the *druzhina* begin to be erased. And, with the propagation of ecclesiastic ideology the combination begins to be viewed as tautological.

\* \* \*

In this chapter we used both documentary data, reflecting everyday reality, and literary works, which are the ideal models of this reality. The laws relating to these two ways of representing life are different, but at the same time their connection, especially in the medieval epoch, cannot be emphasised enough. The man of ancient times is inclined to banish the notion of chance from the world. The latter represents, for him, the result of a certain order which is unknown to him, more mysterious but also more powerful. From this is derived the entire and

---

31. *The Song of Igor's Campaign. An Epic of the 12th Century.* Trans. V. Nabokov. New York: Vintage Books, 1960, p. 51.
32. Ibid., p. 46.
33. Ibid., p. 60.

extensive practice of divination through which that which is random is raised to the level of something which may be predicted. From this point of view an episode of the 23rd song of the *Iliad* (The burial of Patroclus. Games) is worth noting.

The discussion deals with the funeral festivities in honour of the burial of Patroclus. In the sporting competitions, established at the burial, Ulysses and Ajax competed for speed in the race:

> ... and, Ajax, son of Oileus
> took the lead at once,
> with Ulysses as
> close behind him ...

Ajax was all set to win the competition, although ...

> ... Ulysses after Ajax so closely ran;
> treading in his footprints
> before the dust could settle there ... [34]

Homer further develops the content of the tale on two levels: Ajax randomly slips in fresh bull manure and falls on his face. This allowed Ulysses to pass his rival and obtain his first reward. The episode may be understood as a classical illustration of the intervention of the unpredictable in the course of events. However, the poet gives another parallel explanation:

> ... the hero Ulysses prayed inwardly
> to the goddess Pallas Minerva:
> "Hear me," he cried, "and help my feet, O goddess."
> Thus did he pray, and Pallas Minerva heard his prayer.[35]

This dual interpretation provides two equally plausible explanations as: without the aid of Athena, Ulysses would not have won, but he also would not have won without the puddle of bull manure. In this way, the path of causality is opened and at the same time sees in each chance opportunity the direct intervention of the gods.

Homer reaches the synthesis of the idea(s) of godly authority and the unpredictability of events (their informational value) by incorporating the whole chain of the determining factors into the each event: his gods are constantly struggling, and if the outcome of the struggle of the people is explained as the will of the gods, then the outcome of the struggle of gods remains unpredictable; the collision between fate and human will carries the same character and rep-

---

34. Homer. *The Iliad*. Trans. Samuel Butler. Book XXIII.
35. Ibid.

resents a conflict, solved in different ways, yet always disturbing for the Greek authors.

Unpredictable events and their consequences invade the world. These events give impetus to a wide number of further processes. The moment of explosion, as we have already mentioned is, as it were, excluded from time and from it the way is paved towards a new stage of gradual motion, which is marked by its return to the temporal axis. However, the explosion generates a whole chain of other events. The first result of the moment of explosion is the appearance of an entire collection of equally probable consequences. From these it is possible to realise and convert to historical fact just one of them. The selection of that which will become part of historical reality may be defined as random or as the result of the intervention of different regularities, external to the given system and lying beyond its border. That is to say, whilst, from any given perspective, the selection may appear wholly predictable, within the framework of a given structure it represents a chance occurrence. Thus, the realisation of this potential may be described as the non-realisation of a whole range of other possibilities.

This was very sharply delineated by Pushkin, who put into the mouth of Tatyana the words:

"And happiness was ours ... so nearly!
It came so close! ..."[36]

Even more significant (and unique in the history of the novel) are the reflections of the author on the lost future of the dead Lensky:

It may be he was born to fire
The world with good, or earn at least
A glorified name; his silenced lyre
Might well have raised, before it ceased,
A call to ring throughout the ages.
Perhaps, upon the world's great stages,
He might have scaled a lofty height.
His martyred shade, condemned to night,
Perhaps has carried off forever
Some sacred truth, a living word,
Now doomed by death to pass unheard;

---

36. It is characteristic that fate here is interpreted as the result of a random careless act and, therefore, for Pushkin, as an unpredictable event:

   ... But now my fate
   Has been decreed. I may have merely
   Been foolish when I failed to wait ...

(Alexander Pushkin. *Eugene Onegin*. Trans. James E. Falen. Carbondale and Edwardsville: Southern Illinois University Press, 1990, p. 220).

And in the tomb his shade shall never
Receive our race's hymns of praise,
Nor hear the ages bless his days.[37]

In Pushkin's original manuscript, verse XXXVIII continued with an additional stanza omitted in the printed text:

Having filled his life with poison
Having made little much of good
Alas! He could have filled the daily papers
With an immortal glory!
[…]

He could have made a terrible journey
Somewhere to take his final breath
Whilst contemplating his successes
Like Kutuzov or Nelson
Or exiled, like Napoleon
Or even hung, like Ryleev.[38]

Or maybe he was merely fated
To live amid the common tide;
And as his years of youth abated,
The flame within him would have died.

In this version the fate of Lensky:

And in the country he'd have worn
A quilted gown and cuckold's horn,
And happy, he'd have learned life truly;
At forty he'd have had the gout,
Have eaten, drunk, grown bored and stout.[39]

The way of both the individual and of humanity is paved with unrealised opportunities and lost byways. The Hegelian consciousness, which lies almost imperceptibly at the very root of our thoughts, has inculcated in us a piety towards factual reality and engenders a contemptuous relationship towards unactualised potentiality which did not make it to the realm of reality. The Hegelian tradition slights reflections about these lost pathways, treating them as romanticism and counting them amongst those relegated to the path of vain dreams like those, to

37. Alexander Pushkin. *Eugene Onegin*. Trans. James E. Falen. Carbondale and Edwardsville: Southern Illinois University Press, 1990, p. 160.
38. A. Pushkin. Evgenii Onegin. In *Poln. sobr. soch.*, t. VI. Moskva/Leningrad, 1937, s. 612. (Translator's note: English translation my own.)
39. Alexander Pushkin. *Eugene Onegin*. Trans. James E. Falen. Carbondale and Edwardsville: Southern Illinois University Press, 1990, 160.

which the not unknown Gogolian philosopher, Kifa Mokiyevich, gave himself up, whose existence "... was oriented more to the speculative side ...".[40] It is possible, however, to visualise another point of view, according to which it is precisely these "lost" pathways that represent one of the most agitating problems for the historian-philosopher. Here, however, it is necessary to recall the two poles of historical motion.

One of these is connected to those processes which are developed through non-explosive, gradual motion. These processes are relatively predictable. Of quite another nature are those processes which appear as a result of explosions. Here, each actualised event is surrounded by an entire cloud of unactualised events. The pathways which could have sprung out from them prove to be forever lost. Motion is realised not only as a new event but also as a new direction.

This approach is most significant where the discussion relates to historically unique events in which a random incident opens the way for a new and unpredictable system. A genial work of art, which has become a turning point in the cultural history of humanity, would not have been painted, nor would it be worth anything, if its author had died in infancy as a result of an accident. The outcome of Waterloo could not have been predicated exactly, just as at the moment of birth of Napoleon no one could have predicted whether the baby would survive. Nevertheless, once these facts are realised they have, in the historic machine, pressed down on a button which would otherwise have remained unused. In this sense each event can be considered from two points of view.

The work of Pushkin has greatly influenced the transformation of the work of art into an object of trade:

> Inspiration may not be sold,
> But it is possible to sell the manuscript[41]

In this respect, *Eugene Onegin* played a decisive role. However, whether Pushkin had written his novel in verse or even if Pushkin had not been born at all, the process would nevertheless have occurred. But if we look to another historical connection and assume that Pushkin could, by virtue of biographical circumstances, have been removed from the literature during his earliest period, then the entire chain of events which lead to Gogol, Dostoevsky, Tolstoy, Blok and, through them to Solzhenitsyn – as our closest perspective – and thereby strengthened the role of Russian literature (as it was played out in the fates of the Russian intelligentsia and, therefore, generally in the fates of Russia) would not be anything like that which has become known to us.

---

40. Gogol, N. V. *Poln. sobr. soch*, vol. 6, p. 244.
41. A. Pushkin. Razgovor knigoprodavtsa s poetom. In *Poln. sobr. soch.*, t. II, kn. I. Moskva-Leningrad, 1947, p. 330. (Translator's note: English translation my own.)

Thus, one and the same event may be included in both the predictable schema and in the circumstances of explosion. Each "great" event not only opens new pathways but also intercepts a whole host of future possibilities. If this is taken into account, then the description of these lost byways is already, for the historian, no mean reflection on alternative themes.

In such a case, one additional circumstance must be taken into account: different but typologically similar historical movements, for example the Romantic Movement in different European countries or the various forms of anti-feudal revolutions may, at the moment of explosion, take different routes. To compare them would seemingly demonstrate what might occur in one or other country if the results of the explosion in that country were different. This introduces a completely new aspect to the comparative study of cultures: that what has been lost in one historical-national space can be realised in another – with a comparison of each providing a reflection of what might have been, if the historical selection had been otherwise. For example, an analysis of different solutions to one and the same situation through a comparative study of the failed putsch in Moscow[42] and events in Yugoslavia show what might have been if the putsch had not fallen through.

The typological comparison of the different realisations of one event may be considered as a way of studying the "lost" pathways. From this point of view it is possible, for example, to interpret the history of the Renaissance, the Reformation, and the Counter-Reformation as different variations in a singular historical model. Such a view makes it possible to study not only that which did occur, but also that which did not occur but, nevertheless, could have occurred. A comparative study, for example, of economic processes on the one hand, and works of art on the other, gives us not so much cause and effect but rather two poles of a dynamic process neither of which translates to the other but each of which is simultaneously pierced by mutual influences. In the same way we have the antinomy of mass historical phenomena and that which is maximally individual, of predictability and unpredictability: the two wheels of the bicycle of history.

We have already said that the person who lives according to the laws of customs and traditions was, from the point of view of the enterprising hero of the explosive epoch, foolish, and that in the same way, the latter from the point of view of his opponent was considered to be insidious and dishonourable. Now we will try to consider these disputing characters as links in a united chain.

Periods of scientific discovery and technical invention may be considered as two stages of intellectual activity. Discoveries take on the nature of intellectual

---

42. The discussion here relates to the events of August, 1991.

explosions: they cannot be deciphered through the past and their consequences cannot be unambiguously predicted. But at that very moment when the explosion releases its internal energy it is changed by the chain of cause and effect – and enters into the time of technology. Logical development selects from the explosion those ideas whose time has arrived and which can then be used. The remainder passes into oblivion for some time – sometimes a very long time. In this way, in the periodic change of progress of scientific theories and technical successes it is possible to see alternate periods of predictability and unpredictability.

Of course, such a model possesses a high degree of conventionality. In reality a successive chain of explosions and gradual development never exists in isolation. Such a chain is submerged in a cloud of synchronous processes whose lateral influences are constantly interfering with each other and can disrupt the clear picture of alternate periods of explosion and gradual development. However, this does not prevent us from a theoretical examination of this chain of explosions as if they were isolated. This is manifested especially clearly in social and historical processes. We spoke of how the "foolish" knight and "rogue" appear through the eyes of each other. Let us, however, look upon them as the heroes of successive stages of development.

The hero of the *byliny*[43] or the man of the chivalric era, the "good peasant" of the idyllic literature of the XVIII century is a hero of stable or slowly developing processes. The movement in which he is submerged oscillates between the seasonal changes, ceremonies and rituality of repetitive exploits. Under such conditions, for the hero to be victorious requires nothing new. His exclusivity is marked by the sheer scale of his size and strength. He has no need to fabricate, and so invents nothing. However, at this stage he has not yet acquired a negative characteristic. He is not foolish, because the qualities of intelligence or stupidity are not considered relevant.

But then comes the moment of explosion. Regularity and repetition are substituted by unpredictability and the century of strength is substituted by an outburst of guile. We saw how these two types of hero, set before each other, are converted into enemies – spokesmen for the struggle between opposing epochs. But in the chronological sequence they are outlined as two inevitable and interdependent stages. It is interesting to trace the sequence in the fates of a series of historical phenomena.

Thus, for instance, Russian culture of the second-half of the XIX century is developed under the sign of the high value placed on human individuality. This is especially noticeable because of the fact that at the level of self-knowledge it

---

43. Poetic songs about legendary Russian heroes.

is the populist idea that predominates and literature, under the quill of Tolstoy or Dostoevsky and the political struggle personified by populist movements, declared the people as the ideal. The happiness of the people, therefore, was the goal of revolutionary practice, but in this case the 'people' is not the one who acts but rather that for whom they act.

> The spectacle of the calamities of the people
> Is intolerable, my friend;
> The happiness of noble minds –
> Is to see contentment all around.[44]

To Grisha Dobrosklonov:

> ... fate prepared
> The way to glory, the loud name
> Of the defender of the people,
> Consumption and Siberia ...[45]

According to Dostoevsky's intention, Aleksei Karamazov was forced to "lay down his life for his friends" – to end his life on the scaffold for the sins of another person.

In this way, the idea of 'peopleness' (*narodnost*[46]) was expressed in the individual hero just as it was expressed in a host of heroic personalities whose portraits were drawn by Stepnyak-Kravchinsky. The very notion of diversity organised the unity of these portraits. Such a structure was determined by the fact that the epoch prior to the moment of explosion was already enlightened by its 'light'. The fact that the epoch of the explosion generates a diverse range of characters and a widely disseminated individuality is confirmed by the biographies of the people of the Renaissance or of the epoch of Peter the Great.

But here the explosion ends. Revolution turns to stagnation and the ideal of individuality gives way to that of "equality" (*odinakovost*). Thus, from the middle of the 1920s the heroic personality is characterised by a lack of individuality and is poeticised:

> ... a million-fingered hand
> clenched
>         into one fist
>                of shattering might.

---

44. Nekrasov, N. A. *Poln. sobr. soch*: v 15 T. 1982. T. 4, p. 116. 2. T. 5, p. 517. (Translator's note: English translation my own.)

45. Ibid., p. 517.

46. Editor's note: "narodnost'" is a concept with a broad spectrum of meanings, ranging from the "national character" to the "social responsibility for the people" – M.G.

What's an individual?
>> No earthly good.

One man,
>> even the most important of all,

can't raise a ten-yard log of wood,

to say nothing
>> of a house
>>> ten stories tall.[47]

The idea of anonymous heroism was persistently present in the literature which proclaimed heroism in an unheroic epoch from the song of the red cavalry:

We are all anonymous heroes,
All our whole life is a battlefield.[48]

to the poem of Pasternak in the period of the Great war:

You, the nameless heroes
Of towns under siege,
I will conceal you in my heart of heart,
Your valour is greater than words.[49]

It is interesting that neither Pasternak nor his readers of those years felt any dissonance in this text: "will conceal you in my heart of heart" – is a quotation from the speech of Hamlet, where Shakespeare's hero creates the ideal of the noble personality: specifically this (very) personality Hamlet intends to hide in the depths of his heart. In Pasternak's poem this place was assigned to the nameless personalities. It is possible, however, to note that the emergence after the First World War of the ritual of worship at the grave of the Unknown Soldier is also rooted in the unheroic epoch. Let us compare the inscriptions on the graves which oppose the idea of the anonymity of the exploit even when the names of those killed remain unknown. Such is the Parisian inscription on the grave of the heroes of the revolution of the 1830s ("You perished so rapidly, that the fatherland did not have time to memorize your names") or the words which come from the pen of Olga Bergholtz: "No-one is forgotten and nothing

---

47. Mayakovsky, V. V. I. Lenin. In: *Poems*. Trans. Dorian Rottenberg. Moscow: Progress Publishers, 1976, p. 236.
48. The paradoxical impossibility of the poetics around the absence of name in the text from the first person is symptomatic. In the XIX century this word usage would be associated with the tramp or vagrant, who doesn't recall a relationship, and not with the military hero.
49. Pasternak, B. *Sobr. soch*, vol. 2, p. 43. (Translator's note: English translation my own.)

is forgotten" – or the commemorative ribbons on the graves of Jewish children in Prague where a complete list of the names of all the victims is given.

The heroic personality whose name is inscribed in the pages of history and the anonymous 'standard' hero epitomise two of those types of historical development, each of which changes the other.

# Chapter 9
# The text within the text (inset chapter)

In the events examined by us, choice appeared as the realisation of one of several potential possibilities. A generalisation of this kind is, however, no more than a conventional abstraction. We took into consideration a single developing system situated, as it were, in an isolated space. The real picture is a little more complex: any dynamic system is submerged in a space in which other equally dynamic systems exist, together with fragments of those structures which have been destroyed; peculiar comets of this space. As a result, any system lives not only according to the laws of its own self-development but also incorporates a variety of collisions with other cultural structures. These collisions are significantly random in character and it is practically impossible to define them. Nevertheless, to attempt to deny their existence and their significance would be more than careless. In fact, it is here that the distinction between the random and the regular takes place. That which is regular in 'its' own system appears as 'random' in the system with which it has suddenly collided. As a random element it sharply increases the range of further possibilities.

The history of the culture of any population may be examined from two points of view: firstly, as an immanent development; secondly, as the result of a variety of external influences. Both these processes are closely intertwined and their separation is only possible in the modality of scientific abstraction. Furthermore, and taking into account the aforesaid, it follows that any isolated examination of either immanent movement of such influences inevitably creates a distorted picture. The complexity does not, however, lie in this factor but rather in the fact that any intersection of systems sharply increases the unpredictability of future movements. The case where an external intrusion leads to victory over one of the colliding systems and suppression of another is far from characteristic of all such events. Sufficiently frequently the collision produces a third, fundamentally new, phenomenon which is not an obvious, logically predictable, consequence of either of the colliding systems. The matter is made more complex by the fact that the newly formed phenomenon appropriates the name of one or other of the colliding structures, such that something which is, in principle, new lies hidden under an old facade.

Thus, for example, in the reign of the Tsarina Elizabeth Petrovna the culture of the Russian nobility underwent a powerful 'Frenchification'. The French language at the turn of the 18th century established itself as an inextricable part of noble culture (especially in the capital). Above all, it conquered the arena of feminine discourse. Pushkin dealt with this question in great detail and with the accuracy of a culturologist in the third chapter of *Eugene Onegin* where he encounters the question of what language he should use for Tatyana's letter. The question was resolved with a frank and emphatic conventionality: Tatyana, naturally, wrote in prose – whilst the poet translated the prose into the language of poetry which he represented. Simultaneously, he warns the reader that the letter was written in French and that he has translated it for the reader – albeit in a conventional manner – via the Russian language:[1]

> I face another complication:
> My country's honour will demand
> Without a doubt a full translation
> Of Tanya's letter from my hand.
> She knew the Russian language badly,
> Ignored our journals all too gladly,
> And in her native tongue, I fear,
> Could barely make her meaning clear;
> And so she turned for love's discussion
> To French . . . [2]

Two problems of the history of language intersect here. The intrusion of French into Russian, and their fusion into a kind of unified language, generates a wholly functional selection.

Thus, for example, the mélange of French and Russian generates a "feminine" language of an especially "fashionable" variety: see, for example, Pushkin's letter to his brother Lev, dated 24 January 1822, from Kishinev: "First I want to scold you a little. Aren't you ashamed, my dear fellow, to write a half-Russian, half-French letter; you are no Moscow female cousin."[3] "A Moscow cousin" was a term attributed to a provincial follower of fashion, who adopts those clothes and customs which have already become obsolete in Petersburg; a comic personality, a stereotype of scenes from Moscow life (as, for example, Princess Alina in the aforementioned *Eugene Onegin*). The characteristic mixture of French and Russian prompted B. A. Uspensky to identify the language of women of the

---

1. Pushkin first considered representing Tatyana's letter in the form of prose included in a book, perhaps even in French. His chosen decision – a poetic translation into the Russian language – is, semiotically, even more complex in so far as it emphasises the conventional link between expression and content.
2. Alexander Pushkin. *Eugene Onegin*. Trans. James E. Falen. Carbondale and Edwardsville: Southern Illinois University Press, 1990, p. 79.
3. *The Letters of Alexander Pushkin*. Trans. and ed. J. Thomas Shaw. Madison: The University of Wisconsin Press, 1967, p. 90.

"belle monde" of the second half of the 18th century and up to the turn of the 19th century as "mainly macaronic".[4]

French, for the cultivated Russian society of Pushkin's epoch, fulfilled the role of the language of scientific and philosophical thought. At that point in time it also exerted a particular influence in terms of the appearance, in the literature of the French Enlightenment, of a series of scientific books aimed at a feminine audience. The participation of women in scientific reading in Russia, begun by E. R. Dashkova, also contributed to the fact that French was to become the preferred language of science and culture. Not only the woman of fashion but also the educated Russian woman spoke and wrote in French. And, if the characteristics of Tatyana, who

> ... in her native tongue, I fear,
> Could barely make her meaning clear,

bears the nuance of "feminine" language, then in *Roslavlev* Pushkin's heroine already appears as an exponent of high culture which belongs in equal measure to men as well as to the ladies: "This library consisted mainly of the works of eighteenth-century authors. She was familiar with French literature, from Montesquieu to the novels of Crébillon. She knew Rousseau by heart. There was not a single Russian book in her library – apart from the works of Sumarokov, which Polina never opened. She used to tell me that she had difficulty in reading Russian print, and she probably never read anything in Russian, not even the verses dedicated to her by Muscovite versifiers."[5]

It should be noted that the composition of the library characterises the tastes of the educated Russian reader as a whole and not only the female reader; Polina's library belonged to her father. The fusion, in this sense, of "male" and "female" languages is emphasised by the ease with which Pushkin packs into the mouth of his heroine his own dear thoughts: "Here I allow myself a brief digression. It is already thirty years now, thank goodness, since we wretched women were reproved for never reading anything in Russian and for being unable, it would appear, to express ourselves in our native language. [...] The fact is, we would be glad to read Russian; but our literature appears to be no

---

4. Uspensky, B. A. *Iz istorii russkogo literaturnogo yazyka* XVIII – *nachala* XIX *veka*. Moscow, 1985, p. 57. See this for the cultural-historical aspect of this phenomenon. The linguistic analysis of this phenomenon and an interesting collection of examples (in particular, the mixture of French-Danish in the dandy language of the comedy of Holberg) see: Grannes, A. *Prostorechnye i dialektnye elementy v yazyke russkoi komedii* XVIII *veka*. Bergen; Oslo; Tromso.

5. Alexander Pushkin. *Tales of Belkin and Other Prose Writings*. Trans. Ronald Wilks. London: Penguin Books, 1998, p. 93.

older than Lomonosov and is yet extraordinary limited. It of course offers us a few excellent poets, but one really cannot expect from every reader an exclusive liking for poetry. As regards prose, all we have is Karamzin's *History*; the first two or three novels appeared two or three years ago, whereas in France, England and Germany, books appear one after the other, each more remarkable than the last. We do not even see any translations; and if we did then, to tell the truth, I would still prefer to read the originals. Our journals have interest only for men of letters. We are compelled to glean everything, whether news or ideas, from foreign books; thus we also *think in foreign languages* (at least all those who do think and who follow the thoughts of mankind). Our most celebrated men of letters admitted this to me" (italics mine – J. L.).[6]

Griboyedov's attacks on the mélange of languages, as much as Pushkin's protection of it, prove that what lies before us is neither a whim of fashion nor the grimace of ignorance but rather a characteristic feature of the linguistic process. In this sense French represents an organic element of linguistic communication in Russian culture. It is significant that Tolstoy, in *War and Peace*, introduces an abundance of French with the precise intention of reproducing the speech of the Russian nobility. The speech of the French is, as a rule, given in the Russian language. The French language, in this instance, is used primarily as an indicator of linguistic space or as an instance where it is necessary to reproduce the characteristic features of French thought. In neutral situations, Tolstoy does not use it.

In this epoch, a contradictory situation appears in the intersection of Russian with the French language. On the one hand, the mélange of languages forms a kind of unified language of culture but on the other – the use of this language implies a sharp awareness of its artificiality and internal contradictions. This, in particular, appeared in the persistent struggle with this mélange, which was seen as the absence of stylistic skills (cf. Pushkin's reproaches to his brother, discussed above) or even a lack of patriotism or a mark of provinciality. Let us compare this with Griboyedov:

> And does the mixing-up of languages still reign?
> High-French low-Russian conversation?[7]

The intrusion of a "fragment" of text into a foreign language can, however, act as a generator of new meaning. This is emphasised, for example, by the possibility of introducing a discourse in non-existent language, which nevertheless proves to be extremely saturated with meaning. Let us compare, for example,

---

6. Alexander Pushkin. *Tales of Belkin and Other Prose Writings*. Trans. Ronald Wilks. London: Penguin Books, 1998, p. 94.
7. Aleksandr Griboyedov's *Woe from Wit*. Trans. Mary Hobson. Lewiston-Queenston-Lampeter: The Edwin Mellen Press, 2005, p. 27.

Mayakovsky's creation of macaronic language to a conventional "foreign" language:

> The impudent thief stripped jasmine from the linden trees. Give us. Spit! Ticket-nik![8]

or a well-known episode from *War and Peace* describing the conversation of a French and a Russian soldier, as a result of which the latter, wishing to speak in the "foreign" language, resorts to glossolalia.[9]

A typical example of the intrusion of a foreign text is the "text within the text": a fragment of text which is detached from its natural semantic network and mechanically introduced into a different semantic space. Here it may carry out a whole series of functions: it may play the role of a semantic catalyst, change the nature of the basic meaning, remain unnoticed, etc. For us, the most interesting example of this occurs when the unexpected intrusion of a text acquires an essentially semantic function. This is manifested with the utmost clarity in artistic texts.

The "text within the text" is a specific rhetorical construction in relation to which the difference in codification of the different parts of the text starts to reveal the author's construction and the reader's perception of the text. The transfer from one system of semiotic realisation of the text into another across some kind of internal structural boundary becomes, in this instance, the starting point for the generation of meaning. Such a construction, above all, accentuates the ludic quality of the text: from the point of view of a different method of codification, the text acquires features of an increased conventionality and its ludic nature is emphasised – that is, its ironic, parodic, theatrical etc. meaning. Simultaneously, the role of the boundaries of the text, both the external, which separates it from the non-text, and the internal, which divides it into differently coded sections, is high-lighted. The existence of the boundaries is precisely emphasised by their mobility, by the fact that the structure of the boundaries changes as one code or another changes. Thus, for example, against the background of an already prevalent tradition, which places the pedestal or picture frame into the category of the non-text, the art of the Baroque epoch introduced these into the text (for example, by transforming the pedestal into a rock and linking it thematically to the figure in a common composition).

A characteristic example of the introduction of the pedestal into the text of a monument is the rock upon which Falconet placed his statue of Peter the Great in Petersburg. Paolo Trubetskoy, whilst creating the project for a monument to

---

8.  Mayakovsky, V. V. *The Complete Plays of Vladimir Mayakovsky*. New York: Washington Square Press, 1968.
9.  See: Tolstoy, L. *Poln. sobr. soch.* vol. 4, p. 222.

Alexander III introduced a sculptural quotation from Falconet: the horse was also set upon the rock. The reference, however, had a polemical meaning: the rock, which under the hooves of the statue of Peter conferred on it a forward movement, was transformed by Trubetskoy into the precipice and the abyss. His rider galloped as far as the precipice stopping abruptly above the abyss. The meaning of the statue was so obvious that the sculptor was asked to replace the rock with a traditional pedestal.

The ludic moment is accentuated not only by the fact that from one perspective these elements appear to be included in the text, whilst from another they appear to be detached from it, but also by the fact that in both cases the measure of their conventionality differs from that which is inherent in the basic text: when the figures of the baroque sculpture climb or jump down from their pedestal or when the painting leaps out of its frame, this emphasises but does not erase the fact that one of them belongs to material reality whilst the other belongs to artistic reality. The same ludic quality occurs in the perceptions of the audience who experience a different kind of reality when the theatrical drama disappears from the stage and is transferred into the actual everyday space of the auditorium.

The play on the contradiction between the "real" and the "conventional" is characteristic of any instance of the "text within the text". The simplest example of this is the introduction into the text of a fragment which contains the same code as the remainder of the space of the work, with the exception that it is doubly coded. These are, for example, the picture in the picture, the theatre in the theatre, the film in the film or the novel in the novel. The double codification of these defined sections of the text is identified with an artistic conventionality and lead to the primary space of the text being perceived as "real".

Thus, for example, in *Hamlet* we are confronted not only by a "text within the text" but also by *Hamlet* in *Hamlet*. In order to distract the "mad" Hamlet, the king orders that a troupe of wandering actors randomly encountered on the road be brought to Elsinor. In order to verify the skill of the travelling actors, Hamlet asks them to play out a fragment of the first play that comes into his mind. At this moment there is nothing in his head. The choice of play is random (Hamlet simply mentions his favourite play), which testifies to the fact that Shakespeare makes him replace the fragment with another. The witty answer of Hamlet to the foolish observation of Polonius who has interrupted the recitation shows that the connection between the scene being played out by the actor and his own circumstances has not yet been realised by Hamlet, but when the actor pronounces the words:

"But who, O who had seen the mobbled queen..." –

Hamlet's consciousness is instantly illuminated, modifying the meaning of the whole monologue. Furthermore, he (and the spectator) has already linked the monologue of the actor in light of the events in Elsinor and that part of the monologue which has already been delivered acquires a new meaning. Hamlet's insight is further accentuated by the stupidity of Polonius:

| **Hamlet** | 'The mobbled queen'? |
|---|---|
| **Polonius** | That's good; 'mobbled queen' is good. |
| **First actor** | 'Run barefoot up and down, threat'ning the flames |
| | With bisson rheum; a clout upon that head |
| | Where late the diadem stood . . .'[10] |

The fragment, which was a *non-text*, by virtue of its inclusion in the text of "Hamlet", becomes part of this text (it is transformed into the text), but simultaneously it transforms the text into which it has been inserted, as a whole, transporting it to a different level of organisation.

The play, brought about on the initiative of Hamlet echoes in an emphatically conventional manner (first as pantomime, then as the accentuated conventionality of the rhymed monologues, interrupted by the prosaic remarks of the spectators: Hamlet, the king, the queen and Ophelia) the play composed by Shakespeare. The conventionality of the former emphasises the reality of the second[11]. In order to accentuate this feeling in the spectators, Shakespeare introduces metatextual elements into the text: the play's production takes place on stage before us. As if anticipating Fellini's *8½*, Hamlet, in front of the public, instructs the actors on how they should act out the play. Thus, Shakespeare shows us not only the scene within the scene but, and what is more important still, the

---

10. Shakespeare, W. *The Complete Works*. Ed. by Stanley Wells and Gary Taylor. Oxford: Clarendon Press, 1986, p. 752.
11. The characters of *Hamlet* seemingly confer a theatrical effectiveness on the comic actors, and they themselves are transformed into the public off-stage. This explains their passage into prose, and the emphasis of Hamlet's obscene observations, on similar made by the public in the epoch of Shakespeare. In practice, it is not only the "theatre within the theatre" that appears, but also the "public within the public". It is probable that, in order to transmit this effect adequately to the contemporary spectator, it would be necessary for those characters, making their remarks from the public gallery, to remove their makeup and become seated in the auditorium at this point, leaving the scene to the comic actors, who play the role of the "mousetrap". Identification of Hécube with Gertrude is emphasised by the consonance of the forenames, which could be taken as a completely random occurrence, but which, only at this moment suddenly strikes audience. But once the parallel has been drawn, sonic correspondence becomes superfluous and for the parallel between the king (Claudius) and Pyrrhus – it is no longer necessary.

rehearsal of the scene. What is important for us here is the detachment from the "main" narration, which introduces into the text a fragment of another text, which at first glance is completely unconnected with and "foreign" to the text.

Duplication is the simplest way of moving the coding mechanism into the sphere of conscious structural construction. It is not by chance that the myths concerning the origins of art are connected to the act of duplication: the rhyme as a product of the echo, painting as charcoal-traced shadow on stone, etc. The motif of the mirror in painting and cinematography occupies an important place in the production, in the figurative arts, of local subtexts with a duplicated structure.

The motif of the mirror is widely encountered across a wide range of works (see *Venus at her Mirror* of Velazquez, or the *The Portrait of the Banker Arnolfini with his wife* of van Eyck, and many others). However, we immediately encounter the fact that duplication with the aid of a mirror is not a case of simple repetition: it changes the "right-left" axis or, as is more frequently the case, a perpendicular axis is added to the plan view of the canvas or fabric which creates depth or adds a supplementary point of view, which lies outside of the plan view. Thus, on Velazquez's canvas, in addition to the point of view of the spectators who see Venus from the back, there is the added point of view from the depths of the mirror – which reflects the face of Venus. The effect is even more complicated in van Eyck's portrait: the mirror hanging on the wall in the depths of the picture reflects the figures of Arnolfini and his wife from the back (on the canvas they are viewed from the front) and the guests, whom they greet, enter from the side of the spectators, whilst the spectators see them only in the mirror.

Thus, a perspective is cast from the depth of mirror, perpendicular to the canvas (and tilted towards the view of spectators), which falls outside the spatial boundaries of the picture itself. In actual fact the mirror played the same role in the interiors of the baroque opening up the architectural space with the creation of an illusory infinity (the reflection of the mirror in the mirror), duplicating artistic space by reflecting pictures in mirrors[12] or breaking the boundary of the internal/external by reflecting windows in mirrors.

However, the mirror can play another role: duplication distorts things and in so doing reveals the fact that the representation which seems "natural" is but a

---

12. Cf. in Derzhavin:
      ... paintings in mirrors breathed
   Mosaics, marble and porcelain ...
   (Derzhavin, G. R. *Stikhotvoreniya*. Podgot. teksta i red. D. D. Blagogo. Leningrad, 1957, p. 213).

projection which carries within itself a specific language of modelisation. Thus, in van Eyck's portrait the mirror is convex (cf. Lucas Furtenagel's portrait of Hans Burgkmair and his wife Anna, where the woman holds a convex mirror almost at a right angle to the surface of the canvas, which results in a sharp distortion of the reflections), the figures are shown not only from the front and from behind but are also projected on the flat, spherical surface. In Visconti's *Bellíssima* the figure of the heroine, deliberately impassive and petrified, is opposed to its dynamic reflection in the mirror. Let us also consider the staggering effect of the reflection in the broken mirror in Clouzot's *The Crow* or the broken mirror in Carné's *Daybreak*. It would be possible to compare this with the entire literary mythology of reflections in the mirror and beyond the mirror whose roots are to be found in archaic notions of the mirror as a window into the "otherworld".

The literary corollary of the mirror motif is the theme of the double. Just as that which is seen through the mirror represents the estranged world of the everyday, the double represents an estranged reflection of the character. Changing the image of the character according to the laws of mirror reflection (enantiomorphism), the double represents a combination of features, which makes it possible to see their invariant foundation and shifts (the replacement of right – left symmetry may be interpreted in a variety of ways: the corpse as the double of the living, the authentic and the false, the ugly and the beautiful, the criminal and the saint, the negligible and the great, etc.), all of which generates a field full of possibilities for artistic modelisation.

The semiotic nature of the artistic text is fundamentally dualistic: on the one hand, the text simulates reality, suggesting it has an existence independent of its author, to be a thing amongst the things of the real world.[13] On the other, it constantly reminds us that it is someone's creation and that it means something. This double interpretation leads to a game in the semantic field: "reality-fiction", which Pushkin expressed with the words:

My fancy draw sweet tears from me ...[14]

The rhetorical union of "things" and the "signs of things" (collage) in a single textual whole generates a dual effect simultaneously emphasising both the conventionality of the conventional and its unconditional authenticity. The function of "things" (i.e. those realities taken from the external world but not yet created by the author of the text) may appear in the form of those documents-texts whose

---

13. See Derzhavin in his ode "God": I am your creation, Creator! (Derzhavin, G. R. *Stikhotvoreniya*. c. 116). Man as the creation of the creator as the reflection of the deity in the mirror of the material.

14. A. Pushkin. Elegy. In *Lyric Poems: 1826-1836* in *The Complete Works of Alexander Pushkin*, vol. 2, p. 133, Milner and Company Limited, 1999 (Trans. Alan Myers).

authenticity in a given cultural context cannot be doubted. Such are, for example, the insertion into a movie of the characters of a newsreel (cf. A. Tarkovsky's *Mirror*) or the method, which Pushkin used in *Dubrovsky*, of pasting into the narrative a large fragment of an authentic XVIII century judicial case, changing only proper names. More complex are those cases where the sign of "authenticity" is unable to escape the nature of its own sub-text or even contradicts it but in spite of this, in the rhetorical whole of the text, it is precisely to this sub-text that the function of authentic reality is attributed.

From this point of view, let us examine Bulgakov's novel *The Master and Margarita*. The novel is constructed in the form of two independent but interlacing texts: one narrates events which take place in Moscow and is contemporary to the author; the other takes place in ancient Yershalaim (Jerusalem). The Moscow text evokes signs of "reality": it has an everyday feel to it; it is plausibly overloaded with details familiar to the reader and is presented as a direct continuation of all that is familiar to the contemporary reader. In the novel it is presented as a form of primary text on a neutral level. In contrast to this, the narrative about Yershalaim constantly maintains the character of a "text within the text". If the first text is the creation of Bulgakov, then the second is created by the characters of the novel. The irreality of the second text is emphasised by the fact that it is preceded by a metatextual discussion of how it should be written; cf.: Jesus "... in fact, never existed at all. That's where you have to put your main emphasis ... "[15] Thus, if, relative to the first sub-text, they wish to convince us that it has a real denotation, then relative to the second, they demonstratively convince us that no such denotation exists. This situation is reached by a constant foregrounding of the textual nature of the chapters about Yershalaim (first the story of Woland, then the novel of the Master) and the fact that the Moscow chapters are presented as a reality which can be seen and Yershalaim as a story which is heard or read. The Yershalaim chapters are invariably introduced as the tail end of the Muscovite chapters, which become their beginnings, thus accentuating their secondary nature: "He began to speak softly and as he did, his accent somehow disappeared. "It's all very simple: Early in the morning on the fourteenth day of the spring month of Nisan, wearing a white cloak ... " – end of the first chapter; beginning of the second: "wearing the white cloak with a blood-red lining, and shuffling with his cavalryman's gait into the roofed colonnade [...] walked the procurator of Judea, Pontius Pilate". The chapter "The Execution" is introduced

---

15. Mikhail Bulgakov. *The Master and Margarita*. Trans. Diana Burgin & Katherine Tiernan O'Connor. Ann Arbor: Ardis, 1995, p. 5 (Editor's note: the editor Berlioz is giving a young poet "a lecture on Jesus". – M.G.).

as the dream of Ivan:[16] "... and he began to dream that the sun was already sinking behind Bald Mountain,[17] and the mountain was encircled by a double cordon ... " – end of the fifteenth; beginning of the sixteenth chapter: "The sun was already sinking behind Bald Mountain, and the mountain was encircled by a double cordon". Further texts about Yershalaim are introduced as the compositions of the Master: "... Margarita was free to leaf through the pages of the notebooks for as long as she liked, even till dawn. She examined them closely, kissed them, and reread the words again and again, "The darkness that had come in from the Mediterranean covered the city so detested by the procurator ..." "Yes, the darkness ... "– end of the twenty-fourth; beginning of the twenty-fifth chapter: "The darkness that had come in from the Mediterranean covered the city so detested by the procurator."[18]

However, no sooner is the inertia of the distribution between the real and the unreal established, than the author begins to play with the reader through a redistribution of the boundaries between these spheres. First of all, the Muscovite world ("real") is filled with the most fantastic events whilst the "invented" world of the Master's novel is subordinated to the strict laws of everyday verisimilitude. At the level of cohesion of the different elements of the tale the distribution of the "real" and the "unreal" are directly opposed. Furthermore, metatextual elements are also introduced into the narrative of the Muscovite world (albeit rarely, it is true) creating the following schema: the author tells the story of his characters, the characters tell the story of Yeshua and Pilate: "Follow me, reader! Who ever told you there is no such thing in the world as real, true, everlasting love?"[19]

Finally, in an ideological and philosophical sense, this plunge into the "story within the story" is not deemed by Bulgakov to be a move away from reality into the world of wordplay (as, for example, occurs in Jan Potocki's *Manuscript*

---

16. The dream, as well as the insertion of short stories is the traditional method of introducing the text within the text. More complex examples are represented by such works, as Lermontov's "The Dream" ("In the heat of the afternoon, in the valley of Dagestan ...") where the dying hero is seen in the dream of the heroine, who sees the dying hero in her own dream (cf. Lermontov, M. Y. *Works in 6 vols.* Moscow/Leningrad, 1954, vol. 2, p. 197). The alliteration of the first and the last verses creates a space, which form a kind of Moebius's ring, where one surface indicates the dream, and the another indicates reality.

17. Bald Mountain equates to Golgotha ('the place of the skull') of the Gospels, where Christ was crucified. There is also a Bald Mountain near Kiev, where Bulgakov was born.

18. Mikhail Bulgakov. *The Master and Margarita*. Trans. Diana Burgin & Katherine Tiernan O'Connor. Ann Arbor: Ardis, 1995, pp. 12–13, 142–143, 254–255.

19. Ibid., 185.

*Found in Saragossa*) but rather an ascension from the distorted appearance of the so called real world towards the true essence of the mysterious world. A reflective character is established between the two texts, but that which appears to be the real object emerges only as the distorted reflection of that which itself appears to be a reflection.

The compositional frame is also an essential and very traditional method of the rhetorical fusion of texts, which have been coded differently. A "normal" (i.e., neutral) construction is based, in particular, on the framing of text (a picture frame, the binding of a book or the publishing house adverts at the end of it, the clearing of the actor's voice before the aria, the tuning of tools by the orchestra, the words "And now, listen ..." in the oral story, etc.) and is not introduced into the text. It's role is to signal the beginning of the text, but it is itself located beyond the limits of the text. It is sufficient to introduce such a framework into the text to relocate the audience's centre of attention from the communication to the code. The matter is more complex where the text and the frame are interwoven[20] to the extent that each part is, simultaneously, both frame and framed text.

Another construction is also possible where one text is presented as continuous narration and others are introduced in the form of deliberate fragments (quotations, notes, epigraphs, etc.).[21] It is assumed that the reader will unravel the grains of other structural constructions in the texts. Similar inserts may be read as uniform with the surrounding text or as different to it. The more sharply the untranslatability between the codes of the inserted text and the basic code is expressed, the more evident is the specific semiotic character of each of them.

No less multifunctional are those cases of the dual or repeated coding of the whole text. We have had occasion to observe cases where the theatre has coded the behaviour of people, transforming it into the "historical" and "historical behaviour was viewed as a natural subject in painting".[22] In this case, the rhetorical-semiotic moment is at its most accentuated when distant and mutually untranslatable codes converge. So, Visconti in *Belíssima* (a film, made in the 1950s, at the height of the celebration of neo-realism, after the director himself had created *The Earth Trembles*) passed the film through the operatic code in a revelatory manner. Against the background of this general duplication

20. See more on the interlacing of figures: Shubnikov A. V., Koptsik V. A. *Simmetriya v nauke i isskustve*. Moskva, 1972. pp. 17–18.
21. See: Mints, Z. G. *Funktsia reministsentsii v poetike A. Bloka*. Tartu State University. 1973. Iss. 308, pp. 387–417 (*Trudy po znakovym sistemam*) [ V. ] 6.
22. Lotman, J. M. *Stat'i po tipologii kultury*. In *Semiosfera* (2000), St. Petersburg: Isskustvo. See also: Francastel P. *La réalité Figurative*/Ed. Gontleier. Paris, 1965, pp. 211–238.

of the code, which occurs throughout the film, there are montage shots in which a living actor (Franz) is portrayed via a Renaissance fresco.

Culture as a whole may be considered as a text. However, it is exceptionally important to emphasise that this is a complex text, which consists of a hierarchy of "texts within the texts" and which, moreover, generates a complex network of texts. Since the word "text" itself includes the etymology of something that is woven together, we can say that in this interpretation we are returning the concept "text" to its original value.

Thus, the very concept of text undergoes a certain refinement. The idea of the text as a uniformly organised semantic space is supplemented with reference to the intrusion of diverse "random" elements from other texts. The latter enter into an unpredictable game with the basic structures and sharply increase the unpredictability of future developments. If the system did develop without these unpredictable external intrusions (i.e., it formed a unique, enclosed structure), then its development would be cyclical. In its ideal form it would represent a continuous repetition. Taken in isolation such a system, even if it possessed explosive moments, would exhaust them within a specific timeframe. The constant introduction into a system of elements external to it gives it a character at once linear and unpredictable. The union, in one and the same process of these, in principle, incompatible elements forms the basis of the contradiction between reality and our knowledge of it. This is manifested most vividly in artistic cognition: a reality transformed into a plot is assigned such concepts as beginning and end, sense, etc. The well-known phrase of the critics of artistic works "it doesn't happen like that in real life" assumes that reality is strictly limited by the laws of logic whilst art is the domain of freedom. The relationship between these elements is, in fact, much more complex: unpredictability in art is simultaneously a cause and a consequence of unpredictability in life.

# Chapter 10
# Inverse image

In the space, which lies beyond the limits of the norm (which is based on the norm and which disrupts it), we encounter a whole range of possibilities: from abnormality (destruction of the norm) to a whole gamut of positive qualities situated over and above the norm. However, in both cases we are talking, not about a depletion of the norm, a simplification or a fixed view of the latter but rather of "Life's Abundance", to borrow the title of one of Ludwig Tieck's short stories.[1] One of the most elementary methods of evading the limits of predictability is the trope (used especially frequently in the visual arts) by which two opposing objects exchange their dominant features. This method was widely used in an extensive Baroque literature relating to the "inverted world".[2] In many of these texts, the sheep ate the wolf, the horse rode the man, and the blind led the sighted. These inverted subjects were, as a rule, used in satiric texts. The entire poetics of Swift is built on such principles, for example, the transposition of people and horses.

The transposition of such elements whilst retaining their habitual traits is, as a rule, especially agitating for a stereotypical audience. More specifically, this method is most frequently considered to be indecent. Thus, for instance, in one of the satiric periodicals of the end of the last century, the comedy *The Sister of Madame Europe* a sufficiently stereotypical caricature of decadence was given:

> We are the priests of the strange, of the inaccessible.
> For me, the most pleasant of all odours is that of the dead rat,
> of all sounds – I value most the croaking of toads,
> of all women – most amiable to me are those who are bald.[3]

---

1.  It is this very "overabundance" of life, according to Tyutchev, which makes it possible for the Romantics or artists of the Baroque to turn the ugly into aesthetical fact. The impoverishment of life (bluntness, idiocy, physical disgrace) can also be the object of art, but it requires compensation in the form of a negative attitude on the part of the author. This we see in the caricature or, for example, in Goya's engravings.
2.  See, for example: L'image ... 1979; in particular the articles of Francois Pelpech. *Aspects des pays de Cocagne* (pp. 35–48); and of Maurice Lever. *Le Monde Renversé Dans Le Ballet De Cour* (pp. 107–115).
3.  See: *Nashi yumoristy za 100 let v karikaturakh, proze i stikhakh.* [A survey of Russian humorous literature and journalism], St. Petersburg, 1904, p. 143. The fantasy of a mediocre author of Russian satire of the XIX century anticipated the absurd in Ionesco's play *The Bald Singer*. (Translator's note: translation my own.)

However, for us, what is interesting in this case is not so much the work of art where the very possibility of recombination is predetermined by the freedom of fantasy, but rather those facts that relate to a travesty of everyday behaviour.

The inverted world is constructed on the dynamics of the non-dynamic. The everyday realisation of this process is revealed by fashion, which introduces a dynamic principle to those spheres of life which appear to be non-dynamic. In societies, where types of clothing are strictly subordinated to tradition or are dictated by calendrical changes – and anyway do not depend on linear dynamics and the arbitrariness of the human will, there may be expensive and cheap clothing but there is no fashion. Furthermore, in a society of this type, the more highly valued the clothing the longer it is retained and vice versa, the longer it is retained – the more highly it is valued. Such, for example, is the relationship of a society towards the ritual clothing of Heads of State and the hierarchies of the Church.

The regular change of fashion is a sign of a dynamic social structure. Moreover, it is precisely fashion with its constant epithets: "capricious", "variable", "strange", emphasising a lack of motivation and an apparent arbitrariness of movement that makes it a certain metronome of cultural development. The accelerated nature of the movements of fashion is connected with a strengthening of the role of the initiating personality in the process of dynamic change. In the cultural space of clothing there is a constant battle between the tendency toward stability and immobility (this tendency survives psychologically, justified by tradition, habit, morals, historical and religious considerations) and an opposing orientation towards novelty and eccentricity – in short everything that ties into the idea of fashion.

Thus, fashion appears to be the visible embodiment of unmotivated innovation.[4] This allows it to be simultaneously interpreted as both the site of deviant whim and as the sphere of innovative creation. Eccentricity is a prerequisite of

---

4. Examining the history of fashion, we invariably encounter attempts to identify motivation: moral, religious, medical and other considerations explain the introduction of any changes in clothing. However, analysis unconditionally convinces us of the fact that all these motives are introduced from without, post factum. These attempts are to show that which is not motivated as motivated in retrospect. Still, before our eyes, well into the 1950s and the 1960s women wearing trousers were considered to be indecent. One well-known writer expelled the bride of his son from his house because she dared to arrive in "culottes". At this time women in trousers were not allowed into restaurants. It is interesting that moral, cultural and even medical considerations were also used in defence of these prohibitions. In the present day, no-one recalls these prohibitions or motivations.

fashion. The latter is not negated by the periodic resurgence of a traditionally oriented fashion since tradition itself is, in this case, an extravagant form of the negation of eccentricity. To include a specific element in the space of fashion means making it noticeable, allotting significance to it. Fashion is always semiotic. Included in fashion is a continuous process of the transformation of the insignificant into the significant.

The semioticity of fashion is manifested, in particular, in the fact that it always implies an observer. He who speaks the language of fashion is the creator of new information, unanticipated by the audience and incomprehensible to it. The audience must not understand fashion and must be agitated by it. In this lies the victory of fashion. It is another form of victory – incomprehension, linked to disturbance. In this sense, fashion is simultaneously elite and of the masses. If the public is not shocked, fashion becomes meaningless. Thus, one of the psychological aspects of fashion relates to the fear of passing unnoticed and, thus, it feeds itself not by self-confidence but by doubting its own value. Uncertainty hides itself behind the fashionable innovations of Byron. The opposite tendency – the refusal to follow fashion was realised by Chaadaev, "the cold pride of calm" according to Pushkin's expression. P. J. Chaadaev may be an example of refined fashion. His dandyism consisted not in a tendency to strive to be fashionable but in the firm conviction that it was up to him to establish the fashion. However, the eccentricity of his clothing consisted in an audacious absence of eccentricity. Thus, if Denis Davydov, adapting his clothing to the norms of the "national character" of 1812, "... put on a peasant smock (this was possible, of course, only because the action occurred in a partisan detachment. – Ju. L.) let [his] beard grow and, instead of the Order of St Anne, [...] hung an icon of St Nicholas[5] around [his] neck and began talking to the people in their own dialect"[6] then

---

5.  D. Davydov made the following note, indicating that he relied on the specific tradition of the "democratization of the uniform": "Vo vremya voiny 1807 g. komandir Leib-grenaderskogo polka Mazovskii nosil na grudi bol'shoi obraz Sv. Nikolaya-Chudotvortsa, iz-za kotorogo torchalo mnozhestvo malenkikh obrazkov". (During the war, in 1807, the commander of the guard of the Mazovsky regiment bore on his breast the large icon of St Nicholas, the miracle-worker, surrounded by many small icons) (Davydov, D. *Soch.* Predisl., podgot. teksta i primech. V. N. Orlov. Moskva, 1962, p. 536). The act of carrying an icon on the breast had a supplementary meaning in the peasant detachment: the peasants confounded the partisans in hussar uniforms and French marauders, moving along the rear (testified in memoirs). The icon of St. Nicholas thus appeared as a sign of nationality.

6.  Davydov, D. *In the Service of the Tsar against Napoleon. The Memoirs of Denis Davydov, 1806–1814.* Trans. Gregory Troubetzkoy. London: Greenhill Books; Pennsylvania: Stackpole Books, 1999, p. 87.

Chaadaev would have emphasised the extraordinary nature of the situation by his complete negation of any eccentricity in the clothing. That is, non-recognition of the fact that in the field the conditions and burdens of life on the march appear to allow a certain freedom in clothing, in that the requirements for a snow-white collar in the battlefield is not as strict as this might be in the dance hall; and that face, gesture and gait under fire have the right to differ from the gracious movements of mundane society. The deliberate refusal of all that represents the romantic *couleur locale* of life on the march, represented the behaviour of Chaadaev, under marching conditions and under enemy fire, as a form of illusory eccentricity.

Fashion, as with all other forms of behaviour which go beyond the boundaries of the norm, implies a constant testing of the boundaries of the permissible.

The sphere of unpredictability is a complex dynamic reservoir in any or all processes of development. In connection therewith, and of particular interest, is the specific phenomenon of Russian culture: *samodurstvo* (wilful tyranny).

The four-volume academic dictionary of the Russian language explains this word using a quotation from Dobrolyubov: *"The samodur (tyrant) tries to prove in every way possible that no law can hold him and that he will do exactly what he wants.* Dobrolyubov: *The Kingdom of Darkness."*[7]

However, this explanation explains very little and in no way clarifies the historical and/or cultural value of this concept. The word "*samodur*" is, from an etymological point of view, an internal contradiction: the first part, the pronounced "*sam*" (self) signifies a hypertrophied personality (cf.: *samo*derzhavie [autocracy], *samo*vlastie [absolute rule], *samo*lubie [pride], *samo*razvitie [self-development], *samo*dostatochnost' [self-sufficiency]); the second part is connected with the semantics of stupidity. The very union of these two semantic elements is an oxymoron, a semantic contradiction. It may be interpreted as the union of initiative and stupidity or initiative and madness (the word "durnoi" (bad, stupid) in everyday use can indicate both one or the other). The union of these two semantic groups can generate two very different semantic nuances. On the one hand, it may indicate the self-assertion of stupidity. In this case, then, it represents the union of stability and stupidity. The fool behaves eccentrically in order to test the boundaries of his authority and the strength of these boundaries. A classical example of such a *samodur* may be found in Ostrovsky's character "Kit Kitych" Brouskov and the dictum characteristic of heroes of this type: "I will want to, I'll eat it with kasha (porridge), if not, I'll churn it with butter".

---

7. *Slovar' russkogo yazyka v 4 T*. Electronic Ed. Moscow, 1988, vol. 4, p. 18.

On the other hand, the behaviour of the *samodur* may be presented as a senseless and limitless act of innovation, the disturbance of stability for the sake of disturbance. The act is as unpredictable as the behaviour of the romantic madman whose actions reveal no causal connection. From this point of view, the concept of explosion may be defined as a dynamic moment in an otherwise rigid and immobile system. A similar effect may be produced by an excessively retarded mobility, which does not allow dynamic impulses to manifest themselves. The phenomenon of *samodurstvo* is akin to that of *yurodstvo*[8] – the behaviour of the foolish opens something up in the latter. The word "*yurodivye*" just as with "*samodurstvo*" is not translatable in European languages. Thus, the narrative of Gerhart Hauptmann which in Russian is translated as "Vo Hriste yurodiviyi Emanuel Kvint" ("fool-for-Christ") in German resounds as: "Der Narr in Christo Emanuel Quint" as a result of which the translation introduces a semantic nuance which is absent in Hauptmann. However, as Panchenko correctly notes, amongst the Russian *yurodivye*, a significant place was occupied by newcomers from the West, including Germans.[9]

Thus, the very concept of *yurodstvo* contains a contradiction: the interference of the stranger, frequently a foreigner and always a newcomer "not from this place" creates a typically Russian phenomenon which also is difficult to translate into the languages of other cultures.[10]

Ivan the Terrible serves as a convenient example of how from the point of view of the dynamics of culture this sphere of contradictions appears. Here, it is appropriate to touch upon some of the marginal aspects of Ivan the Terrible's behaviour. If we examine this behaviour from the point of view of the semiotics of culture, it represents itself as a conscious experiment aimed at overcoming all taboos. In this case, what interests us are ethical taboos and everyday behaviour. The latter represents an area in which behavioural excesses cannot be justified by any political or innovative considerations. However, in relation to the activities of Ivan the Terrible, this sphere occupies such a vast expanse that historians, from Karamzin to Klyuchevsky, Platonov and S. B. Veselovsky, even if they

---

8.  Translator's note: yurodstvo is a concept which encapsulates the idea of divine "folly"; yurodivyi=holy "fool-for-Christ".
9.  See: Panchenko, A. M. 1984. *Smekh kak zrelishche.* In Likhachev, D. S.; Panchenko, A. M.; Ponyrko, N. V. *Smekh v Drevnei Rusi.* Leningrad, p. 73.
10. It would be possible to compare this with the case, where the foreigner plays the role of the catalyst in a specific culture or is the carrier of specific features in its uniqueness. See, for example: the foreign teacher in the landowner's family – from the Frenchmen in the satiric literature of the XVIII century to the touching Karl Ivanovich in Tolstoy's *Childhood.*

were studying the problems of politics, social conflicts, statehood, inevitably found themselves implicated in a discussion of the psychological riddles of Ivan the Terrible. From our point of view, what is interesting is not so much the individual psychology of Ivan the Terrible as a unique and possibly pathologic personality but rather the mechanism of his cultural behaviour.

The perception of the personality of Ivan the Terrible, both by his contemporaries and by historians, is divided by a line drawn at the end of 1560, the period when the epoch of the reformation became the epoch of terror. Leaving to one side the extensive literature on this question and without adding to conjecture as to the reasons for the sharp break in the behaviour of the tsar, it is possible to note the following: the first period is organically-bound up in the epoch of the reforms, begun even in the time of Ivan III, and is characterised by a gradual, logically-sequential movement. State rule bears perceptible features of collectivity and moderate traditionalism. The personality of the tsar is manifested in the fact that he follows a specific progressive process; the second period differs sharply from the first, firstly by the unpredictability with which both the state and the behaviour of the tsar are brought to their limits. The *samodurstvo* (tyranny) and *yurodstvo* (foolishness) of which we spoke earlier have reached their optimal limits.

Many hypotheses – from Kurbsky to contemporary historians – have been put forward in relation to the reasons for this strange behaviour. However, before evaluating them, it is necessary to recall that the phenomenon of Ivan the Terrible is not so unique. The fact that absolute monarchism can fall into the excesses of reckless despotism is a sufficiently common phenomenon in world history although it obtains each time its own national-historical aura. The elevation of the tsar to the level of God, possessor of the full weight of authority, unavoidably caused on the one hand his identification with the devil, and on the other – the need for constant self-verification. Ivan the Terrible broke all ethical taboos one after the other, moreover he did so with a unique sense of pedantry that involuntarily causes us to stop and ask the question: what is the primary motivation here – the desire to satisfy unbridled desires in relation to which the theories are thereby adapted, or the experimental realisation of a theory, in the course of which the passions cease to be controllable and pass beyond the limits of the permissible? Does physiology shape an "obliging" semiotics that suits its purpose or does semiotics give space to physiology?

The real excesses of history are unlimited in their variety, yet the alphabet of any semiotic system is limited (or is perceived by us to be somewhat limited). This leads to a situation where the description of historical events sharply increases their repetitiveness. What is heterogeneous becomes homogeneous at the level of description. Isomorphism, too, is frequently generated by the mechanism of description; in the behaviour of Ivan the Terrible the following roles are clearly delineated:

1. *The role of God.* Ivan the Terrible assigns to himself the function of the Almighty, taking the metaphor of "unlimited authority" quite literally (in general, the tsar characteristically interprets the metaphor as a carrier of direct meaning). Such an interpretation of authority transforms the bearer of this authority into God Almighty. In this sense the words of Vasily Gryaznoi: "You, Sire, are like God . . ."[11] – had a much greater meaning, literally speaking, than we are now inclined to suspect.

2. *The role of the devil.* The idea of absolute authority (in the literal sense) generated a complex and practically insoluble question: Is this authority given to Christ or to the devil? Given that the bearer of absolute authority could not answer the question as to whether his personality was of God or of the devil, sharp deviations in behaviour were inevitable. Ivan the Terrible's unpredictable and confusing switches from holiness to sin and vice versa was, noted many sources, not the consequence of excesses in his personal psychology but an inevitable result of his absolute authority. Most of the executions conducted by Ivan the Terrible were reproductions of infernal punishments and, correspondingly, Ivan the Terrible lived his role both as the ruler of hell and as omnipotent God. One should add to this that a strong Manichean influence was perceived in the ideas and behaviour of Ivan the Terrible such that it was possible to view the devil as a plenipotentiary substitute of God in control of a culpable humanity.[12]

3. *The role of the fool for God (yurodivyi).* The combination of the roles of God, devil and the sinner generated one additional character in the behaviour of Ivan the Terrible: the divine fool (*yurodivye*). The concept of *yurodstvo* permitted the compatibility of the incompatible: the ability to live the life of sinner and saint at one and the same time, a fact incomprehensible to the "simple" but clear to the pious. The disgraceful behaviour of the fool (*yurodivyi*) was a result of his humility and he who wishes to understand the riddle of *yurodstvo* must be more humble than he who plays the fool: hence the idea of such secular feelings as fastidiousness, the love for cleanliness, are creations of the sin of pride. The fool (*yurodivyi*) may be dragged through faeces and see in this the highest cleanliness

---

11. *Poslaniya Ivana Groznogo.* Moscow/Leningrad, 1951, p. 567.
12. Elements of similar behaviour can be seen in the legend of Dracula. It is not by chance that the creator of the Russian version in 1481–1486 was the heretic Fyodor Kuritsyn, whose views were clearly influenced by Manichaean elements.

of spirit.[13] His behaviour is closed and contradictory, constantly posing a riddle to the world and this is clearly visible in the behaviour of Ivan the Terrible.

4. *The role of the exile.* The absolute sovereign is a defenceless exile – Ivan the Terrible constantly exhibits contradictory behaviour. He appropriates to himself all forms of authority. His tendency to amplify his spheres of competence, to enter into religious debates, and to formulate ideas of state is tied to this. The very meaning he ascribes to authority is that it is infinite. Therefore, in principle, he does not consider the possibility that any affairs of State could be entrusted to another. At the same time, Ivan the Terrible constantly developed the role of the defenceless exile. Here, we are talking not only about his plans to marry the English queen in order to have a place of refuge should he be forced to flee from Moscow, but also about his monkish mask and his frequently repeated words about his future ordination. Moreover, the very excess of the *oprichnina* (Ivan the Terrible's state troops) includes a dual psychology: the exile surrounded by enemies who searches for safe refuge and the autocratic ruler with absolute authority. Even in this case, the incompatibility of these two mutually contradictory concepts not only did not confuse Ivan the Terrible but, on the contrary, recreated a contradictory space that was natural to him. We can see a combination of these tendencies in his letters to Kurbsky where the voices of the defenceless victim of unrighteous persecutions and of the absolute ruler are indivisibly interwoven.

In the sphere of interest to us, the contrast of these incompatible tendencies led to the fact that out of the very roots of the behaviour of Ivan the Terrible "*samodurstvo*" ("wilfulness") was elevated to the level of a State norm: his behaviour was not translated into a sequential, internally justified policy but it did present itself in the form of a number of unpredictable explosions. "Unpredictability" in this case should be understood as the absence of internal political logic;[14] however, in the domain of personal behaviour the alternation between explosive bursts of cruelty and excesses of repentance allows us to speak of a form of regularity, represented by the field of psychopathology.

Exit beyond the boundaries of a structure may be realised as an unpredictable movement into another structure. In this case that which from a different point of view may be considered as systemic and predictable and within the limits of this structure is actualised as the unpredictable consequence of explosion.

---

13. See: *The Legend of St. Julian the Hospitalier* of Flaubert, where the last test of the sinner consists in overcoming feelings of fastidiousness and the fear of being infected: Julian embraces and warms the leper, who turns out to be Christ, with his own body.

14. For a critical analysis of the many attempts of the historians to introduce the notion of "state wisdom" or even simple logic into the activity of Ivan the Terrible, see: Veselovsky, S. B. *Issledovaniya po istorii oprichniny*. Moscow, 1963, p. 11–37.

Of particular interest, from this point of view, are those cases where there is a change in the functions of the sexes, since a non-semiotic structure is deliberately absorbed into the space of the semiotic game and a level of unpredictability is introduced into the system which is completely independent of the human will. In this case we will not dwell on the problems of the changing role of the sexes in the homosexual sense, although the semiotic function of similar phenomena could become a rich object for discussion.[15] Our attention will focus on the cultural role of secondary sexual functions: on those cases where the woman, in specific cultural contexts, assigns to herself the role of the man or vice versa; and to even more subtle situations, for example, where the woman plays the role of a woman in an accentuated manner.

A special variant is the case where the dominant role of articulation according to gender is generally abolished and concepts of the type "person", "citizen", "comrade" are introduced. Such terms as an "uncomradely attitude towards a woman" characteristically appeared at the time of the revolution of 1917. This expression was interpreted as a view of woman as the object of love or sexual desire. However, the real content of this "abolition of the sexes" was revealed by the fact that "human" was actually identified with "man". Woman apparently equated to man.

Thus, for instance, "revolutionary clothing" was designed to transform men's clothing into common clothing suitable for both men and women. Consequently, in the posters of the 1930s, this began to be converted into an ideal of sexless clothing. This may also be compared with the emphatic "chastity" of Soviet cinematography in the second half of the 1930s. By way of contrast, let us compare this to the marked feminine image of freedom in Barbier's *Iambic Verse*:

> Liberty is a strong woman with thrusting breasts
> Who, with her bronzed skin and her flashing eye...
> Takes her lovers only from among the people.[16]

Those cases, where men change their sex into a role, such that they merge with the norm in social consciousness are, as a rule, not reflected in the texts. The

---

15. See, for example, the expansion of homosexuality in the antique world and the obvious connection of this, in particular, to the humble position of the woman in classical Greece or the unique games of Nero, which involved women dressing like men in order to increase their sexual attractiveness. The very idea of these "games" was to introduce a variability in a structure that is, by nature, devoid of variability.

16. le Barbier, Auguste. *La Curée (The Quarry)*, 1831. In Boime, Albert, Art in an age of counterrevolution 1815–1848, University of Chicago Press: Chicago (2004) (Trans. E. de Mirecourt, Horace Vermeet, Paris, 1855), p. 254.

latter cannot be said about those cases where the fulfilment of the female role is assigned to a man. Usually this is connected with homosexual psychology and, therefore, appears to move beyond the limits of semiotics in its strictest sense. However, cases would also be possible where a man who has no apparent homosexual tendencies "plays the role of a woman".

Here we may, for example, recall the mysterious Chevalier d'Eon – an adventurer, a spy, who worked for Louis XV and played an eminent part in the diplomatic intrigues of that epoch (in particular, in the history of Russian-French relations). Since the Chevalier d'Eon, as he was called in Russia, repeatedly appeared in many intrigues in both female and male guise, after his death (he died in London in 1810) his body was looked at by the doctor who testified that the knight was a normal man. Moreover, at certain moments of his intricate adventurer's biography the Chevalier d'Eon clearly showed a preference for male behaviour. Thus, once he left behind the role of the woman of intrigue and as spy (parallel to the Milady of Dumas in real life) in order to enter France under the royal standards, to battle valiantly, to obtain a heavy wound and to merit a military reward. This behaviour did not prevent him from soon again changing into woman's clothing and returning to his usual role of adventurer.

It is interesting that in transferring secret letters from Louis XV to Empress Elizabeth the knight hid them in the skilfully prepared binding of the "Spirit of the Laws" by Montesquieu. Catherine II, would, in this case, certainly have appreciated the unintentional irony of the situation, whereas Elizabeth hardly paid attention to the elegant book the Frenchman presented to her.[17] Meanwhile, she could see in the book those thoughts which were important to her: for example, the interesting parallel between the extremes of despotism and democracy. Referring to the opinion of historians in regard to this, Montesquieu writes: "If to this we add the example of England and Russia, we shall find that they succeed alike both in moderate and despotic governments". It is difficult to determine whether this statement would be considered flattering by Elizabeth. But then, she might think well of herself in terms of the following words: "By the constitution of Russia the Czar may choose whom he has a mind for his successor, whether of his own or of a strange family. Such a settlement produces

---

17. Or Frenchwoman? Despite the fact that in sources dedicated to d'Eon, proceedings about the fact that in Petersburg the Chevalier fulfilled his secret diplomatic functions in female clothing are inflated, the latter appears groundless. The motivation provided by one of the early French biographers, that this detail was necessary in order to more easily enter into the bedroom of the Empress, misses the fact that the latter was in no way compulsory.

a thousand revolutions, and renders the throne as tottering as the succession is arbitrary".[18]

Constantly changing between the image of man and woman, the Chevalier d'Eon at the end of his life conducted himself in a very strange manner. Whether he got entangled in the problems of his own gender or, desiring to personify in himself both extremes, he, being an excellent swordsman, and having been deprived of all possible sources of income from his adventurist activities, became a teacher of fencing in London where, however, he carried out these lessons in women's clothing.

As a mirror reflection of behaviour of this type, we could add those cases where women appropriate men's clothing. Women's adoption of men's clothing (transformation into the man) has typically been associated with bellicose behaviour. The tragic role that this change of clothing played in the fate of Joan of Arc is well-known. This obligatory change into men's clothing, which Joan was forced to do, and the fraudulent nature of this action, formed the basis of the evidence against her in the judgement process, since such activity was considered to be a blasphemous disturbance of the distribution of the roles given by God. To the latter, in particular, is connected the medieval, but long held idea of the perverse nature of the acting profession. The very fact of an arbitrary change of clothing seemed suspicious from the point of view of a consciousness which did not separate expression from content. From this point of view, a change in appearance was perceived as the equivalent of a perverse spirit.

A change of sex on stage was prohibited even more. The widespread prohibition of women appearing on stage in general, which obliged the actor in the female role to change their clothing, created a permanently sinful situation on stage. The appearance of a female-actor did not resolve the problem but rather lent it an even more subtle nature. Perversity became not the change of sex but the change of the sign of the sex: the change of clothes, which turned the actress into the queen and the actor into the king, converted not only the stage but also the off-stage reality into a world of signs. Hence the countless themes based on the erosion of the boundaries between the theatre and life.

It was not only the theatre that provoked a change in the signifying functions of clothing. Palace coups in Russia during the XVIII century headed, as a rule, by women were accompanied by a ritual changing of clothing where the pretender to the throne would dress in a uniform which was in the first place designed for the male and in the second place for the Guards, and thirdly, belonging precisely to that regiment which played the leading part in the coup. Men's clothing and

---

18. Montesquieu, Charles de Secondat. *The Spirit of Laws*. Trans. Thomas Nugent, LL.D., vol. 1. New York: The Colonial Press, 1900, pp. 108, 61.

riding habits became the required accessories of the ritual transformation of the pretender into the empress. On the eve of the Decembrist uprising, Ryleev and Bestuzhev wrote, in their agitational song:

> You say, speak,
> Of how, in Russia, the tsars
> > reign.
> You say, more quickly,
> How, in Russia, the tsars
> > are strangled
> How corporals sent Peter off
> the courtyard in silence
> But his wife before the palace
> Galloped by, proudly
> > dashing.[19]

The picture drawn by the poets is entirely mythological: the coup occurred on the way to Peterhoff, not in Petersburg and the episode according to which Catherine accompanied troops astride a horse, is considered to be apocryphal. But this, for us, only serves to strengthen the value of the text written in verse which converts a historical episode into myth. In reality, this mythologized picture corresponds to the pretender to the throne's change of clothes into a male Guard's uniform. The ritual nature of this gesture is obvious. In the description of Dashkova, the beginning of the coup is marked precisely by this change of clothes into male garb: "... I lost no time in donning a man's greatcoat". The very declaration of Catherine herself, as empress, appears as a chain of changes of clothes: "Suddenly I noticed that she was still wearing the Order of St Catherine and had not yet put on the blue ribbon of the Cross of St Andrew.[20] [ ... ] I ran to Mr Panin to borrow his blue ribbon, which I put on the Empress's shoulder."[21] The last phrase is full of meaning: the expression "put it on the shoulders" indicated not a simple dressing but a ritual elevation. By this, Dashkova hints that Catherine

---

19. Ryleev, K. *Poln. sobr. stikhotvorenii*. Leningrad, 1934, p. 310. (Editor's note: Both Peter III and Paul I were strangled, 'sent Peter off' – this refers to Peter III's farewell to his loyal Holstein Guards after his deposition from the throne, 'his wife' – Peter III's wife, the future Catherine the Great, who had led the palace coup to become the Empress) (Translator's note: translation my own.)
20. Until Paul I, empresses (the wives of emperors) did not wear the order of Saint Andrew (this order was only founded in the era of Pavel), but only the female order of Saint Catherine. By changing the order of Catherine to that of Andrew this indicated the transformation of Catherine from the wife of the emperor into the empress. Simultaneously, there occurred a substitution of both sex and title.
21. Panin – the uncle of Dashkova, was implicated by her in the plot.

is obliged to it by the throne. "After a light dinner we proposed to go with the troops to Peterhof. The Empress and I decided to wear the uniform of the one of the Guards regiments; she therefore borrowed Captain Talyzin's uniform for the purpose and I that of Lieutenant Pushkin, as these two officers were roughly similar to us in height. [...] I went quickly home to change."[22]

Fonvizin, in the satire *Universal Court Grammar*, demonstratively divided "female nature" and "feminine sex":

> *Question.* What is the gender[23] of the court?
> *Answer.* There is a difference between the masculine and feminine soul. This difference does not depend on gender, since in court sometimes woman is worth more than a man, but another man is worse than a woman.

Let us consider the use of grammatical gender as employed by Fonvizin in the text: "Having as sovereign (*monarkhinya*) an honest person (*chelovek*) ..."[24] This is also typical of a change of a grammatical gender in an analogous situation in Shcherbatov's reflections on Elizabeth: "Yes, whether it was this (the fall in morals – J. L.) or it could be otherwise, when the Sovereign himself did everything he could to embellish of his person, when he as a rule, had himself to put on a new dress every day and sometimes two or three a day and I am ashamed to say how many but can assure you that several tens of thousands of different robes remained after her death'.[25] The combination of male type verbs and the enumeration of details of feminine clothing creates an especially interesting effect. Several lines further on Shcherbatov, passing from the rhetorical style to the neutral, transports Elizabeth into the grammatical feminine gender.

Examples of the fact that female emancipation in the XIX century, in effect, awarded itself the male role through the adoption of male clothing can be exemplified by Georges Sand who is linked to the adoption of a male pseudonym and men's clothing, or the famous "cavalry maiden" Durova. N. A. Durova's memoirs enraptured Pushkin, as in her notes she describes her "transformation into a man" as the adoption not only of men's clothing but also of man's fate – as the finding of the freedom: "And so I'm at liberty. Free! Independent! I have taken the freedom that is rightfully mine – the freedom that is a precious gift from heaven, the inalienable prerogative of every human being! I have found

---

22. *The Memoirs of Princess Dashkov*. Trans. Kyril Fitzlyon. London: John Calder, 1958, p. 70, 73, 74.
23. Translator's note: i.e. in grammar – English translation my own.
24. Fonvizin, D. I. *Sobr. soch. v 2 T.* Collected text, publication and commentary by G. P. Makogonenko. Moscow/Leningrad, 1959, vol. 2, pp. 50, 274. (Translator's note: translation my own.)
25. Shcherbatov, M. M. *Soch. knyazya M. M. Shcherbatova* [ v 6 T. ], St. Petersburg, 1898, vol. 2, p. 219. (Translator's note: translation my own.)

a way to take it and guard it from all future claims against it; from now to my grave, it will be my portion and my reward!"[26]

In spite of a somewhat pathetic tone, this exclamation was undoubtedly sincere.

A woman's change of clothes into men's clothing could take on another meaning, if it was accompanied by a man's change of clothes into female clothing. This may be considered as one version of emancipation: if men's clothing only emphasised the piquant features of the appearance of a young and harmonious beauty (this, for example, ties in with Elizabeth's love of male clothing), it also gave them a certain nuance of ambiguity,[27] so that a man's change of clothing into that of the female invariably reduced his rank, turning him into a kind of comic hero. Let us compare numerous cases of men's forced change of clothing into women's clothes in the novels and comedies of the XVIII century. The contemporary reader may recall the flight of D'Artagnan from the bedroom of Milady or *The House in Colomna*:

> "... But where is Mavrusha?" "Gone, and how depraved!
> She – just like my lamented spouse – she shaved!"[28]

Amongst the papers of Catherine II is a plan of entertainment, intended for the small circle of visitors to the Hermitage. In the spirit of the French "inverted ballets" at the end of the XVI and the beginning of the XVII century, in the farcical masquerade planned by Catherine, the women had to change into men's suits, and the men – into female dresses. The appearance of the giant Orlov brothers (Grigory Orlov, with a scar on his cheek took the guise of a bandit, according to N. K. Zagryazhskaya[29] ) or of a one-eyed Potemkin in women's garments not only had to cause laughter, but was also a comic lowering of their social role.

The retention by the woman of the "female role" could also acquire an element of eccentricity. However, in this case, some special socio-cultural position

---

26. Nadezhda Durova. *The Cavalry Maiden. Journals of a Russian Officer in the Napoleonic Wars*. Trans. Mary Fleming Zirin. Bloomington/Indianapolis: Indiana University Press, 1989, p. 18.
27. It is possible to compare this with a young gentlewoman's change of clothes into peasant dress: this allowed the other, a considerably more accessible type of behaviour, and it simultaneously allowed a man a high degree of freedom, see "The Miss-Peasant Woman" of Pushkin. For interesting details of this see further in the description of A. Orlova-Chesmenskaya's behaviour.
28. Alexander Pushkin. *Three Comic Poems*. Trans. William E. Harkins. Ann Arbor: Ardis, p. 81.
29. Pushkin's note: "Il avait l'air d'un brigand avec sa balafre" (*Poln. sobr. soch.*, t. XII, 176).

was required, which sharply set one apart from average female stereotypes. For Russia in the first half of the XIX century, examples of this can be shown by two polar opposites, that of Anna Alekseevna Orlova-Chesmenskaya and Sofya Dmitrievna Ponomareva.

A. A. Orlova-Chesmenskaya was the only daughter of Count Aleksei Orlov, one of Catherines dignitaries, who advanced together with his brothers during the revolution which overthrew Peter III and was a participant in the murder of the former emperor. The early childhood of the countess took place in her father's house. The fairytale wealth of Aleksei Orlov, the open, truly lordly lifestyle (Orlov was richer than many of the crown heads of Europe) was tied to adherence to the way of life of the common people:

> I go off riding to the Swings;
> I stop at taverns for some spirits
> Or, if this too becomes a bore –
> My nature does incline to changes –
> I set my cap at jaunty angle
> And fly atop a sportive steed.[30]

To these verses Derzhavin added a note: "It refers also to him [to Potemkin ], and all the more to Count Al. Gr. Orlov ..."[31]

Anna Alekseevna received a good education – she spoke three European languages fluently; and foreign governesses had inculcated in her the norms of secular behaviour. Her childhood was lived out in the company of her father who was very attached to her and in the company of adults belonging to the highest circle of Moscow nobility, enriching her early impressions about the life of the court. The death of Catherine and accession of Paul I turned the position of the Orlovs to one of disgrace, one that was even dangerous. Aleksei Orlov, together with his daughter, left for foreign parts – for reasons of safety. Aleksei Orlov's conversation with Zagryazhskaya at this time, later recorded by Pushkin, testifies to the mood of the Orlov brothers at this time: "Orloff était régicide dans l'âme, c'était comme une mauvaise habitude.[32] I met with him in Dresden, in an out-of-town garden. He sat down next to me on the bench. We chatted about Pavel I. "That freak! How can they suffer him?" – "Ah, batushka, well, what would you have me do? After all, we could not strangle him, could we?– "And why not, matushka?" – "What! And you would agree that your daughter Anna

---

30. Derzhavin, G. R. Felitsa. In: *Poetic Works. A Bilingual Album*. Ed. A. Levitsky. Trans. Alexander Levitsky and Martha T. Kitchen. Brown Slavic Contributions, vol. 12. Providence: Brown University Press, 2001, p. 30.
31. Derzhavin, G. R. *Soch. v 9 T.* St. Petersburg, 1863–1883, vol. 3, p. 598.
32. Orlov's vocation was regicide, it was like a bad habit (Fr.).

Alekseevna could be mixed up in such a thing?" – "Not only would I agree, but I would be very pleased". Such was the man!"[33]

Life in the paternal house carried on in a very tense, contrasting manner. According to the evidence of a biographer, A. A. Orlova-Chesmenskaya[34] frequently ran away from the noisy festivals of the paternal house and could be found praying in the church. However, we have other evidence, correcting the somewhat iconographic style of the memoirist: "At the will of her father and for the pleasure of the guests she danced the dance with the shawl, with the tambourine, the Cossack dance, the Gypsy and the Russian dance, etc. In some cases, two servants carried out some of the steps in her place, those which were considered to be insufficiently decent for the young countess, whilst the guests sat around her in a reverential circle."[35]

This period of the life cycle of Orlova is very little documented. A valuable source on her are the letters of the sisters Martha and Catherine Wilmott from Russia published by G. A. Veselov. In the letters and the diary Martha Wilmott noted the absence of pretentiousness and the natural simplicity in the behaviour of Orlova. On the 16th of March, 1804, she wrote in her diary on a trip to the countryside: "The charming Countess Orloff was the only Woman who drove,

---

33. A. Pushkin. *Poln. sobr. soch.*, t. XII. Moskva-Leningrad, 1949, p. 177. (Translator's note: translation my own.)

34. See: Elagin, N. *Zhizn' grafini Anny Alekseevny Orlovoi-Chesmenskoi.* CPb, 1853, p. 21.

35. Pylyaev, M. I. *Staraya Moskva: Rasskazy iz byloi zhizni pervoprestol'noi stolicy.* Moscow, 1990, p. 148. However, the image described, is probably the result of exaggerations or gossips. At least, sufficiently stiff Englishwomen M. and K. Wilmott found in the dances of the Countess nothing reprehensible. In a letter to her father Martha Wilmot reported: "I told all our proceedings in my last letter to my Mother. Since that we have been at Count Orloff's ball which was superb, and what pleased me more, it was in the Russian fashion. We began with a country dance (this is after the Polonaise which is always danc'd first, or rather walk'd). There were five country dances, and between each Countess Orloff danc'd figure dances which exceeded everything I ever beheld (even in pictures) for Grace, Elegance and beauty. Lady Hamilton's attitudes are absolutely vulgar compar'd to the Sylph like beauty of Countess Orloff – 'tis a sin they are not preserv'd on Canvas – and added to this is such sweetness I never beheld before. The Shawl dance in every moment was a picture of the most exquisite beauty …" (*The Russian Journals of Martha and Catherine Wilmott. 1803-1808.* Edited by the Marchioness of Londonderry and H. M. Hyde. London, Macmillan, p. 70–71; the Russian edition: Dashkova, E. R. *Zapiski. Pis'ma sester M. i K. Vilmot iz Rossii.* Translated from the French by A. Yu. Bazilevich, G. A. Veselov, G. M. Lebedev, with commentary by G. A. Veselov. Moscow, 1987, p. 240).

and she was her father's Charioteer, driving 4 in hand. The Carriage was preceded by two Horsemen in scarlet, a Postillion guided two horses & the Countess 4. The Carriage was a high light Phaeton like a shell & uncommonly pretty."[36]

After the death of her father, the countess did not want to endure guardians over her (which resulted in a quarrel with her uncle – the youngest of the Orlov brothers) and she began to live the extravagant life of a young, independent girl without patron or male protector. The extravagance, to which her unprecedented wealth gave her the right, did not scare her. She rejected fiancés and, after one love which ended tragically for her, she apparently decided to remain single. It is likely that, here, she exhibited the most Orlovian of traits – the search for unlimited freedom. On 9 January, 1808, M. Wilmott noted in her diary a fateful entry for the countess: "This morning Count Orloff was buried". Following on from this, she added: "The Charming young Countess Orloff his daughter is afflicted beyond all expression, but she is a most superior creature. She makes none of the parade of woe so usual here. She has however had constancy & courage enough each day to visit the cold remains of her father while no one was present of the tribes who have been as usual to kiss the body. Her entire life has been pass'd amidst scenes which would have corrupted a common mind; hers has preserv'd all its purity & risen superior to every seduction."[37] The property of this most enviable bride of Russia was so great, that neither she nor her envious contemporaries could calculate its worth. The Englishwoman suggested 300 thousand roubles (40 thousand pounds), not including treasures or land, repeating aloud that in the basements besides diamonds, pearls and other treasures, were stored three enormous trunks of ducats. Russian sources, clearly more reliable, asserted that "... the yearly income of the inheritance stretched to 1,000,000 roubles, the value of her immovable estate, excluding diamonds and other treasures which were valued at 20,000,000 roubles, reached about 45,000,000 roubles."[38]

After burying her father, the Countess led a quiet life, moderate in both expenditure and behaviour, providing little fodder for the gossips. The best evidence of this is the silence in these years about her in the communications of her contemporaries. The unhappy love she experienced, whose details are almost unknown to us and possibly, the Orlovian family trait – the incapacity to obey someone, were a reason for her decision not to marry. However, she reveals no mystical impulses at this time; a journey, for example, to the holy places was accomplished with great convenience: "They are travelling with 9 carriages or

---

36. *The Russian Journals of Martha and Catherine Wilmott* ... , p. 86.
37. Ibid, 315.
38. Pylyaev, M. I. *Staraya Moskva*, p. 147.

Carts, Kitchen, food, Hay, in short like a moving Colony ..."[39] Simultaneously she received, to use Pushkin's expression, a succession of rewards and ranks. In 1817 she was made a lady-in-waiting, on which occasion, Alexander I gave her a portrait of the empress decorated with diamonds, and under Nicholas she received the ribbon of the order of Saint Catherine; in 1828 she accompanied the empress on a prolonged trip through Russia and Europe; but all this was seemingly an outer, showy aspect of her life. Having everything, the Countess, apparently, secretly dreamed of throwing it all away: she aspired to an unlimited freedom, and thirsted for an unlimited obedience. Half-measures and common sense did not entice her and Orlova sought out a severe leader. Behind such maximalism lay the thirst for adventure. In another epoch she possibly would have found her lack of compromise in entirely different, perhaps rebellious, expression.

As a spiritual mentor, she chose for herself the monk Anfilofi, who took care of saint's relics in the monastery.[40] The old man soon passed away and after this Orlova crossed paths with Photius. Photius (Pyotr Nikitich Spassky) was born in 1792 into a poor family. His father, the dyachok of Spassky cemetery (hence his surname), was a terrible son beater. In the seminary, where he learned badly, they also beat him. After finishing seminary, he entered the Saint Petersburg seminary but he did not learn well and was forced to leave within a year.

After seminary he became an instructor in the Aleksandr Nevsky seminary. It seemed that fate appointed him to the role of a spiritual Akaki Akakievich – the eternal toiler, suffering the permanent torment of the unlucky wretch. But circumstances proved otherwise. In the seminary, he entered into the confidence of the archimandrite Innokenti – a severe ascetic. Photius himself later acknowledged that he diligently noted all Innokenti's words, his behaviour, his opinions and actions. In 1817 he accepted monastic dignity and was appointed as a teacher of religion in the Second Cadet Corp. The children who learned in this building came from the kind of social world that was closed at that time to Photius. The inaccessible was made accessible. Photius's behaviour began to be provocatively extravagant. It is possible that he actually suffered mystical visions, leading himself through ascetic exercises, in chains and by fast to the highest levels nervous tension. But it is indisputable and that some of his mystical experiences were rough simulations and what is more that he used them with great skill and craftiness.

His ambition was limitless. Finding himself in Petersburg, with the help of A. N. Golitsyn, against whom he secretly plotted, he gained access to the

---

39. *The Russian Journals of Martha and Catherine Wilmott*, p. 361.
40. See: Pylyaev, M. I. *Staraya Moskva*, p. 148.

sovereign and he knew how to produce a strong impression before the emperor. Subsequently Photius adopted the behaviour of a fanatic and a schemer. Skilfully changing masks, he relied on different strengths. In the society of the court, he appeared in the mask of the severe censor, the ascetic, ostentatiously coarse and playing the role of the mystical mediator of God. His coarseness sharply separated him from the background of the remaining church hierarchy of the Alexandrian epoch. He even ventured into censure of such bluntness that it created around him a halo of apostolic simplicity. The behaviour of Photius influenced the court and permitted him to enter into that circle, skilfully using his contrasting influence as much with secular society as he did within the church hierarchy – who were either intimidated or sincerely devoted to him. The behaviour of Photius, including his impudent censure, also influenced the emperor.

Photius was soon permitted an audience with Alexander as his intimate col-locutor, a role he used skilfully. However, the "courage" of Photius (including the celebrated episode in which he proclaimed anathema for his patron and abso-lute protector Golitsyn) was wholly calculated. It was not by chance that Photius chose for himself the Novgorod Yurievsky monastery: thus, he was able to be-come the nearest neighbour of Arakcheev. The monastery was transformed into a spiritual fortress for military colonies. It is difficult to tell whether Arakcheev used Photius in order to bring down the hateful Golitsyn or whether Photius used Arakcheev to strengthen his position; however, it is obvious that they formed a closed alliance to their mutual advantage. Arakcheev was sentimental but he was not characterised by a religious fervour and his sacrificial libations of wine at a bust of the emperor Paul I resembled the pagan cult of the emperor. In his meetings with Photius, he undoubtedly removed his mystical mask.

Such was the man whose influence in the 1820s turned Countess Orlova-Chesmenskaya almost into a slave. She became an obedient executor of his authority and sacrificed enormous amounts of money to his monastery (Photius demonstrated his personal unselfishness and an apostolic austerity in his way of life but he zealously enriched his monastery). The Orlovian traits of *samodurstvo* (wilfulness), pride and a thirst for an unlimited scope of action, psychologically motivated the idea of rescuing the soul in the form of voluntary servitude. This was violence on the self.

In society there were widespread rumours about an amorous connection between Orlova and Photius. These epigrams are attributed to the young Pushkin:

A CONVERSATION BETWEEN PHOTIUS AND COUNTESS ORLOVA

"Oh, harken, what I am averring:
I've a eunuch's body, the soul of a man."

But what are you doing with me then?
"I'm body into soul transforming".

TO COUNTESS ORLOVA-CHESMENSKAYA
One woman, pious on the whole,
To God devoted full her soul,
But gave her sinful flesh
To Archimandrite Photius.[41]

However, the actual relations between Orlova and Photius are here distorted by translation into the language of Voltairian satire. The Countess's voluntary enslavement to Photius stretched so far that she even tolerated the ambiguous relationship of Photius with Photina. The old residents of Moscow preserved this scandalous story in their memory in the following form. One day, into the cloister hospital appeared "the young girl, Photina, who served as a dancer in the Petersburg ballet; not anticipating a great future for herself in the theatre, she decided to play an eminent role elsewhere. After arriving at the hospital, she declared herself to be obsessed by an unclean spirit and Photius began to treat her. After prayers and during convulsive motions the cries: "I will leave, I will leave!" were heard – and then the girl fell into unconsciousness. Coming back to herself, she declared herself free from her demons. They led her to some accommodation next to the monastery.

Photius worried about her . . . ". The new saint then fell into all manner of debauchery. However, the scandal connected with this did not stop Photius, who was, apparently, attracted by the connection between asceticism and ambiguous behaviour. In the monastery it was established that: ". . . all young women living in the environments of the monastery would be gathered together for the evening rule at the monastery and, dressed in identical clothing to the monks, would accomplish prayers".[42] The Countess Orlova was caught up in this Sabbath and, apparently, took it to be one additional test of obedience. In this manner, the impulse of independence was turned into an impulse of voluntary servitude.

In conclusion, it remains to be considered into whose hands in the final analysis the mystical refusal of the sin of wilfulness has led the Countess. The first and obvious answer is Photius. However, Photius himself could only obtain this level of importance because he played Arakcheev's game.

In the meantime, it doesn't follow that we should emphasise this well-trodden path to logic. We must recall the words of Krylov:

---

41. Alexander Pushkin. *Epigrams & Satirical Verse*. Ed. and trans. by Cynthia Whittaker. Ardis: Ann Arbor, 1984, p. 112.
42. Pylyaev, M. I. *Staraya Moskva*, p. 150. (Translator's note: translation my own.)

And how did all the beasts this sad result explain?
The Lion does his best: 'It's all those wolves again.'[43]

The conviction of many historians, that in these years Alexander confided all in Arakcheev and was himself immersed in a mystical fog, is only partly correct and the main thing is that this coincides with the persistent tactics of the emperor: to hide behind just another "favourite" on whose head falls the whole of public dissatisfaction.

The first to become disillusioned was Photius. In the place of Golitsyn they appointed Shishkov. He was a very successful choice. This was a man from the camp of the Archaists[44] in policy and religion, but at the same time he was the narrow-minded but honest leader of the "Beseda" Society (Colloquy of Lovers of the Russian Word). He was completely alien to that group of "traders in the temple" which surrounded Photius. It is significant that the choice of Shishkov and the corresponding impact on Golitsyn were sympathetically perceived in liberal circles:

> Having, finally, thought through his good intentions,
> Our good tsar has chosen an honest minister,
> We see that Shishkov has already assumed management of the sciences
> This old man is dear to us: a friend of honour, a friend of people,
> He is glorious by the glory of the twelfth year . . . [45]

After the fall of Golitsyn and all the changes surrounding this moment, behind Arakcheev's, the profile of Alexander himself is clearly visible. Metternich believed that he had pulled the wool over the eyes of the tsar, Photius assumed that he deceived Alexander with his mystical spectacles, everyone in Russia thought that the country was actually governed by Arakcheev and the tsar played merely a passive role in politics.

However, it is possible to assume that Alexander, as always, having hidden behind the spin-doctoring of his dummies held authority in his hands at the last minute. Alexander went, it seemed, for the realisation of his utopia: a militarily-

---

43. Krylov, I. A. Speckled Sheep. In: *Krylov's Fables*. Trans. Bernard Pares. Westport, Connecticut: Hyperion Press, 1977, p. 270. (Editor's note. The plot of Krylov's fable is as follows: the Lion King hates speckled sheep, but does not dare to destroy them publicly. The Fox recommends entrusting the protection of the sheep to the wolves. "The plan worked out so well that, as the days went on, / The speckled sheep were nearly gone, – / The plain ones too were going." – M.G.).
44. Editor's note: adepts of linguistic, literary and political conservatism in the early 19th century Russia. – M.G.
45. A. Pushkin. Vtoroe poslanie k tsenzoru. In: *Poln. sobr. soch.*, t. II, kn.I. Moskva/ Leningrad, 1947, p. 368. (Translator's note: English translation my own.)

settled Russia, believing that in this way he would throw off all these shameful bonds and again appear as the rescuer of Russia and Europe, who reconciled freedom with the will of God. The Countess Anna Orlova was only a small step in this immense phantasmagorical concept.

Another method for the talented woman of that time to show her individuality was connected with the literary salon. The culture of the salon bloomed in XVII–XVIII century France. It was, in principal, an unofficial and informal culture. In this sense it opposed the Academy. In the salon of Madame de Rambouillet unofficial trends in politics and literature merged. This tradition passed into the philosophical salon of the Enlightenment. The model of philosophical salon was constructed as a meeting of celebrities, skilfully selected, with similar tastes so that an excessive identity of ideas would not destroy the possibility of discussions but simultaneously so that these discussions would be the dialogues of friends or at least companions-in-arms. The skill of intellectual conversation was culti-vated in this salon as a refined game of minds which draws together intellectual enlightenment and the elite. The sun amongst all these planets was the lady, the mistress of the salon. She, as a rule, belonged to an age which prevents amorous enthusiasm. On the social scale she most frequently stood above devotees. She personified that world in which philosophers were submerged and which they energetically undermined. Encyclopaedists hurried the destruction of this world, but, happily for them, the majority did not exist prior to this desired epoch.

Out of this arose the well-known legend of Cazotte, who allegedly prophe-sised to all participants in the salon the philosophical future of which they all arduously dreamed. In his prophetically inspired vision he described to them the as yet uninvented guillotine and the terror that awaited them all.

This entire episode is, of course, legendary in nature and was elaborated retrospectively. It may be compared with Repin's picture *Kakoy Prostor!* (What Freedom!). The artist's canvas depicts an ice floe inundated by waves, upon which two students (a boy and a girl) are enthusiastically holding hands. They greet the beginning of the floating ice and the unlimited space opened before them with a stroke of the hand. The artist obviously shares their happiness. In the same way, the members of the Enlightenment in France and the Russian intellectuals at the beginning of the XX century joyfully greeted the dawn of the new century.

The salon in the Russia of the 1820s was a unique phenomenon, reflecting the Parisian salon of the pre-revolutionary epoch and at the same time substantially different from it. As in Paris, the salon is a unique solar system revolving around the chosen lady. However, if in the French salon it was only by way of exception that the mistress might be a charming woman who introduced into the life of the salon a nuance of gallanterie, then in the Russian salon this was a requirement.

The mistress of the salon possesses a sharpness of mind, is artistically inclined, beautiful and attractive. Visitors to the salon are more quickly attached to her not by those bonds which connected the Encyclopaedists to the mistresses of various salons, but by the collective service of knights to their chosen lady. Such were the salons of Sofya Ponomareva from 1820–1823 or Zinaida Volkonskaya's in the second-half of the 1820s.

Sofya Dmitrievna Ponomareva's salon was studied by. V. E. Vatsuro, whose captivating analysis reveals the "life novel" of this remarkable woman who knew how to raise everyday life to the level of art.[46] We can call the salon of Ponomareva a work of art because it was something unique: it copied nothing and could not be perpetuated.

In the many extensive poetic reflections on Sofya Ponomareva, she is first of all characterised as unpredictable and capricious in her behaviour.[47]

Oh, wilful Sofya! –

wrote Baratynsky[48] Of the numerous poems given to her by devotees and later dedicated to her, the constant epitaph is that of the image of the woman-child. Her pose – the playful child, who plays at life:

She flowered and shone
She was happiness before our eyes;
Like a child

She played at life ... [49]
She played an earthly life, like a baby with its toy.

Yet soon it broke: hopefully she has consoled herself beyond the grave.[50]

The "childish" behaviour of an adult woman cites infantilism as a certain individual and, in this exceptional case only, the acknowledged norm. This is that which is permitted "only to her" and cannot be imitated nor reproduced. The uniqueness of this infantilism is determined by the fact that it is combined with a unique talent and female attractiveness. This unpredictable woman-child, alternately appears first in the female, then in the child's hypostasis. Her devo-

46. See: Vatsuro, V. E. *S. D. P. Iz istorii literaturnogo byta pushkinskoi pory.* [*The history of literary life in Pushkin's time.*] Moscow, 1989.
47. See: Watteau's Hermitage picture "La Boudeuse", personifying on the canvas the integral "program" of the capricious behaviour of the lady. Whim – early form of the fight for the right to individuality.
48. Baratynsky, E. A. *Poln. sobr. stikhotvorenii.* T. 1, p. 98.
49. Gnedich, N. I. *Stikhotvoreniya.* 2nd ed. Leningrad., 1956. p. 135.
50. Del'vig, A. A. *Poln. sobr. stikhotvorenii.* (*The Poet's Library. Large series*) Ed. and annotated by B. V. Tomashevsky, 2nd ed. Leningrad, 1959, p. 180. (Translator's note: translation my own.)

tees agonisingly try to distinguish whether they are dealing with the capricious child who naively leads them into ambiguous situations without suspecting their ambiguity or with the passionate woman who rushes into enthusiasm as the butterfly rushes into the flame.

The issue of unpredictability is supplemented by the fact that the heroine of this novel possesses a sharp mind and sharp language. Her life, woven from unexpected contingencies, is crowned by unexpected death as the perfect composition of an artistic work – at the very apex of her youth and success.

If the life of Sofya Ponomareva is realised in the poetry of behaviour, then the creative participation of poets in her life, beginning with Aleksandr Efimovich Izmailov, Orest Somov, Vladimir Panayev, Boris Fyodorov (the notorious "Bor'ka"), M. l. Yakovlev, N. Ostolopov to Gnedich, Delvig and Baratynsky, transformed this poetic life into poetic texts. Having passed trial in Sofya Ponomareva's salon and then in the Izmailov's literary society, these texts appeared little by little in the pages of periodicals and almanacs and were gradually converted into literary facts. Only the congeniality of Sofya Ponomareva, as convincingly shown by Vatsuro, transformed life into art with the same talent with which her devotees transformed the facts of art into their amorous confessions.

A different atmosphere reigned in the salon of Zinaida Volkonskaya, which bloomed in Moscow in the middle 1820s. Born into the family of Prince Beloselsky-Belozersky and noted for her frivolity and literary dilettantism she had, since childhood, received the most refined education. She spoke and wrote in five languages. Rich and happy-go-lucky, Princess Volkonskaya combined the style of European salons with the light touch of Bohemia and an unconcealed political independence. Even the fact that she later placed, in her Roman palace, a marble bust of Alexander I alongside antique marble pieces dedicated to Pushkin and Venevitinov was not deprived of a rebellious nuance. This respectful gesture towards the deceased emperor only served to emphasise her opposition to the reigning one.

Nicholas I forced the princess to leave Russia. In doing so, he was punishing her for her "provocative" conversion to Catholicism but, probably, also for the demonstrative nature of her opposition. In reality, the salon of princess did not have a political nature, however, it was an island wherein an artificial atmosphere of the cult of beauty and fine arts was generated and one which acquired, against the background of Nicholas's regime, an unexpected meaning that was in no way neutral. Let us recall Pushkin's words, enunciated much later (1836) about true freedom:

To be dependent on a king, or on a nation...
Is it not all the same? Good riddance! But to dance
To no one else's fiddle, foster and advance

One's private self alone; before gold braid and power
With neither conscience, thought, nor spine to cower;
To move now here, now there with fancy's whim for law,
In Nature's godlike works to take delight and awe,
And start before the gifts of art and inspiration
With pangs of trembling, joyous adoration –
There's bliss for you! There are your rights ... [51]

The "aesthetised" independence of the princess was clearly visible in her farewells to Maria Volkonskaya who was herself leaving for Siberia, following her husband who had been exiled to penal servitude. One should recall that the mother of Volkonsky, a lady-in-waiting in the court of the widowed empress, had rejected her son, sentenced to penal servitude, and had left at the same time for Moscow in order to participate in the celebrations of the coronation of Nicholas I. Against this background Zinaida Nikolaevna had organised, in Moscow, a noisy demonstrative send-off for her sister-in-law, having invited well-known Italian musicians and singers and the entire spectrum of intellectual society, including Pushkin. Maria Volkonskaya wrote: "In Moscow, I stayed with Zinaida Volkonskaya, my third sister-in-law who accepted me with such tenderness and kindness that I will never forget: she surrounded me with concerns, attention, love and compassion. Knowing my passion for music, she invited all the Italian singers who were then in Moscow and several talented girls. I very much admired the excellent Italian singing and thinking that I might be hearing it for the last time made it all the more excellent for me. I said to them: "Again, again, just think, indeed, I may never hear music again!" Pushkin, our great poet, was also there."[52]

The celebration arranged by Zinaida Volkonskaya for the daughter-in-law was not a sign of political sympathy towards the Decembrists. It demonstrated something else: the independence of art from authority but, in the situation that existed then, indifference to politics was transformed into a political position.

The image of Volkonskaya's salon as an "enchanted island", on which were gathered the devotees of the arts with different views and different talents is reflected in the well-known picture Of G. G. Myasoedov, creator of the mythological scene of the meeting of the "priests of art". In G. G. Myasoedov's painting, Zinaida Volkonskaya sits at the feet of the statue of Venus de Milo, surrounded by Venevitinov, Pushkin, Khomyakov, Vyazemsky and Pogodin. The compositional centre of the painting is given over to the figures of Chaadaev and Mickiewicz

---

51. A. Pushkin. From Pindemonte. In *Lyric Poems: 1826–1836* in *The Complete Works of Alexander Pushkin*, vol. 3, p. 248, Milner and Company Limited, 1999 (Trans. W. Arndt).

52. *Zapiski knyagini Marii Nikolaevny Volkonskoi*, St. Petersburg, 1914, p. 61.

each of whom stands on one of the two extremes of the painting: the former is presented in a reflective pose, the latter enthusiastically recites verses. Whatever the real relationship between the pleiad of artists drawn together for these evenings, the painting very accurately reflects the historical mythology of the meetings in Zinaida Volkonskaya's salon. In his recollections of Mickiewicz, Vyazemsky wrote: "In Moscow, the salon in Zinaida Volkonskaya's house was an elegant meeting place for all the eminent and elite personalities of contemporary society. All the representatives of high society gathered here: dignitaries, beauties, young and old, intellectuals, professors, writers, journalists, poets, artists. Everything in the house bore the imprint of a devotion to the arts, and to thinking. Readings, concerts by dilettantes and by lovers of Italian opera took place there. Amongst the artists, and at their head, stood the mistress of the house herself. Having heard her, it was impossible to forget the impression she provoked with her full-bodied, sonorous contralto and her animated interpretation of the role of Tancred in the opera of Rossini. I can still remember, and hear, how, in the presence of Pushkin, on the first day of her acquaintance with him, she sang his elegy, put to music by Genishta:

> "The daily star has gone out,
> At sea, the dark-blue fog of dusk is falling".

Pushkin was extremely touched by this artistic charm and refined coquetry. As usual, he blushed. It goes without saying that Mickiewicz, as soon as he arrived in Moscow was a frequent visitor and was numbered amongst the most favourite and most honoured guests in Volkonskaya's salon. He dedicated a poem to her which went by the name Pokoj Grecki (The Greek Room)".[53]

Volkonskaya's salon had, as is assumed of societies of this type, its own legend. This legend concerned the unrequited love of Venevitinov for the mistress of salon; a love, which was tragically interrupted by the death of the young genius. Such a legend was a required embellishment to the atmosphere of salon. However, on the whole, the unifying factor in the meetings in Zinaida Volkonskaya's salon was not that of love but rather the cult of art. This cultivated aestheticism gave Volkonskaya's salon a somewhat cold nature. This climate is reflected particularly well in the stereotypical salon described in the elegant poem of Pushkin, dedicated to Volkonskaya:

> In Moscow's dissipated rabble,
> Where whist and bridge and gossip lead,
> And balls are rife with idle battle,
> You love an Apollonian creed.

53. Vyazemsky, P. A. *Vospominaniya o Mitskeviche.* In *Sobr. Soch. T. VII.* St. Petersburg, 1878–1896, p. 329.

Of Muses and of beauty queen,
Within your gentle grasp is seen
Enchanted sceptre to inspire,
And on your meditative brow
That's wreathed with double garland now,
There throbs and flashes genuis' fire.
This captive poet, when he pays
Poor tribute – do you not decry;
But listen smiling to my praise,
As Catalonians passing by
Hear wandering gypsy in her ways.[54]

Between the very surnames of Ponomareva (born Poznyak) and Volkonskaya (born Beloselskaya-Belozerskaya) – there is an eloquent difference which clearly speaks of the differences in their social position and the entire atmosphere that lies between these two, so chronologically close, salons. And what is even more striking is the correlation of their opposition to everyday reality. In both salons we see an attempt to rise above the vulgar.[55]

Another way in which a woman could, to paraphrase Pasternak, rise above "the shameful life" was a way, which society considered reprobate. In poetry (for example, under the pen of Lermontov) this was portrayed as the romantic image of the prostitute:

Oh, let the world torment and hate us
And probe our secret with a knife,
And let it rob you of the status
Of a respected, honest wife!
We both despise the proud and idle –
The rabble's gods of love and hate;
Let someone else create an idol
To bow before and venerate.[56]

In everyday reality, this image lost its romantic aura and in literature it will only return in the form of "those who are humbled and insulted" – in the social interpretation of Nekrasov and the religious interpretation of Dostoevsky.

---

54. A. Pushkin. To Princess Z. A. Volkonskaya. In *Lyric Poems: 1826–1836*, in *The Complete Works of Alexander Pushkin*, vol. 3, p. 45, Milner and Company Limited, 1999 (Trans. J. Higgs); (Editor's note: Pushkin refers to the famous Italian opera singer Angelica Catalani (1780–1849) who visited Russia in 1820 and was delighted by the Moscow Gipsy singers' art. – M.G.) (Translator's note: translation my own.)
55. Here: beyond the limits of norm (Fr.).
56. Mikhail Lermontov. The Pact. In M. Lermontov. *Major Poetical Works*. Trans. Anatoly Liberman. Minneapolis: University of Minnesota Press, 1983, p. 249.

The romanticised revolt of woman in the Russia of the first half of the XIX century found its expression in the image of the romantic heroine. In the language of romanticism, decency became "convention" and the revolt against this assumed two faces: poetic freedom in literature and amorous freedom in real life. The first was "naturally" clothed in male behaviour and was actualised on paper, the second was actualised in the "female" and realised in private life. Such is the dual nature of the image of Zakrevskaya. In Pushkin's verses, she was portrayed as follows:

> When she, that soul of fire, appears,
> O women of the North, among you,
> It is a radiant challenge flung you,
> Your dull conventions, worldly fears.
> And spends herself as, brightly daring,
> She flies, disdainful of those bars,
> How like a lawless comet flaring
> Among the calculated stars![57]

In the poetic world, conversations with Zakrevskaya found an echo in Pushkin in the poem *Napersnik* (The Confidant), where the "entrancing language" of her "reckless and rebellious passions" frightened the poet by their unrestrained nature:

> But curb, dear girl, your recollection,
> Your dreams keep to yourself alone.
> I dread their fiery infection,
> I dread to know what you have known![58]

In male behaviour, no matter how sincere the passion[59], it was, nevertheless, all literature. However, the relationship between literature and life in terms of male behaviour at that time were complex and created the possibility of the most varied of interpretations. Pushkin was sincere, when he wrote these verses, but he was also sincere when, in correspondence with Vazemsky he included ambiguous jokes about the "copper Venus" (this was how Zakrevskaya was referred to in correspondence between Pushkin and Vyazemsky) or when, together with the same Vyazemsky his correspondence alternated between passion and jealousy. The image of Zakrevskaya was not compromised in any way, even when Pushkin

---

57. A. Pushkin. Portrait (1828). In *An Anthology of Russian Verse. 1812–1960.* Ed. by Avrahm Yarmolinsky. New York: Doubleday & Co, 1962, p. 15.
58. A. Pushkin. The Confidant. In *Lyric Poems: 1826–1836* in *The Complete Works of Alexander Pushkin*, vol. 3, p. 80, Milner and Company Limited, 1999 (Trans. W. Arndt).
59. For example, Baratynsky's love for Zakrevskya was deep and tragic.

put on the mask of her master of love. In a letter to Vyazemsky from Petersburg on 1 September, 1828, he wrote: "If it were not for your bronze Venus,[60] I would have died of ennui. But she is consolingly amusing and sweet. I am writing verses to her. And she made me one of her panders (to the doing of which I was drawn by my usual inclination and the present condition of my own well-intentioned,[61] about which one may say the same as was said of its printed namesake: "The intention is good, but, by golly, the fulfilment is bad")".[62]

Opposed to the "artistic" and "amorous-romantic" feminine behaviour in Russia at the beginning of the XIX century was an artistoctratic notion of *comme il faut*, the main feature of which was anonymity. Let us give two surprisingly close descriptions, one of which sketches out an everyday scene, the other belongs to literature. Both texts depict high society. The similarity between them is dictated by the fact that, at this level, uniqueness is an equivalent of indecency.

The first example is taken from A. F. Tyutcheva's memoirs and describes the salon of Sofya Karamzina. The salon of Ekaterina Andreevna and Nikolai Mikhaylovich Karamzin was one of the cultural centres of Petersburg in the first decade of the 1800s during the writer's life; its uniqueness was further emphasised by the fact that directly above it, on the third floor, the young members of the Decembrist movement were gathered in the office of Nikita Muravyev. Now – in the 1830s – the picture changed sharply and all the more noticeably, since the mistress of the salon was convinced that she should preserve the traditions of her father. The salon of Sofya Karamzina was thus deprived of its intellectual cultural centre. It became the well-oiled machine of a faceless aristocratic society. "... the clever and inspired leadership and the soul of this hospitable salon was undoubtedly Sofya Nikolaevna, the daughter of Karamzin from his first marriage with Elizabeth Ivanovna Protasova, who herself passed away in the generation of his daughter. At the beginning of the evening, Sofya, like an experienced General in the field of battle and ever the scientific strategist set down large red armchairs and between them light straw chairs creating comfortable groups for the collocutors; she knew how to arrange things so that each of the guests, completely naturally and as if by chance, happened

---

60. Zakrevskaya.
61. Editor's note: "well-intentioned" – there is an obscene hint at decreased sexual capacity in Pushkin's words; *Blagonamerennyi* (Well-Intentioned) was a literary magazine published by the fable-writer Izmailov, who first maintained a friendly relationship with Pushkin and later entered the confrontation with the poets of Pushkin's circle. The quotation is the poet M. V. Milonov's witticism on Izmailov's periodical. – M.G.
62. *The Letters of Alexander Pushkin*. Trans. and ed. by J. Thomas Shaw. Madison: The University of Wisconsin Press, 1967, p. 357.

to be in that group or next to this or that neighbour best suited to them. In this respect, she was a total organisational genius. Poor, dear Sofya, she was, in reality, like a busy bee, buzzing from one group of guests to another, connecting some, separating others, catching an ingenious word, or an anecdote, noting a fashionable makeup, organising a game of cards for the old men, or jeux d'esprit[63] for the young people, entering into conversation with any lonely mother, or encouraging a shy and modest debutante, in brief, demonstrating the art of developing society as a work of art and almost of virtue".[64] The image described in Tyutcheva's memoirs is so evocative of a scene from Tolstoy's *War and Peace* that it is difficult to forego the conclusion that the as yet unpublished memoirs of Tyutcheva were available to Tolstoy. The emotional accent in Tolstoy's novel is the direct opposite, but this only serves to emphasise the similarity of the image. The root of this similarity lies in a fundamental orientation towards a lack of originality as the highest ideal of the salon. It is also typical that whilst Karamzina's salon is shown to us in the 1830s and that of Anna Pavlovna Scherer – in the 1800s; despite this, a completely identical atmosphere reigns in them:

> She likes the stately disposition
> Of oligarchic colloquies,
> Their chilly pride in high position,
> The mix of years and ranks she sees.[65]

"Anna Pavlovna's reception was in full swing. The spindles hummed steadily and ceaselessly on all sides. With the exception of the aunt, beside whom sat only one elderly lady, who with her thin careworn face was rather out of place in this brilliant society, the whole company had settled into three groups. One, chiefly masculine, had formed round the abbé. Another, of young people, was grouped round the beautiful Princess Hélène, Prince Vasili's daughter, and the little Princess Bolkonskaya, very pretty and rosy, though rather too plump for her age. The third group was gathered round Mortemart and Anna Pavlovna.

The vicomte was a nice-looking young man with soft features and polished manners, who evidently considered himself a celebrity but out of politeness

---

63. Salon games (Fr.).
64. Tyutcheva, A. F. *Pri dvore dvukh imperatorov. Vospominaniya i fragmenty denvnikov freiliny dvora Nikolaya I i Aleksandra II.* Moscow, 1990, p. 22.
65. Alexander Pushkin. *Eugene Onegin.* Trans. James E. Falen. Carbondale and Edwardsville: Southern Illinois University Press, 1990, p. 198.

modestly placed himself at the disposal of the circle in which he found himself. Anna Pavlovna was obviously serving him up as a treat to her guests. As a clever maître d'hôtel serves up as a specially choice delicacy a piece of meat that no one who had seen in the kitchen would have care to eat, so Anna Pavlovna served up to her guests, first the vicomte and then the abbé, as peculiarly choice morsels".[66]

The romantic and secular salons seem to personify two opposite tendencies of female secular behaviour of that epoch. If, in the romantic epoch, woman's freedom was thought of as a *feminine* freedom, then in the period of democratic upsurge of the second-half of the XIX century the role of woman was accentuated as that of *a human being*. In the vulgar behaviour of the everyday this was expressed in the right to sport a man's hair-do, to take up a male profession, male gestures and manners of the speech (the habit of adopting men's clothing was, as we said, in Georges Sand, an example that seemed also too extravagant). This contrast was actualised as the battle between the fashionably worldly ball gown, for example crinoline, and the modest garment of the "working woman".[67]

Thus, for instance, the satires of A. K. Tolstoy imitated the stereotypical character of the language of the nihilists, i.e., the instantaneous transformation of explosion into the stereotype:

> The Torrent was terrified, and fled from beauty,
> And they vehemently exclaimed:
> "Ah, how vulgar! Ah, how undeveloped!
> There is nothing contemporary there!"
> But the Torrent replied, having fled to the yard:
> "Look what happened on the Bald Mountain,
> Only whilst the witches went naked and barefoot,
> At least, they had long tresses!"[68]

As we see, the lengthy period of female emancipation which went under the slogan of equal rights for woman and man was actually interpreted by society

---

66. Tolstoy, Leo. *War and Peace*. Trans. Louise and Aylmer Maud. New York: Simon and Schuster, 1942, p. 11.

67. See in *The Death of Tarelkin* by Sukhovo-Kobylin: "... when they declared progress, thus it was and it went before progress – so that already Tarelkin was in front, and progress came from behind! – When it came to the emancipation of women, then Tarelkin cried, that he was not a woman in order to remove crinoline in the face of the public and to show himself... as is necessary for emancipation" (Sukhovo-Kobylin A. Pictures of the Past. Moscow, 1869, p. 400–401).

68. Tolstoy, A. K. *Poln. sobr. stikh.* L., 1984. T. 1, p. 177. (Translator's note: translation my own.)

as the right of woman to occupy "male" public roles and professions. Only in the second-half of the XIX century did the fight begin not for woman to be the "man", but so that man and woman would be received as equivalent in the united concept of the "person". This was required so that at least one woman could prove her superiority in those spheres which were traditionally considered as a male monopoly. In this sense not only for the Russian but also in the whole history of European culture the appearance of such people as Sofya Vasilyevna Kovalevskaya was a truly historical turning point, which can be compared only to the equality of the role of man and woman in the political struggle of the Narodovoltsy (the Populists).

The Korvin-Krukovsky sisters (by marriage: Jaclard and Kovalevskaya) appeared to realise both possibilities. Anna Vasilyevna Korvin-Krukovskaya rejected Dostoevsky's love. Dostoevsky requested her hand but was refused: her choice was the Parisian communard who escaped death only by fleeing from prison. Dostoevsky, according to A. G. Dostoevskaya's memoirs, spoke of her thus: "Anna Vasilyevna was one of the best women I have ever met in my life. She is extremely clever, erudite, educated in literature, and she possesses an excellent and good heart. This is a girl of high moral qualities; but her convictions are diametrically opposite to my own, and she cannot yield them, she is too straightforward. That is why I doubt whether our marriage could ever be happy. I gave her back my word and with my whole soul I hope that she will meet a man who will share her ideas and with whom she can be happy!"[69] Her younger sister, Sofya Kovalevskaya, was precisely that type of personality which ripens at moments of steep turns in culture.

Certainly, it is not by chance that the Renaissance gave birth to richly endowed people, whose talents could not be accommodated by any single sphere of culture. Not by chance that the following explosion, at the turn of the XVII and XVIII centuries, caused the occurrence of the Encyclopaedists in the life of France and Lomonosov in Russia: the explosion resulted in an outburst of versatile talents. In the cultural function of the woman, this explosion occurred at the end of the XIX century and gave birth to the likes of Sofya Kovalevskaya.

A mathematician, a professor and a writer who generated her own artistic works in several languages, it was precisely her versatility in her cultural activities that drew attention to Kovalevskaya. The fact that Kovalevskaya had obtained the academic rank of professor (1884) and her designation as the Head of the Department of Mechanics at Stockholm University can only be compared

---

69. *Dostoevsky v vospominaniyakh sovremennikov*: V 2 T./ Sost. A. Dolinin. M., 1964. T. 2, p. 37.

with the action of the government of Alexander III who gave Sofya Perovskaya an equal right of execution alongside male Populists (members of the populist organization "People's Will"). Women ceased to receive exceptional treatment both scientifically and politically. In the latter situation, Alexander III unexpectedly conducted himself as a kind of Robespierre, who had proved that the guillotine knows no difference between man and woman. Pushkin also wrote about equality "in the last, terrible minute" of the "majestic martyr", and his executioner, of Charlotte de Corday and the charming du Barry, of the madman Louvel and the rebel Berton (XI, 94–95).

The chair of the professor and the gallows of Petersburg signified the absolute equality of man and woman. Only, for the first it was necessary to go to Stockholm, whilst the second was achieved in-house. This paradoxical equality between "our" land and foreign land was noted by Archpriest Avvakum, who said that martyrs, in order to complete their exploits, had to go "to Persia" only to continue, with bitter irony, to declare that in Russia they had their very own "Babylon!"[70]

Equality was thus affirmed. Henceforth, it was no longer necessary for a woman to be rendered incapable of playing the role of the man. This had an unprecedented effect: and at the beginning of the XX century, a whole pleiad of brilliant women poets burst onto the scene of Russian poetry. Both Akhmatova and Tsvetaeva not only did not hide the feministic nature of their Muse – they emphasised it. Even so, their verses were not "female" verses. They emerged in the literature not as poetesses but as poets.

The apex of achievement for women of a pan-humanistic position did not become the Valkyries of the "rights of women" nor were they proponents of lesbianism but rather they were women who displaced men in politics and the state activity ("Lady Thatcher" in the politics and science of the XX century). However, the most vibrant, almost symbolic picture appears before us in the opposition between Marina Tsvetaeva and Boris Pasternak. The matter does not even lie in the fact that in their personal relations, Tsvetaeva manifests courage, whereas Pasternak exhibits a certain "femininity". What is more important is how their epistolary and literary romance was reflected in poetry.

In the lyric poetry of Tsvetaeva, with her hypertrophied female fervency, the feminine "I" receives traits which are traditionally male: an offensive spirit, the perception of poetry as labour and craft, courage. Here, however, the man is assigned an auxiliary and unpoetic role:

---

70. See: *Pamyatniki literatury Drevnei Rusi: XVII vek*. Kn. 2, p. 388.

With the toll of immortal banality
Poor man, how do you cope?[71]

Attributes of Tsvetaeva are a "courageous sleeve" and a work-table. Probably, there is not a single poet in whom we will find regret as to the fact that love steals time from work[72] which, for the poet, is the only authentic existence:

Youth – to love,
Old age – to warm:
There is no time – to be,
Nowhere to go.[73]

We are quits: you have eaten me
I have painted you.
They will place you at the dinner table –
And me – they will place on the escritoire.
Because, happy in one iota,
I knew of no other meals.[74]

It is difficult to find other verses, in which femininity was doused by such contempt; the "twittering" and the cost of it is found alongside:

But maybe, amongst the twittering and the calculations,
Tired of these endless feminine regulations –
You will recall my hand devoid of rights
And my masculine sleeve[75]

This – leaping over the epoch of Pushkin – brings us to the XVIII century, and to Lomonosov for whom poetry is "poor rhyming work" and to Merzlyakov who calls poetry "holy work" (cf. the "sacred craft" in Akhmatova").[76]

Against the background of this poetry the fundamental femininity of Pasternak's position acquires a contrasting meaning; that of who "is equal to the female destiny ". The femininity of his poetry is manifested not even in its topicality but in its fundamental sensibility and "passivity". This poetry does not seize, it does not rule, it does not tie, but it returns to the spontaneous, the supra-personal; its

---

71. Tsvetaeva, M. An Attempt at Jealousy. In *The Burden of Sufferance. Women Poets of Russia*. Ed. and trans. by Pamela Perkins and Albert Cook. New York & London: Garland Publishing, 1993, p. 114.

72. Cf. young Pushkin's audacious verses: But labour is cold and empty; a poem never costs the smile of the most voluptuous of lips (*Poln. sobr.soch.* II, 41).

73. Tsvetaeva, M. I. *Sobr. soch*, p. 275. (Translator's note: translation my own.)

74. Ibid., 302.

75. Ibid., 194.

76. See: Akhmatova, A. A. *Stikhotvoreniya*. Leningrad, 1976, p. 207. See: Lomonosov, M. V. *Poln. sobr. soch v 10 T*. Moskva/Leningrad, 1953, p. 545.

only victory lies in the fact that it "is conquered by all". Tsvetaeva erupts on the world through her language and is blind to everything that is not of her emanation, Pasternak absorbs the world into himself. Tsvetaeva is submerged in what is "hers", Pasternak, as Doctor Zhivago, is always constant because he is always immersed in the "alien". This does not exclude the notion, however, that in Russia the precise idea of the equality of man and woman subsequently became a form of oppression of women because the natural difference was sacrificed to an unrealisable utopia which, in practice, was converted to exploitation.

As we have seen, the problem which interested us is located on the border between physiology and semiotics: and in this case the centre of gravity is constantly moving first into one, then into the other sphere. As a semiotic problem, it cannot be artificially isolated from other sociocultural codes, in particular, from the conflict of physiological and cultural aspects. In Japan, this led to the contrast between the woman of the family and the geisha – a woman for enjoyment. In the Middle Ages, in Europe – in the private life of the royal families – this led to the legalised antithesis of the wife, whose function is procreation, and of the mistress, who gives enjoyment. The separation of these two cultural functions resulted, in a whole series of cases, in the antithesis of "normal" and homosexual love.

The propagation of homosexuality in the officer schools of Petersburg had, most likely, a physiological root, since it was connected with the isolation of a large number of adolescents and young people. But this acquired another character in cases where homosexual love was transformed into a unique regimental tradition. Gogol ironically emphasised differences in the specific character of the regimental guard: "The infantry regiment of P*** was not at all of the sort to which many infantry regiments belong; and, even though it was mostly quartered in villages, it was nevertheless on such a footing that it would not yield to certain cavalry regiments. The majority of the officers drank *vymorozki* and knew how to pull Jews by their sidelocks no worse than hussars; several of them even danced the mazurka, and the colonel of the P*** regiment never missed an opportunity of mentioning it when talking with someone in society. "I have many," he used to say, patting himself on the belly after each work, "who dance the mazurka, sir. A good many, sir. A great many." To better show readers the cultivation of the P*** infantry regiment, we shall add that two of the officers gambled terribly at faro and would lose uniform, visored cap, greatcoat, sword knot, and underwear to boot – something not always found even among cavalrymen."[77]

---

77. Gogol, N. Ivan Fyodorovich and his Aunt. In *The Collected Tales of Nikolai Gogol*.
   Translated and annotated by Richard Pevear and Larissa Volokhonsky. New York:

That which, over the long term and in the everyday may be considered a fault, in semiotic terms may become the sign of social ritual. In the epoch of Nicholas I, homosexuality was a ritual defect of the cavalry just as unrestrained alcoholism was a ritual defect in the hussars.[78] Hence, for instance, the scandalous liaison between Van Heeckeren and D'Anthès, the royalist-emigré, the handsome man without a penny to his name who gathered to himself all the defects of the old aristocracy scattered throughout foreign territories,[79] elegant, always merry, frivolous – the liaison, which would be impossible against the background of the sedate and strict morals of Petersburg society, if he had not taken part in the ritual deficiency (homosexuality) of the cavalry guards. In official Petersburg it was customary to take the pretence that this "deficiency" simply did not exist. Let us compare Pushkin's words about the fact that the truth:

> ... does not punish errors,
> but requires them to be secret.[80]

However, unofficially, ritual deficiencies were perceived as signs of dedication. In this case, homosexuality was given a fin-de-siècle delicateness. The spicy "end of the century" spirit of French emigrants was thus introduced into the Petersburg salons long before the word "decadence" was heard in Russian criticism.

---

Pantheon Books, 1998, p. 109. Notes, p. 430: Vymorozki: "a concentrate produced by allowing wine to freeze and then removing the frozen portion".

78. According to the interesting observation of G. V. Vilinbakhov, a unique example of the ritual vices of the guard was the stirring song "Zhura, zhura-zhuravel".

79. Thus, for instance, the marquise-aristocrat, who escaped from France and who found refuge in the Russian provincial noble house, pursued the homosexual love of Vigel, which played a subsequently fateful role in the fate of this person.

80. A. Pushkin. Kogda tvoi mladye leta... In *Poln. sobr. soch.*, t. III. Moskva-Leningrad, 1948, p. 205.

# Chapter 11
# The logic of explosion

We are immersed in the space of language. Even in the most basic abstract conditions, we cannot extract ourselves from this space, which simply envelops us, and yet it is a space of which we are also a part and which, simultaneously, is part of us. And as a result of this, our relationship with language is far from ideal: we need to exert a tremendous effort to push ourselves beyond the limits of language and it is precisely to language that we ascribe our lies, deviations from the norm, and the majority of our defects and perversions. The struggle with language is as old as language itself. History convinces of its hopelessness on the one hand and of its unlimited potential on the other.

One of the foundations of the semiosphere is its heterogeneity. Sub-systems with variable speeds of cyclic motion are drawn together on a temporary axis. Thus, if in our time female fashion in Europe has a durational speed of change of a year,[1] then the phonological structure of language changes so slowly that we are inclined to consider it, on the basis of our common sense, as constant.

Many systems encounter others and in the midst of flight change their appearance and their orbits. Semiological space is filled with the freely moving fragments of a variety of structures which, however, store stably within themselves a memory of the whole which, falling into a strange environment, can suddenly and vigorously restore themselves. Semiotic systems, encountered in the semiosphere, display an ability to survive and to be transformed and, like Proteus, become 'others' whilst remaining themselves so that to speak of the complete disappearance of something within this space must be something which is done only with extreme caution.

Completely stable invariant semiotic structures do not exist at all, generally speaking. If we allow such a hypothesis, then it is also necessary to recognise, albeit theoretically, the limits of their possible combinations.[2] Then Lermontov's

---

1. The limit of velocity is, on the one hand, established by the oldest criteria – the revolution of the calendar cycle, and on the other hand, the sufficiently dynamic potentials of the technologies of tailoring.
2. The intersection of a variety of closed systems can be one a source of enrichment in these closed systems. The phonological system represents one of the most stable systems. However, the foppish dialect of 18th century Russian language permitted new vowels to be borrowed from the French. Pushkin's heroine "pronounced a Russian *n* as slightly/ As *n* in French … and through the nose" (Alexander Pushkin. *Eugene Onegin*. Trans. James E. Falen. Carbondale and Edwardsville: Southern Illi-

ironic epigraph "Les poètes ressemblent aux ours, qui se nourrisent en suçent leurs patte"[3] should be taken literally.

However, it is necessary to emphasise the fact that the boundary, which separated the closed world of semiosis from extra-semiotic reality, is permeable. It is constantly transgressed via intrusions from the extra-semiotic sphere which, when bursting in, introduce a new dynamic, transforming the bounded space and simultaneously transforming themselves according to its laws. At the same time, semiotic space constantly ejects all the layers of culture from itself. The latter form layers of deposits beyond the limits of culture and await their time to re-enter the closed space by which time they are so 'forgotten' as to be conceived of as new. Such exchanges with the extra-semiotic sphere create an inexhaustible reservoir of dynamic reserves. This "perpetual motion" cannot be exhausted – it does not yield to the laws of entropy since its variability is constantly being fed by the permeability of the system.

However, the source of variety could become a generator of chaos if the opposing structures were not connected.

An essential difference of contemporary structural analysis when compared to formalism and the early stages of structural studies lies in the very isolation of the object of analysis. The concept of the separate, isolated, stable, self-sufficient text was the cornerstone of the latter schools. Text was the constant, and the beginning and the end, of the study. The concept of the text was, actually, *a priori*.

Contemporary semiotic study also considers text as one of the basic research concepts, but text itself is considered as a functional rather than a stable object with constant properties. Both the individual work, its parts, the compositional group, the genre, in the final analysis – literature as a whole, may emerge as a text. The point here is not that the possibility of expansion is introduced to the concept of the text. The difference is much more fundamental in nature. The presumption of author and audience is introduced into the concept of the text and the latter, thus conceived, does not necessarily coincide with the real author and the real audience.

Let us recall the heated but completely unproductive debate that flared up in the domestic history of literature not so long ago about the so-called "canonical" versions of texts. It is characteristic that the supporters of this insipid idea

---

nois University Press, 1990, p. 61). This is read in Russian as: "i russkii [nash] kak [en] frantzuskii" – And Russian "Nash" as the French N" ("nash" ['our'] – is the Church-Slavonic name for the letter "N").

3.  Their poets resemble bears, who feed themselves by sucking their paws. (Fr.) See: Lermontov, M. Yu. *Sobr. soch.*, vol. 2, p. 145.

were those Moscow literary scholars who had had more success in the administrative than in the scientific spheres. It received a negative response from the experienced textualist and scientist B. V. Tomashevsky.[4]

The contemporary point of view rests on the concept of the text as the intersection of the point of view of the author of the text and the audience. A third component is represented by the presence of specific structural features which are understood as text signals. The intersection of these three elements creates optimal conditions for the perception of the object as a text. However, the sharp manifestation of some of these elements can lead to a reduction of the others.

Thus, from the position of the author, the text may appear to be unfinished, to be situated in a dynamic state, whilst the external point of view (reader, publisher, editor) will attempt to assign to the text a state of completion. Numerous cases of conflict between author and publisher have appeared on this basis. Leo Tolstoy refused to consider proofs as finalised texts, seeing in them only one stage of a continuous process. For him, the text actually represented a process. Pushkin began to rework the poem *The Bronze Horseman* and, having half-finished the work required by the censor, this turned out to be an artistic process for the poet who then gave up the reworking. Thus, one of Pushkin's most important works is deprived of the so-called author's last will. The publisher, with one eye on the reader, is obliged to compromise when bringing together the two stages of development. The exploratory position gives us the text as it is grasped at the moment of formation. The finality of the author's will is a figment of the imagination. The works of M. O. Chudakova revealed the mutli-layered process of the work of Bulgakov on his novel *The Master and Margarita*. This process also did not achieve final completion. And herein lies the conflict between the experimentation (the author's) and publishing (the reader's) point of view.

It is precisely this contradiction, lying at the very heart of the question, which creates the need for different types of publication. Academic publication is distinguished not only by the authority of its researchers or by the splendour of its design, but by its fundamental orientation to the perception of the author.[5] The contemporary perception of the text as an element in the artistic process implies an internal contradiction in the scientific approach.

---

4.  On this, see: Eichenbaum, B. M. *Tekstologicheskie raboty B. V. Tomashevskogo* // Tomashevsky, B. V. *Pisatel' i kniga. Ocherk tekstologii*. Moskva, 1959, p. 3–22.
5.  Here it is essential to consider the problem of "point of view". On this, see: Uspensky, B. A. *Poetika kompozitsii*, Moskva, 1970; and, similarly: *Istoriya russkogo literaturnogo yazyka* (XI–XVII vek). Munchen, 1987 (Sagners Slavistische Sammlung, Bd. 12).

One of the fundamental questions posed by the text can be outlined as follows. In a number of European languages there is the category of articles which group nouns into those which are immersed in the restricted world of objects, personally familiar and intimately related to the speaker, and the designation of objects which are abstract generalisations reflected in the national language. The absence of articles in the Russian language does not indicate the absence of a given category. The latter is simply expressed by other means.

It is possible to assert that the world of a very young child, which is extremely limited by the three-dimensional sphere of personal experience, is filled with unique things. In language, this is reflected by the supremacy of proper names and by a tendency to receive an entire vocabulary through this prism. We have already given an example of the childhood language of Vladimir Solovyev.[6] The tendency to transform the world into a space of proper names was manifested in the latter in a particularly acute way. Let us also compare the epic motif of naming the world, which occurs in many national epochs and which always fulfils a singular function: the transformation of chaos in space.

The world of proper names with its intimacy (a unique linguistic parallel to the idea of the maternal bosom) and the world of proper nouns which carries the idea of objectivity emerge as two registers, united in conflict. Discourse flows freely from one sphere into another but the latter do not merge. On the contrary, the contrast between them is merely emphasised.

As soon as we consider the limits of the artistic text, the relations between these lingual mechanisms take on a fundamentally new form. The novel is especially interesting in this respect in that it creates the space of the "third person". In linguistic terms, the latter is objective and external to the world of the reader and the author. Nevertheless, the space is simultaneously experienced by the author as something created by him, i.e. intimately coloured, and by the reader as something personal. The third person is emotionally enriched by the aura of the first person. Even here we are talking not about the possibility of the author to lyrically experience the fate of his hero or of the reader to react to the tone or digressions in the author's narration. The most objective construction of the text does not contradict the subjectivity through which the reader experiences the text. Such a possibility is potentially located in language.

A newspaper article about a spontaneous catastrophe at the other end of the world is experienced by us differently to those communications which concern regions which are geographically closer to us and in an entirely different manner again where they directly concern us and those closest to us. The fact is that, here, communication shifts from the space of common nouns to the world of

---

6. See this publ. p. 37.

proper nouns. And news from the latter world is primarily experienced in an emotional and intimate way.

The artistic text transforms this tendency into one of its most important structural elements. In principle, it forces us to experience any space as the space of proper nouns. We oscillate between the subjective world, which is personally familiar to us, and its antithesis. In the artistic world, the "alien" is always our "own" but at the same time our "own" is also always "alien". In this way, the poet, having created a work riddled with personal emotions, experiences this as a catharsis of feelings, as a liberation from tragedy. Thus, Lermontov said of his "demon" that ". . . he had been delivered from it – through his poetry".[7] However, artistic release itself may become not only the end of one contradiction, fraught with explosion, but also the beginning of another.

Thus, for example, the entire artistic space of Charlie Chaplin may be considered as a unitary work. The extraordinary individual talent of the artist and the direct linking of each film to a unitary space beyond the screen completely justifies this perception.

However, no less substantive is the view of Chaplin's heritage as a route to the exchange of independent, enclosed texts. Chaplin's early screen debuts (such films as *Making a Living*, 1914) were built on the contradiction between traditional cinematographic clichés of the era and circus technology. The virtuoso use of gesture and the language of pantomime produced an unexpected effect on screen and created what was, for cinema, a completely new language. The subsequent phase developed the achievements of the first but, at the same time, was based on a fundamentally unpredictable transfer to a new system of artistic language. The films *Tramp, Conscript* (1915), *A Dog's Life*, and *To Arms!* (1917–1918) took the circus motif to such a point that it transported the viewer into a world of a completely different genre. Contradictions between the technology of gesture and topical collisions (seen very clearly in *To Arms!* where the hero is transported into the situation of life in the trenches during the First World War) create a sharp transfer into a different system of film language. Such a transfer is not a simple, logical continuation of the previous one. It takes the shape of the constant and surprising, from the spectator's perspective, change in film language – the manner, which further becomes typical for Chaplin's evolution. It is no accident that each critical moment will be accompanied by the bewilderment of the public and the creation of a "new" Chaplin.

In *Gold Rush* such bifurcation becomes a leading artistic principle. The principle is intensified by the foppish upper clothing and the rags which the hero wears below the belt. Contradictions between clothing and gesture also

---

7.  Lermontov, M. Yu. *Sobr. soch*, T. 4, p. 174.

assume an active role. Whilst the hero is dressed in the rags of a tramplike gold-prospector, his gestures portray a gentleman beyond reproach. But, no sooner does he become a millionaire and adorns himself in luxurious clothing, than he is transformed into a tramp: the vulgar scratching of different parts of the body, the clumsy gestures – everything evokes the non-conformity of clothing and role. Here we see the method, which would become so important in later films, of loss and reinstatement of memory depending on the role played by the hero in the film.

The episode of the dancing doll, made up of two loaves, which Charlie causes to carry out refined dances and diverse movements do not, it would seem, have any direct relation to the subject (it was inserted for amusement, in which the poor hero who waits in vain for his guest, the coquettish heroine, is involved). However, in actual fact, this episode is the key to the entire film. Through it, the "internal" Charlie appears to the viewer, the personification of refinement and artistic taste, reviving the rough and primitive comic structure. The entire episode represents the victory of substance over appearance. Without it, the satisfying ending of the film would be a primitive tribute to cinematographic convention. It gives the end of the film the character of a utopian hope in the possibility of happiness.

This springboard made possible the phase of serious, topical films of a type that was certainly not predictable in the prevailing film language of Chaplin. The film *The Great Dictator* took the internal contradiction of method to the limit – the hero splits into two antithetical characters who simultaneously mutually influence each other. The sense of satire lies in the unmasking of sublime showiness. This transformed the element of comedy from the technical method of the organisation of language into its content.

Two socio-philosophical films, *City Lights* and *New Times* (1931, 1935) shot in the era of the Great Depression completed the creation of the new language which was built on the contradiction between substance and appearance. The language of film comedy achieved philosophical universality because it rendered itself a means of recreating tragedy. The cycle of films created between 1947 and the beginning of the 1950s were also met with incomprehension. The critics spoke of Chaplin's decline. His appearance without his moustache and the characteristic mask of Charlot, minus the conventional costume of masquerade, appeared to renounce the great achievements of the previous period. In reality such films as *Footlights* (1952) and *A King in New York* (1957) were a new departure. The mask of Charlot was so connected to Chaplin's method and so entrenched in viewers' expectations that it was possible to abandon it. Moreover, in *Footlights* Chaplin audaciously introduces self-citation. In the film, an old actor forced to earn a living on cheap stages suffers complete failure. It is

Chaplin himself, appearing without the mask. The final outcome sees Chaplin and that other long-forgotten cinematic genius, Buster Keaton, appear on stage without make-up, playing themselves. They transform their lives and failures, turning them into subject and role, playing out before the public the tragicomedy of real experience. That which was language becomes plot and the contradiction between Chaplin and Charlot allows the old drama of "actor and man" to be tragically renewed. The mask survives and lives an independent life, displacing the man, like Andersen's Shadow.

Explosion can also be realised as a chain of sequential explosions, each of which changes the other, creating a dynamic, multi-levelled unpredictability.

The problem of predictability-unpredictability is central to the resolution of such fundamental questions as authentic and surrogate art. Artistic creation is invariably immersed in the vast space of surrogates. The latter should not be understood as a simple condemnation. Artistic surrogates are harmful in their aggressiveness. They have a tendency to envelop authentic art and to displace it. Where it is a question of commercial competition, they always have the victory.

However, reduced by their limits, they are not only necessary but also useful. They perform a broad educational role and represent the first step towards an understanding of the language of art. Their annihilation is impossible and, furthermore, would be as disastrous as the seizure by them of authentic art. They can perform those tasks uncharacteristic to art, which, nevertheless, society imperatively places before the artist: educational instruction, propaganda, moral training, etc.

Those quasi-artistic works which, in actual fact, represent tasks to be resolved, occupy a special position. Such works as folkloristic riddles and, in the art of most recent times – the wide expanse of the detective novel. The detective novel is characterised by a task which simulates art. The subject of the detective novel outwardly resembles the subjects of the novel or the tale. A chain of events is played out before the reader and in a situation which is typical of artistic prose he is called upon to make a choice so that the subject will make sense.

In Chesterton's novel *The Man Who Was Thursday* the reader encounters two poets. One of them is an anarchist, the other a police detective. The matter is made more complex by the fact that both wear masks. The police detective is portrayed in an almost gentlemanly manner, whilst the mask of the anarchist is more complex: in order to avoid suspicion, he pretends to be an anarchist, a bloodthirsty windbag whose nature is already common to society. The essence of both is manifested by their artistic tastes. The anarchist curses the prose of the movement of the railways, where the sequence of the stations is prescribed. He sees poetry in the unexpected and the unexpected brings explosion. To this the detective objects: "... every time a train comes in [to the station. – M.G.]

I feel that it has broken past batteries of besiegers, and that man has won a battle against chaos. You say contemptuously that when one has left Sloane Square one must come to Victoria. I say that one might do a thousand things instead, and that whenever I really come there I have the sense of hair-breadth escape. And when I hear the guard shout out the word 'Victoria', it is not an unmeaning word. It is to me a cry of a herald announcing conquest. It is to me indeed 'Victoria'; it is the victory of Adam."[8] The piquancy here lies in the fact that we find ourselves in a world where normal, peaceful existence is less probable than murder. Consequently, the absence of an event is more informative than its presence.

In this way, Chesterton seemingly introduces us to the world of unpredictability and, consequently, creates a text which is subjugated to artistic laws. However, in actual fact, this is no more than a brilliantly constructed mystification. As is the case when a task has only one correct solution and the art of the audience lies in finding this solution; the Chestertonian subject leads us to a singular truth. The intricate web of the plot lines is designed to disguise this way, making it accessible only to the reader who manages to unravel the secrets of the unique solution.

Such a situation is fundamentally opposed to art, whether we are speaking of its brilliant or its mediocre manifestations.

In this regard, the example of the tales of Edgar Allan Poe is interesting. The reader seems implicitly to realise that the terrible riddle proposed by the author offers only one "correct" solution and the composition of the tale is constructed according to a stable schema: the riddle, which it is possible and necessary to solve, lies submerged in the frame of fantastic horrors. It is precisely along this schema that the contemporary narratives of Clive Barker are constructed. In actual fact, the artistic strength of the works of E. A. Poe consists precisely in the fact that he lays before the reader riddles which cannot be solved. These are not modern problems packed in the fantastic candy wrappers of plot but the fantastic itself that is insoluble. E. A. Poe opens before the reader a way without end, a window onto unpredictability, lying on the other side of logic and worldly experience. His tales do not imply any sly or simple "explanations".

The artistic text does not have a singular solution. This special characteristic is clearly revealed by some external signs. A work of art can be used an infinite number of times. It would be absurd to say: "I won't go into the Rembrandt gallery, I've already seen his pictures – or: I've already heard this poem or symphony". But it would be completely natural to say: I've already completed

---

8. Chesterton, Gilbert Keith. *The Man Who Was Thursday*. New York: The Modern Library, 2001, p. 11.

this task. I've already guessed this riddle. Texts of this second type are not subject to repeated use. But we read Chesterton a second time because it is not merely a detecting task but also a work of artistic prose, which is far from being reduced to its topical solution. Over and above this is another level – the poetry of paradox is nourished by unpredictability. The best science fiction authors of the second half of the 20th century attempt to transfer us into a world that is so alien to everyday experience that it stokes up the emaciated forecasts of technical progress in the sea of unpredictability.

Thus, art enlarges the space of the unpredictable – the space of information – and simultaneously creates a conventional world experimenting with this space and proclaiming mastery over it.

# Chapter 12
# The moment of unpredictability

The moment of explosion is the moment of unpredictability. Unpredictability should not, however, be understood as constituting a series of unlimited or undefined possibilities for movement from one state to another. Each moment of explosion has its own collection of equally probable possibilities of movement into a sequential state beyond the limits of which lie only those changes which are flagrantly impossible. The latter are excluded from the discussion. Each time we speak of unpredictability we have in mind a specific collection of equally probable possibilities from which only one may be realised. In this way, each structural position represents a cluster of variant possibilities. Up to a certain point they appear as indistinguishable synonyms. However, movement from the point of explosion causes them to become more and more dispersed in semantic space. Finally, the moment arrives when they become carriers of semantic difference. As a result the general collection of semantic differences is continually enriched by ever-newer semantic nuances. This process, however, is regulated by an opposing tendency: the limitation of differentiation through the transformation of cultural antonyms into cultural synonyms.

In his description of the possible variations of the future of Lensky, Pushkin, as was previously indicated, places the reader before a whole gamut of potential trajectories relating to the future course of events at the very moment when Onegin and Lensky drew near to one another, pistols raised. One should consider that Lensky (a student of the German university) had to have been able to shoot very well.[1] At this exact moment, it is impossible to unequivocally predict what will follow.

In a situation where the participants in a duel are not intent on exchanging a pair of pistol shots only to make peace afterwards, having accomplished the necessary ritual in the defence of honour but have decided, rather, to pursue a 'duel to the death' of their opponent, the natural tactic lies in not hurrying to make the first shot, especially whilst moving. Shooting whilst moving reduces by

---

1. This was referred to by Boris Ivanov in his *The Distance of the Free Novel* (M., 1959); it is generally a strange book and one which caused it, at the time of its publication, to receive a critical response from the author of this book, but which reveals in separate questions a sound knowledge and some noteworthy ideas. See also: V. Nabokov's commentaries in: *Eugene Onegin. A Novel in Verse by Alexander Pushkin*. Translated from the Russian, with a commentary, by Vladimir Nabokov, vol. 1–4. London, 1964.

more than half the possibility of defeating an opponent, especially if the duellist has a specific intention, for example – aiming for the knee or the shoulder, so as to heavily wound the opponent without killing him; or aiming at the head or the chest, so as to fell him on the spot. Therefore, the opportunist – i.e. the cold-blooded and prudent duellist causes the opponent to shoot whilst he's on the move. Thereafter, he can approach the 'barrier', himself calling the opponent to the barrier and may, then, at his discretion and without error settle his opponent's fate. An analogous situation is found in the duels of Pushkin and D'Anthès.

Such were the tactics of Pushkin who firmly decided to kill or heavily wound D'Anthès as this was the only way he could destroy the tangled web which surrounded him. Such a resolution of the duel brought with it the threat of exile to Mikhailovskoe (he was not part of the military and, therefore, he could not be degraded to the rank of the soldier; and exile to the village could only occur if it was preceded by ecclesiastic repentance). Natalya Nikolaevna, naturally, would have had to accompany him. But this was exactly what Pushkin wanted! D'Anthès left Pushkin no other choice. Despising his opponent (the ugly husband of a beautiful woman – a traditionally comic figure), the frivolous and mundane D'Anthès saw the duel as yet another entertaining opportunity and, undoubtedly, did not assume that he would be obliged to discard his pleasant, merry life and the rapid advancement of his career in Petersburg.

Pushkin, like Lensky, was in no hurry to make the first shot. However, whilst Onegin shot first and from a distance this, obviously, was because he did not wish the matter to come to a bloody end.[2] D'Anthès' tactic was, however, different: an experienced duellist, he anticipated Pushkin's tactic and shot first, so as to precipitate the shot of his opponent, hoping to kill him with a bullet whilst he was on the move. We may note, in light of this, that even a perfect shot, as D'Anthès invariably was, let off a shot whilst moving and whilst under the muzzle of Pushkin, and was unable to hit his opponent in the breast, hitting him, rather, in the stomach, which did not exclude the possibility of a heavy, but not a fatal wound. This situation was equally unacceptable to both participants of the duel.

These reflections are necessary if we are to consider, following Pushkin, what potential possibilities remained unrealised at that moment when Onegin's bullet was still located in the cannon of his pistol. Pushkin strives to show us how the tragic outcome of the duel is framed against the background of those possibilities which are not realised but which are nevertheless capable of being realised. But no sooner had Onegin shot, than:

---

2.  In just the same way, Pierre shot first in *War and Peace* and, without bloody intention, heavily and only by chance avoided mortally wounding Dolokhov.

... the hour fated
Had struck ...[3]

In the novel the death of Lensky was predetermined by the poet's intention; in real life, at the moment when the shot takes place, there is no predetermined future – there is only a cluster of equally probable "futures". Which of these is ultimately realised cannot be predicted beforehand. Chance is the interference of an event from another system. For example, it is not possible to exclude the possibility that D'Anthès (or Onegin) could, at the very moment when their finger pulls on the trigger, slip on the trampled snow, which would cause a light and almost imperceptible vibration of the hand. The killer's bullet would fly by. And then, another bullet, from the pistol so wonderfully shot by Pushkin (or the former German student, Lensky) would have proven fatal. Then it would have been necessary for Lensky to mourn his dear friend and the life of Pushkin would have followed other, unpredictable roads.

Thus, the moment of explosion creates an unpredictable situation.[4] A very curious process then occurs: the event, once completed, casts a retrospective reflection. In this way, the character of that which has occurred is completely transformed. It should, however, be emphasised here that the view from the past into the future on the one hand and from the future into the past on the other completely changes the object under observation. Looking from the past into the future, we see the present as a complete collection of a series of equally probable possibilities. When we look into the past, reality acquires the status of fact and we are inclined to see it as the only possible realisation. Unrealised possibilities are transformed into possibilities which could not be realised. They acquire an

---

3. Alexander Pushkin. *Eugene Onegin*. Trans. James E. Falen. Carbondale and Edwardsville: Southern Illinois University Press, 1990, p. 156.
4. Reflections of the type: Pushkin was doomed, and had it not been D'Anthès' bullet, then some another situation would have led him to a tragic end, and this being the case, therefore, this example cannot be considered as a matter of chance – resting upon an incorrect substitution of events. Actually, if we examine Pushkin's fate from the perspective of the last two years of his life, then it becomes wholly predictable in *general terms* and cannot be considered as random. But we mustn't forget that in this case we have now changed the perspective and thus have changed the object in question. From this perspective, we are evaluating a much larger range, in which, in reality, the event will be perceived as predictable. However, if we examine a single event – the duel, then the nature of predictability and unpredictability changes sharply. It is possible to say that the Pushkin of Petersburg in the 1830s is doomed. However, it cannot be said that at that moment, when he took the pistol into his hands, he was already doomed. One and the same event, depending on the range within which it falls, may change its level of predictability.

ephemeral character. Hegelian philosophy, for example, is constructed on just such a premise.

Pasternak committed an error in the quotation, attributing to Hegel a statement made by Schlegel[5] but this error is extremely significant:

> Once upon a time, unintentionally
> And, probably, hazarding a guess,
> Hegel called the historian a prophet,
> Predicting in reverse.[6]

The ingenious statement, which drew Pasternak's attention, actually very deeply reflects the fundamental concepts of Hegelian philosophy and Hegel's attitude towards history.

The retrospective view allows the historian to examine the past from two points of view: being located in the future in relation to the event described, he sees before himself a whole chain of completed actions; transporting himself mentally into the past and looking from the past into the future, he already knows the results of the process. However, it is as if these results had not yet been completed and they are presented to the reader as predictions. In the course of this process the element of chance disappears completely from the historical process. The historian may be compared with the theatrical spectator who watches a play for the second time: on the one hand, he knows how it will end and there is nothing unpredictable about it for him. The play, for him, takes place, as it were, in the past from which he extracts his knowledge of the matter. But, simultaneously, as a spectator who looks upon the scene, he finds himself once again in the present and experiences a feeling of uncertainty, an alleged "ignorance" of how play will end. These mutual but also mutually opposing experiences merge, paradoxically, into a certain feeling of simultaneity.

Thus, the event that has occurred presents itself in a multilayered fashion: on the one hand, it is aligned to the memory of the explosion it has recently experienced and on the other – it acquires the features of an inevitable destination. The latter is psychologically connected with the tendency to turn back to that which has occurred and to subject it to a "correction" in the memory or in its retelling. This is why we should examine in detail the psychological basis of written memoirs and what is more, the psychological substantiation of historical texts.

---

5. This fact was first noted by N. Pustygina.
6. Pasternak, B. *Sobr. soch.* T. 1, p. 561. The given quotation is attributed to an early version (1924). (Editor's note: English translation by Vadim Z. Rogovin in the introduction to *1937: Stalin's Year of Terror*, Mehring Books.)

The reasons, which impel culture to recreate its own past, are complex and varied. For now, we will examine just one of them, which, until now has possibly attracted less attention. We are referring, here, to the psychological need to alter the past, to introduce corrections and, moreover, to treat this corrective process as genuine reality. Thus, we are talking about the transformation of memory.

Many and varied are the anecdotal stories about liars and dreamers who fooled their audience. If we consider a similar behaviour from the point of view of cultural-psychological motivation, then it may be interpreted as a duplication of the account and its translation into the language of memory not, however, with the aim of fixing it in reality but rather for the purpose of recreating reality in a more acceptable form. A similar tendency is inseparable from the very concept of memory and, as a rule, from that which is incorrectly referred to as a subjective selection of the facts. However, in some cases, this area of memory may suffer hypertrophy. An example of this may be found in the well-known memoirs of the Decembrist D. I. Zavalishin.

Dmitry Irinarkhovich Zavalishin lived a tragic life. He was, unquestionably, a talented individual who possessed a diverse knowledge, which distinguished him even amongst the Decembrists. Zavalishin, in 1819 brilliantly finished military school, completed a round-the-world journey by sea and, early on, drew himself to the attention of the authorities by virtue of his brilliant talents, in particular in mathematics. The son of a General, he had, however, neither sufficiently solid relationships, nor wealth. Nevertheless, his education and his talent opened up to him the most optimistic prospects for successful promotion up through the ranks. However, Zavalishin had one character trait that completely changed his fate. He was a liar. Pushkin once remarked that "A tendency to lie when found in children endowed with a lively fancy does not prevent them from being sincere and frank."[7] In this sense, Zavalishin remained a child his entire life. Although his life began quite brilliantly, this wasn't enough for him. Compared to his imagination, it was dull and uninteresting. So, he embellished it with lies.

And so, he wrote a letter to Alexander I, in which he sketched out for the tsar the organisation of a global monarchist plot (Alexander, through Shishkov, made it clear that he didn't find the realisation of such a project amenable[8]) and simultaneously projected the creation of an extensive colony whose capital would lie on the western shore of North America. Not long before the uprising of the Decembrists he obtained some information about the existence of a secret

---

7. A. Pushkin. Delvig. In *Critical and Autobiographical Prose* in *The Complete Works of Alexander Pushkin*, vol. 13, p. 399, Milner and Company Limited, 1999.
8. See: *Notes of the Decembrist D. I. Zavalishin*. 1st Russ. ed. St. Petersburg, 1906, p. 86.

society and attempted to join it, but Ryleev did not trust him and prevented his penetration into the Decembrist circle. Whether Zavalishin was accepted into the secret society or not remains questionable. At the very least, he did not participate in the real life of the Decembrist's Northern society. This did not prevent him from enlisting several young people into "his" fantastic society, which he represented as a powerful and extremely decisive organisation. It is possible to visualise how rapturously he sketched completely fantastic pictures of a decisive and bloody plot to his audience.

His boasting did not pass with impunity. In spite of his completely insignificant participation in the Decembrist movement, Zavalishin was sentenced, as one of the most dangerous conspirators, to life imprisonment.[9] He did not abandon his fantastic tales even during penal servitude. In his memoirs he first of all narrates the division of the exiled Decembrists to the Democrats (as head of which, naturally, he set himself) and the aristocrats, then writes about the attempt to flee from Siberia through China towards the Pacific Ocean. It is possible to assume that conversations of this type could appear among the exiled Decembrists, but their realisation, naturally, remained in the realm of fantasy. However, in the consciousness of Zavalishin such conversations are transformed into a deliberate, thoroughly prepared plan which only by chance remains incomplete.

The apex of his fantasy lies in those memoirs written at the end of his life. Zavalishin "recalls" not the tragic, complete failures of his life which were the reality but the bright, successful life of his imagination. His entire life is surrounded by enthusiasm and acknowledgement; his childhood stories (for example, the episode with Bernadotte[10]) vividly resemble the story of General Ivolgin in Dostoevsky's *The Idiot* about his meeting with Napoleon. According to his stories, Zavalishin, on entering the secret society, is immediately made head of the organisation. He "recalls" fantastic scenes of numerous stormy secret sessions where members were gathered solely "to listen to Zavalishin". Ryleev envies him. Ryleev's organisation in Petersburg is in a pitiful state, while he, Zavalishin, knew how to organise large underground centres in the provincial cities. He presents his trip to Simbirsk on the eve of the uprising as an inspection mission for the secret society with the purpose of verifying the preparation of the province for the uprising. Even as he approaches

---

9. Editor's note: The Supreme Criminal Court established 11 categories of punishment for the Decembrists, according to their guilt, yet Nicholas I mitigated the sentence and substituted capital punishment for life imprisonment in the first category, except for 5 supreme criminals. – M.G.

10. Ibid., pp. 30–31.

Simbirsk, the rejoicing conspirators meet him to inform him of their activities.

At the same time, the memoirs of Zavalishin are a most valuable source, not only for studying his psychology, but also for investigating the political history of the Decembrist movement. It is only necessary to make a few corrections to make it possible to re-establish reality.

The study of similar representations of the lie is interesting not only from a psychological point of view. Karamzin once wrote, speaking of poetry:

> What is a poet? A skillful liar:
> To him is glory and the crown![11] –

and elsewhere:

> Lie, untruth, the spectre of truth!
> Be now my goddess … [12]

The formula – the "spectre of truth" is especially important: it lays a bridge between the lie of Zavalishin and poetry.

Karamzin's expression, the "spectre of truth" connects together what, at first, appear to be opposing concepts. Firstly, the lie is connected with the truth, but, in the second place, the truth occurs not in the lie, but in its spectre, i.e., by an apparent doubling. Already this unexpected link between truth and lie forces us to think on two questions: is a lie only evil and if it does fulfil some essential function besides the tendency of people to deceive each other, then what?

Animals hunting or protecting can use fraudulent tactics. However, the lie, i.e., an unmotivated and disinterested untruth is alien to them. Gogol, having created the image of Khlestakov, went on to create an entire poem based on the lie, conceived of as pure art, a lie which finds pleasure in itself and which is overindulged by its own poetry. Khlestakov is able to use the fruits of his lying in a mercenary way (Osip does it so much better), but he doesn't lie out of self-interest. He lies because he possessed "an unusual lightness of thought."[13] His thoughts have the ability to become detached from reality and of forming their own, unconfined and uncontrolled, world. The lie gives Khlestakov a certain degree of freedom, which raises him above the futile reality of a minor Petersburg official. And the fact that the lie is unexpectedly linked to freedom, forces us to give it serious thought.

---

11. Karamzin, N. *Poln. sobr. stikhotvorenii* (*The Poet's Library. Large Series*). Annotated by J. M. Lotman. Moskva/Leningrad, 1966, s. 195. (Translator's note: translation my own.)
12. Ibid., p.151.
13. Gogol, N. V. *Sobr. soch*. T. 4, p. 49.

In the era of Pushkin, his contemporaries guarded the memory of the great liars as masters of a special art. At the beginning of the XIX century, a famous liar, who entered into the legends of his time, was Prince D. Tsitsianov. P. A. Vyazemsky recalled him as follows: During the pouring rain he arrived at a friend's house. "Did you come by coach?" – they asked him. "No, I arrived on foot". – "You did, and why are you not completely soaked?" – "Oh, he answered, I know very well how to dodge deftly between the drops of rain". Tsitsianov told him, ". . . that in the village a peasant woman gave birth, after a long pregnancy to a seven-year-old boy, and his first words, in the hour after the birth, was: "give me a vodka!"[14] Vyazemsky saw in this the special "poetry" of story.

Pushkin introduced into his *Table Talk* the image of the liar, whom he compared with Shakespeare's Falstaff (it is possible he was referring to B. Fyodorov): "Here is a feature from the domestic life of my honourable friend. His four year old son, the double of his father, a little Falstaff III, once, in his absence, repeated all by himself: "How papa is brave! How the tsar loves papa!" Overhearing this, they called the boy: "Who told you this, Volodya?" – Papa, answered Volodya".[15]

In *The Idiot*, Dostoevsky sketches an uncommon scene. The liar and dreamer, General Ivolgin, impudently writes the history of his fictitious intimacy with Napoleon, a history not only deprived of probability but absolutely impossible. Prince Myshkin, Ivolgin's interlocutor, understanding that he is lying, suffering in his soul for the shame of his interlocutor and out of sympathy for him, at the same time perceives in his story some kind of unreal reality.

> 'This is all extremely interesting,' the prince said, in a very hushed tones. 'If that's how it all really happened . . . that's to say, I mean . . . ' he hurried to correct himself.
>
> 'Oh, Prince!' exclaimed the general, intoxicated with his own story to a point where he might now be unable to hold back even the most extreme indiscretions. 'You say: "It all happened!" But there was more, I assure you, there was much more! All that is just wretched political facts. But I repeat to you, I was a witness of that great man's nocturnal tears and groans; but absolutely no one saw that, except me! Towards the end, it's true, he didn't weep at all, there were no tears, he merely groaned sometimes; but his face seemed more and more clouded by darkness. It was as though eternity were already spreading the dark wing over him. Sometimes, at night, we spent whole hours alone, in silence – the Mameluke Rustan would be snoring in the next room; that man slept awfully soundly. "But he's loyal to me and to the dynasty," Napoleon would say of him. On one occasion

---

14. Vyazemsky, P. A. 1929. *Staraya zapisnaya knizhka.* [Old Notebook]. (Ginzburg, L., ed. and annotated.) Leningrad. pp. 111, 223.
15. A. Pushkin. *Poln. sobr. soch.*, t. XII. Moskva, Leningrad, 1949, pp. 160–161. (Translator's note: translation my own.)

it all became too terribly painful, and he suddenly noticed the tears in my eyes; he gave me a look of tender emotion: "You feel sorry for me!" he exclaimed. "You, a child, and perhaps there's another child who feels sorry for me – my son, *le roi de Rome*; all the others, they all hate me, and my brothers will be the first to sell me into slavery!" I began to sob and rushed to him; at that point he himself broke down; we embraced, and our tears mingled. "Write, write to the Empress Josephine!" I sobbed to him. Napoleon gave a shudder, thought, and said to me: "You have reminded me of another heart that loves me; I thank you, *mon ami!*" He sat right down and wrote the letter to Josephine with which Constant was dispatched the next day.'

'You did well,' said the prince. 'Amidst cruel thoughts, you led him to kind feeling.'[16]

Thus, the lie comes out not only as a distortion of genuine reality, but also as a sphere of free and completely independent speech. This brings it together with the sufficiently vast space of "speech for speech", a sort of "pure art". It is not difficult to note that speech for the purpose of information by no means occupies the complete space of our discourse (*rech*). A substantial part of this discourse is self-sufficient in nature. It is worth thinking on this.

It occurred to me to observe the sleeping state of animals, a thing which sufficiently rarely attracts the attention of naturalists. Once I noticed that my dog, which several days before, whilst on a walk, had been chasing a hare (which, thankfully, escaped), reproduced in his sleep in a thin sleepy voice that same kind of the barking, emitted by a dog in pursuit of a hare. In the meantime, his paws repeated not the gestures of a rapid run but an indisputable playful imitation thereof. It was possible to assume that the dog was reliving a repetition during his sleep of the pursuit it had experienced in reality. Moreover, this was precisely a repetition, i.e., a certain imitation, which included not only features of similarity but also differences.

In societies of oral culture, enormous layers of information, which rested both on the inventive collective culture and on the isolation of the individual "geniuses" of memory, were stored and transferred from generation to generation. Written language made a substantial part of this culture superfluous. This was especially evident in the epistolary-diaristic culture. Already, in comparatively recent times, the progress of oral forms of communication – the telephone and radio – have caused the degradation of epistolary culture. In exactly the same manner, the dynamic expansion of newspapers and radio has led to the degradation and simplification of whole domains of traditional culture.

---

16. Fyodor Dostoevsky. *The Idiot*. Trans. David McDuff. London: Penguin Books, 2004, p. 585.

The displacement of the culture of dreams from the realm of conserved information has been more than compensated for in the separation of the word from reality. Speech has become a closed and fully autonomous realm. The possibility of a range of variations in imaginary discourse has separated the vulgar lie from the subtle mechanism of human consciousness.

# Chapter 13
# Internal structures and external influences

The dynamics of culture can be represented as neither an isolated immanent process nor the passive sphere of external influences. Both these tendencies are realised in conditions of mutual tension from which they cannot be abstracted without the distortion of their very essence.

Intersection with other cultural structures may be achieved in a variety of ways. Thus, an "external" culture in order to enter into our world must cease to be "external" to it. It must find for itself a name and a place in the language of the culture into which it seeks to insert itself. But in order to change from "alien" (*chuzhoi*) to "own" (*svoi*) this external culture must, as we can see, submit to a new name in the language of the "internal" culture. The process of renaming does not take place without leaving a trace of that content which has received the new name.

Thus, for example, in the feudal structure, which emerged from the ruins of the ancient world, old designations were widely used. In particular we may cite, for example, the denomination of the Holy Roman Empire or the aspiration of the barbaric kings to call themselves emperors and to appropriate for themselves the symbols of Roman imperial authority. The fact that the old symbolism did not conform to the new political reality meant very little. This divergence from reality troubled no one because no one looks for reality in ideological symbolism. That which was inherited from the past was perceived as a prophecy for the future. When Pushkin, turning to Napoleon, wrote:

> Did your eagles fly, long ago,
> Over this defamed land?[1] –

he was not simply reproducing conventional symbolic clichés but rather he was setting out a concept, "connecting the extremities of time" – the Roman and the Napoleonic empires. The words "your eagles" can be understood as ceremonial but it is impossible to delete the symbolic content expressed within them – which the epoch employed to decode its reality.

The adoption of one symbolic language or another actively influences people's behaviour and the path of history. Thus, the wider cultural context absorbs the elements that invade it from without.

---

1. A. Pushkin. Napoleon. In *Poln. sobr. soch.*, t. II, kn. 1. Moskva-Leningrad, 1947, S. 213. (Translator's note: translation my own.)

But the opposite may occur: the intrusion can be so energetic that it introduces itself not as a separate element of text but as an entire language, which can either completely supplant the language it invades or which may form with it a complex hierarchy (cf., for example, the relationship between Latin and the national languages of medieval Europe).

Finally, it may play the role of the catalyst: without participating directly it may, nevertheless, accelerate the dynamics of the process as represented, for example, by the intrusion of Chinese art into the structure of baroque. In this latter case, the intrusion will take the form of a fashion, which appears, interferes in the dynamics of the basic culture, only then to disappear without trace. Such, in essence is the function of fashion: it is intended to act as a metronome and catalyst of cultural development.[2]

As has been said elsewhere, the intrusion into the sphere of culture from without is accomplished through naming. External events, however active they might be in the extra-cultural sphere (for example, in the fields of physics, or physiology, in the material sphere, etc.), do not influence the consciousness of man until they themselves become "human", i.e., acquire semiotic meaning.

For human thought all that exists is that which falls into any of its languages. Thus, for instance, purely physiological processes such as sexual contact or the impact of alcohol on the organism represent physical and physiological realities. But it is precisely these examples which manifest an essential law: the more distant by its very nature this or that domain is from the sphere of culture, the more effort is applied to introduce it into this sphere. Here it would be possible to highlight the extent of that space which is allotted in culture, even in its highest form – poetry, to the semiotics of wine and love. Poetry, for example, transforms the consumption of wine (and, for other cultures – the use of narcotic drugs) from a physio-chemical and physiological fact into a fact of culture. This phenomenon is so universal and is surrounded by so many prohibitions and prescriptions, by poetic and religious interpretations, and it is so tightly enfolded in the semiotic space of culture that man cannot separate his perception of the effects of alcohol from the psycho-cultural domain.

Culture is traditionally represented as a specific regulated space. The true picture is much more complex and disorderly. The randomness of individual human fates and the interlacing of historical events, which occur on many different levels, populate the world of culture with unpredictable collisions. The harmonious picture sketched out by the researcher of a single genre or an individual closed historical system is an illusion. This is a theoretical model whose

---

2.  See greater detail on this in the chapter: "Inverse image".

eventual realisation at best represents an average of different non-realisations but, more often than not, it is generally not realised.

We never encounter "pure" historical processes, equivalent to the realisation of a theoretical schema. Moreover, it is precisely this disorderliness, this unpredictability, this "spread" of history, which so grieves the researcher that represents the true value of history as such. Specifically, it is these things that fill history with unpredictability; collections of random events, i.e., information. Specifically, it is these things that transform the science of history from the domain of schoolroom boredom into the world of artistic variety.

In a way, it is possible to present culture as a structure which, submerged in a world external to itself, draws this world into itself and expels it in a re-elaborated form (organised) according to the structure of its own language. However this external world, which culture looks on as chaotic is, in reality, also organised. Its organisation is accomplished in accordance with the rules of some language unknown to this culture. In the moment that the texts of this external language are drawn into the space of culture an act of explosion occurs.

From this point of view, explosion can be interpreted as the moment of the collision of two opposing languages: the assimilating and the assimilated. An explosive space appears: a cluster of unpredictable possibilities. The particles expelled by the explosion initially follow such close trajectories that they may be described as synonymous routes of one and the same language. In the artistic world these continue to be recognised as part and parcel of one and the same phenomenon albeit painted with insignificant variations. But subsequent movement along different trajectories causes the particles to move further and further away from each other to the extent that variations of *one* object are transformed into a collection of *different* objects. Thus, the various protagonists created by Lermontov have their genetic roots in one common point of explosion, but are subsequently transformed into not only different, but also contrasting, types.

From this point of view, we may say that the explosion does not form synonyms, although the external observer is inclined to combine different trajectories into synonymous groupings. Thus, for instance, the foreign reader of Russian literature of the XIX century is inclined to create for himself conventional generalisations of the type: the "Russian writer of this epoch". Everything that falls within this framework will be considered from a similar point of view, as synonymy.

However, from an internal point of view for this culture, *the works of one writer cannot be considered as being synonymous with the works of another* (at least, if we are talking about an original work). Each of them is separately individual and unique in their own way. This does not prevent them from being included into some generalised categories. Pushkin's Lensky, from a certain

point of view, might be considered as "representative" of some kind of generalised classification but Pushkin had the right to write, in connection with his
loss:

> However, reader, we may wonder ...
> The youthful lover's voice is stilled ...[3]

Here we see a switch from the category of common nouns to that of proper
names.[4]

For the observer external to this culture, the writers – as is the case for the
general with his soldiers – are identified by common nouns. However, in their
neighbourhood, for their own 'family' they belong to the category of proper
names and have no plural. Herein, by the way, lies the radical difference between the two methods of cultural perception. Those, who share the author's
point of view, consider both the people of a culture and their artistic works to be
in the category of proper names. However, the tradition of cultural studies, which
appeared vividly, for example, in the Hegelian school and which has won for
itself an enduring place in the criticism and teaching of literature, in principle,
transforms proper names into common nouns. The writer becomes a "product"
and his hero – a "representative". This transformation has frequently been criticised and mocked; but we must not forget that we have no other knowledge
mechanism than transformation of "our" (own) (*svoi*) into the "other" (alien)
(*chuzhoi*) and the subject of knowledge – into its object.

Neither the world of proper names nor the world of common nouns, taken
separately, can encapsulate genuine reality. Reality is given to us in dialogic
form and in this, once again, we see the need for art.

The world of common nouns gravitates towards processes of gradual development, which are inextricably linked to the mutual changeability of its elements. The space of proper names is the space of explosion. It is no accident
that historically explosive epochs push "great people" to the surface, i.e., they
actualise the world of proper names. The history of the disappearance of proper
names in those domains where, it would seem, they could not be substituted
with anything, might offer a special theme for further research.

The link between the world of proper names and explosive processes is further confirmed by the following consideration. The history of language and the
history of literary language may be considered as disciplines of a single order.
They are usually considered to form a part of the general science of historical linguistics. At the same time, we cannot fail to note an essential difference between

---

3. Alexander Pushkin. *Eugene Onegin*. Trans. James E. Falen. Carbondale and Edwardsville: Southern Illinois University Press, 1990, p. 161.
4. See more detail on this in the chapter "The world of proper names".

them: the history of language studies anonymous processes, which processes are simultaneously characterised by gradual development. The ideas of N. J. Marr concerning explosions in linguistic processes were roundly criticised in the Fifties. The history of language gravitates towards anonymity and gradual development.

The history of literary language, meanwhile, is characterised by its indissoluble links to the individuality of each writer and the explosive nature of the process. And therein lies the difference between these two related disciplines: one has a tendency towards predictability and the other to unpredictability. There is, however, an even more important aspect: the development of language does not assume self-knowledge as a necessary element. Self-knowledge in the form of the creation of grammar and elements of meta-description invades language from without, from the domain of general culture. The sphere of literary language, meanwhile, rests on the foundation of self-knowledge and presents itself as the beginnings of individual creativity. From this point of view, the explosive nature of the domain of literary language appears completely natural. We may recall that the innovative attempts of Juri Sergeyevich Sorokin who, even as early as the end of the Forties, raised the question as to whether, in principle, the study and teaching of literary language should relate to the individual works of the writer, was perceived by some traditional linguists as an attempt on the historic foundations of language. In respect of the latter the notion of anonymity was viewed as an inalienable quality.

Thus, the dynamic development of culture is accompanied by the constant transposition of internal and external processes. The same can be said of gradual and explosive processes.

# Chapter 14
# Two forms of dynamic

The correlation between different forms of dynamics determines the specific character of two fundamental types of processes. We have defined the difference between them as the opposition between explosion and gradual development. Nevertheless, we would, however, once again warn against a literal understanding of these concepts – based on the dictates of everyday experience. The concept of explosion, in particular, is only connected with the everyday content of this word in certain isolated instances. Thus, for instance, repetitive cyclical movements (such as the calendrical cycle) regardless of the many changes connected therewith, cannot be regarded as explosive. What is important here is quite another factor – that as a result of this development, which can take shape in the stormiest of environments, the system returns to the starting point. Thus, a pulsating development cannot be considered explosive, even if it includes some isolated incidents of a turbulent nature.

The history of literary criticism in the 1920–30s brought about two concepts of Romanticism. The author of one of them, V. M. Zhirmunsky, proposed a model of the history of literature which was based on a chain of constant replacements of two basic types of art. Zhirmunsky wrote: "We will define them conditionally as Classical and Romantic art ... We," noted the author, "are now talking not of the historical phenomenon in its individual wealth and uniqueness but of a certain constant, timeless type of poetic creation." Further V. M. Zhirmunsky explains a similar position: "The Classical poet has before him an objective task: to create an excellent work of art, a complete and perfect, self-sufficient world, subordinated to its own specific laws. On the contrary, the Romantic poet, in his work, attempts first of all to describe himself to us, "to open his soul". He confesses himself and introduces us to the emotional depths and the unique humanity of his personality. The poems of Homer, the tragedies of Shakespeare and Racine (which are, in this sense – equally "Classical"), the comedies of Plautus and Molière, Pushkin's *Poltava* and his *The Stone Guest* and *Wilhelm Meister* and *Herman and Dorothea* of Goethe provide no inclination on the part of the reader to extract perfection from the leaves of the completed work of art in order to search out the living, human personality of poet; his "sincere" biography. The poems of Byron and Alfred de Musset, the *New Heloise* of Rousseau and the *Faust* of the young Goethe, the lyric poetry of Fet and Aleksandr Blok and the latter's dramatic works (*The Stranger, The Rose and the Cross*) cause us to "commune" with the true spiritual world, which lies beyond the strict boundaries of art."[1]

In this way, the antithesis: "Classicism – Romanticism" includes within itself not only the opposition of two styles, but also a principally different resolution of the question: "art and life". For us, it is important to note that these two models of culture, in Zhirmunsky's opinion, comprise a universal constant regardless of whether they change each other or coexist chronologically. Another element is just as important: that they are regarded as types of culture which are constantly present, and not included in historical dynamics.

In contrast to Zhirmunsky, G. A. Gukovsky proceeded on the basis of the development of literature in phases. From his point of view,[2] literary movement presents itself as a temporally sequential series of typological phases each of which succeeds the other. In this way, the uniqueness of the text is generated by the intersection of typology and chronology and is not separated from the historical approach.

We will not concern ourselves with the historical criticism of each of these concepts. In their time they played a positive role in the development of the theory of literature. For us, now, it is essential to focus attention on the differences which lie at the root of their methodologies. V. M. Zhirmunsky studied literature as a change of states, completely free from explosions, G. A. Gukovsky studies it as a chain of explosions. It is interesting to note that however much Gukovsky attempts to disguise this, the passage from one stage to another is accomplished "suddenly" with a decisive break.

Another example is also curious. It is known that the concept of qualitative breaks in the development of language proposed by N. J. Marr and founded on Hegelian dialectics contrasted sharply with the reality of linguistic development, which, as a rule, possesses a gradual nature. This circumstance was emphasized in the critiques of Marrism (by Stalin, and Vinogradov). It is all the more re-markable then, that where the ideas of Marr returned to their native domain – to the region of culture, folklore and literature, they no longer appeared to be quite so absurd.

The theory of the development of culture by stages, which we touched upon in connection with Gukovsky, was also shared by Zhirmunsky. A special session of the Departments of Literature of Leningrad State University was held in

---

1. Zhirmunsky, V. M. *Voprosy teorii literatury: Statyi 1916–1926.g.* Leningrad, 1928, p. 175–177. See the new publication: Zhirmunsky, V. M. *Teoriya literatury. Poetika. Stilistika.* Leningrad, 1977. Here and throughout we cite the first edition.

2. See: Gukovsky, G. A. *Ocherki po istorii russkogo realizma. Part 1 (Pushkin i russkie romantiki).* Saratov, 1946, p. 6–10 and further.

1949 to address questions relating to the development of culture by stages. Zhirmunsky and Gukovsky were the principal speakers at the session. This session subsequently fell to unscientific criticism, as a result of which a rash of political charges was dropped on the speakers and a scientific resolution of the problem did not take place.

O. M. Freidenberg drew attention to the explosive nature of processes in culture, folklore and literature. The works of the "marrists", dedicated to the problems of cultural processes, not only lacked the arbitrary nature noted in the late linguistic works of Marr but also preserved a scientific interest in the topic until our time. Such, for example, is the work of Freidenberg in "Tersit" which contains a scientific analysis of the function of the fool in folklore and literature across the centuries. In her polemic with the Formalists, Freidenberg focuses her attention on the impossibility of separating the text from the myth and the latter from everyday behaviour: "... this is not simply a literary device and literary topic, but a replica of social ideology: indeed it is precisely in life (of the court – especially) that the fool who took on the appearance of Tersit; a man, born with a hump and with other specific features of deformity, often became a fool, consequently, the literary view was contiguous to the everyday view. Both were caused by the general semantics of the term "fool", which was one of the metaphors of death, just as "tsar" was one of the metaphors of life ... " Subsequently, Freidenberg examines the movement of the image of the fool through the stages of the genre: "Later, in the following stage, invective becomes a ritual act, in particular a military rite, and the tsar fulfils the functions of the fool; in order to raise the spirit of leader or the troops, whom he swears publicly – and thus renews the martial spirit". Freidenberg formulates her conclusion as follows: "Paleontological semantics take shape in the form of the schematic structure of plot; the structure of the plot creates a content, which is alien to this structure; and one state passes into another."[3]

History is rich in paradoxes, and oppositions frequently gravitate towards each other. In this sense it is an interesting task, and not outwith the bounds of historical irony, to trace how the deep movements of thought of O. M. Freidenberg and M. M. Bakhtin gravitate towards rapprochement, breaking through the polar opposition of the terminologies, views and personalities of the authors.

The latter relates to the distant stages of scientific development. It is all the more interesting, therefore, to note their continued fruitfulness and to highlight the deep roots of contemporary scientific ideas.

---

3.  Freidenberg, O. M. Tersit. *Yafeticheski Sbornik VI.* Leningrad, 1930, pp. 233, 241, 253.

Although it may seem strange, the mechanisms of gradual processes have been the subject of much less study. It would seem that, here, the problem itself is absent; it is quite simply the retarded development, the gradual nature or even the absence of dynamics in various phenomena. Meanwhile, gradual processes represent an exceptionally important aspect of historical movement. Above all, it is necessary to renounce any idea of their stability.

Those movements, which cannot even be defined as processes, are especially interesting as, in them, the start and end points of the cycle coincide. However, complex movements can occur between these basic points. Calendrical cycles are a particular example of this. The latter are, without doubt, the source of the idea of cyclic changes in the linear development of the consciousness of man. However, calendrical processes themselves represent just one of the most noticeable manifestations for mankind of the pulsating cyclic recurrence which penetrates both cosmic and elementary levels. The significance of these slow and pulsating processes in the general structure of human existence is not inferior to the role of the explosive one and it should be added that, in historical reality, all these types of processes are interwoven and act upon each other, first accelerating, then slowing down general movement.

# Chapter 15
# The dream – a semiotic window

The moment a temporary space (the pause) between impulse and reaction appeared represented a turning point in the history of consciousness. The basic biological schema is shaped in the following way: "stimulus – response". In this case, the space between these elements is, in an ideal sense, instantaneous, i.e. it is determined by physiological time, which is necessary for the realisation of an immediate response. Such a schema characterises everything living and preserves its authority, even over humanity. Upon this notion rests the entire sphere of impulses and instantaneous reactions. On the one hand, they are associated with immediate actions, on the other, with instantaneous reactions, those for which ordinary semiotic communication appears to be too slow.

A fundamentally new stage occurs with the appearance of a temporary break between the receipt of information and reaction to it. This state, above all, requires the development and improvement of memory. Another important result is the transformation of the reaction to an immediate action into a sign. The reaction to information becomes an independent structure capable of assimilation into an ever more complex and self-developing mechanism.

At this stage, the reaction, having lost its immediate impulse, is not yet totally free and therefore, remains potentially controllable. Its mechanism is, as before, conditioned by the physiological impulses, which lie outside of the conscious will of the speaker, but which, to all intents and purposes, is already sufficiently independent. A prime exponent of this stage is the dream.

It is possible to assume that, in a psychological state where thoughts and behaviour are inseparable, dreamy visions represent a sphere where it would be impossible to break these down into independent, isolated experiences. Speech and gesture, and wider still, the whole sphere of language with all its possibilities, triggered much more powerful mechanisms and muffled the potential of the dream to develop into a sphere of self-sufficient consciousness. However, this domain has not surrendered its position without a fight.

It is quite evident that ancient man possessed a much greater culture of the dream, that in truth, he 'saw' his dreams and memorised them with greater ease and coherence. And we mustn't forget that the Shaman culture, indisputably, possessed a method of controlling dreams, to say nothing of their ability to retell and interpret them coherently. Retelling in the culture of dreams, as P. Florensky showed, plays an enormous role because this also organises the system of dreams, giving them, in particular, a temporary linear composition.[1]

The development of speech pushed aside this sphere to a second level of culture and resulted in its primitivisation. The progress and dynamics of other realms of thinking caused an unavoidable regress in such spheres, necessarily causing the latter to cede their key position. In this way, for example, the development of written language indisputably caused the degradation of oral culture. The need for a developed mnemonic system (in particular, such mnemonic devices as singing and poetry), which for a long time occupied a position of extreme importance, was eliminated.

We will not concern ourselves with the fairly complex and knotty problem of the Freudian concept of sleep. Let us just pause upon the parallel between this method and the earliest interpretations of dreams which goes all the way back to the pre-cultural era.

Entering into the world of dreams, ancient man, who had not yet not developed a written language, found himself confronted by a space which was similar to real space but which, simultaneously, was not reality. It was natural for him to assume that this world had a meaning, but its meaning was unknown. These were signs of who knew what, i.e., signs in their pure form. Their meaning was indeterminate and it was necessary to establish a meaning for them. Consequently, in the beginning there was a semiotic experiment. Apparently, it is in this same sense that we should understand the biblical assertion: *in the beginning was the word*. The word preceded its meaning, i.e., man knew that this *was a word*; that it *had a meaning*, but he did not know what that meaning was. He, as it were, spoke in a language incomprehensible to himself.

The perception of the dream as a form of communication begs the question: what is the source of this communication? Subsequently, in more developed mythological structures, the dream is identified with the *alien's* prophetic voice, i.e., represents the turning of *her/him to me*. It is possible to assume that, at an early stage, something resembling our experience of cinematography occurred, that first and third person merged but were not distinguished from each other. "I" and "He" were mutually identical. In the following stage the problem of dialogue appeared. We may also observe a similar sequence in children's mastery of language. This property of the dream as a pure form allowed it to become a space ready to be filled: a Shaman interpreting dreams is as "knowledgeable"

---

1. This thought was, later, substantially corrected by B. A. Uspensky in the article: "History and semiotics" (see: Uspensky B. A. 1988. Istoriya i semiotika (Vospriyatiye vremeni kak semioticheskaya problema). *Trudy po znakovym sistemam* 22: 71–72.)

as the experienced Freudian. Sleep is a semiotic mirror and each of us sees in it the reflection of our own language.

A fundamental property of this language lies in its extreme unpredictability. This makes it inconvenient for the transfer of constant communications, but, on the other hand, it is extremely well suited to the generation of new information. The dream was perceived as communication from a mysterious *other*, although in reality, it was little more than an information-free transfer of "text for text". In much the same way that art realised itself, having won the right to be free of meaning and any other exterior goal ("engagement" comes later, when culture realises that it must "engage"), the possibility of being interpreted precedes the concept of correct interpretation. However, the need for a collectively comprehensible transmission of information prevailed sharply over the tendency to enlarge the boundaries of linguistic invention. This was a competition the language of dreams could not sustain.

In the movement of languages, culture systematically creates periods where simplified, but adequately understood, languages are celebrated over and above those languages which are richer in content but only individually understood. Thus, at the end of the XX century we are witnessing a retreat of the languages of art (especially of poetry and of cinema) before the strong advance of those languages which support technical progress. In Europe, in the first half of our century, the relative strengths of the latter were completely the opposite. Of course any "victory" in culture is little more than a displaced accent in the dialogue.

A confusion of functions has occurred: the dream, precisely because of those qualities which rendered it inconvenient for the functioning of practical communications, passed naturally into the realm of contacts with deities, divination and predictions. The entrance of poetry into the sacral sphere signified the beginning of the displacement of the monopoly of the dream, although the link between poetic inspiration and the mystical dream is a universal phenomenon for many cultures. The dream was pushed out to the periphery of the sacral space.

The dream-prediction (a window into the mysterious future) gave way to the notion of the dream as a way into the self. In order that the function of the dream could change, it was necessary to change the location of the mysterious space. From the external it became internal. Our comparison of the Freudian and the Shaman is not at all pejorative. It is an indication of the ability, at different cultural moments, of magic as well as the sciences; and of prediction and medicine as a means to recovery, to carry out identical functions – to become objects of faith. But faith exerts an extreme influence over man and can actually generate miracles. If a patient believes, then the remedy helps him.

Emile Zola, in his novel *Doctor Pascal* described a doctor who invented a universal medicine which miraculously helped all patients. Both patients and doctor were seized with enthusiasm and piously believed in the wonderful ability of medicine. Then, one day, Doctor Pascal gave distilled water to a patient by mistake. The effect was just as health-giving as with the medicine. Patients so deeply believed in the injections that they got better from distilled water. Faith is not the "opium of the people", but it is a powerful means of self-organisation. Faith in the mysterious meaning of dreams is based on faith in the meaning of communication as such. You might say that the dream is the father of semiotic processes.

The dream is characterised by polylingualism: it does not immerse us in visual, verbal, musical and other spaces but rather in the space of their coalescence which is analogous to real space. This is the "unreal reality". The translation of the dream into the languages of human communication is accompanied by a decrease in the level of uncertainty and by an increase in the level of communicability. Subsequently, this way will be transferred over to art. The moment that the dream took a step towards linguistic communication with the deities, it was perfectly natural that the latter should pass into the language of riddles and mysterious sayings possessing a high level of uncertainty.

In light of the aforesaid, the new concept of "primitive syncretism" has emerged, drawing the attention of the academic A. N. Veselovsky. This does not consist of the dramatic performance of certain texts, but rather pertains to the reproduction of an event in a different, but extremely similar language. It concerns the radical articulation of the space of life and death, which we are living even now as the antithesis of practical reality on the one hand, and a polyphonic space, into which the diverse modelling systems fall on the other, which in the pre-archaic stage, was reduced to the binary lingual structure: practical language – sleep.

Of course, such a picture represents only a rough sketch; in reality, this sphere is being shaped in the form of a complex and contradictory semiotic web (*klubok*),[2] which floats in semiotic space.

As we already noted, the dream is a form of communication with a concealed source and this zero space may be occupied by different carriers of communication depending on the type of interpreting culture involved. The guilty brother in Schiller's *Brigands* repeated the Helvetian formula: "dreams are of the stomach"; Schiller himself believed that the dream is the oppressed voice of the conscience of man, a concealed internal judge. The ancient Romans regarded

---

2. Translator's note: The word *klubok* in Russian has the basic meaning: 'wool ball' (or a mass of wool). However, it also carries with it notions of 'tangle', 'web' or 'mass' such that the kind of ball referred to here might be best understood a kind of clump of elements being brought together in an almost organic way.

dreams as the prediction of the gods, and contemporary Freudians see them as the voice of suppressed sexuality. If we generalise all these interpretations by attributing to them a certain general formula, then we will gain some idea of the hidden power, concealed in the mysterious depths, which controls man. This power speaks to man in a language which requires an interpreter in order to be understood.

The dream requires an interpreter – whether this be a contemporary psychologist or a pagan priest. The dream has one additional special feature – it is individual and it is not possible to penetrate the dream of another. Consequently the dream is, fundamentally, a "language for one person". And therein lies the extreme complexity of communicating in this language: to verbally narrate a dream is as difficult as, let us say, it is to narrate a musical work through the medium of the word. This inability to communicate the content of a dream makes any memorisation, together with its transformation, little more than an approximation of its essence.

Thus, the dream is surrounded by numerous limitations, which make of it an extremely brittle and polysemantic way of storing information. But it is precisely these "deficiencies" which make it possible to assign to the dream a special and extremely essential cultural function: to become the reserve of semiotic uncertainty, a space which must, of necessity, become filled with meaning. This renders the dream an ideal *ich-Erzählung*, capable of being filled up with diverse interpretations, both mystical and aesthetical.

# Chapter 16
# "I" and "I"

At the beginning of *Confessions*, Rousseau wrote: "I alone.[1] I know my heart, and I am acquainted with mankind. I am not made like any one I have seen; I dare believe I am not made like any one existing."[2] From *Emile* to *Confessions*, Rousseau made great progress. The "I" in *Emile* is a pronoun designating he who expresses the essence of discourse in the first person. In *Emile* the discussion deals with the essence of man as such. Therefore, the narrator is portrayed as the embodiment of natural reason and the pupil as Nature which finds itself.[3] In *Confessions*, "I" is a proper name, which has no plural and cannot therefore be appropriated by a unique and irreplaceable human personality. The epigraph: "Intus et in cute" – "internally and under the skin"[4] (quotation from the ancient Roman poet, Aulus Persius Flaccus). Rousseau thus moved away from the pronoun "I" to the proper name "I". This is one of the basic poles of human thought.

Tradition has led us to believe that the path of human consciousness leads from the individual (unique) to the universal (general). If we understand the individual as the ability to increase the number of differences, to find in one and the same thing that which is different, then this, of course, represents one of the basic tenets of cultural progress. It is necessary only to note that the ability to see difference in sameness and sameness in difference represents the two inseparable halves of the unity of consciousness. The non-differentiation of that which is different does not emphasise but rather destroys similarity as, generally speaking, it eliminates comparison.

The structure of the "I" is one of the basic indices of culture. "I" as a pronoun is much simpler in structure than "I" as a proper name. The latter is not a well-defined linguistic sign.

Different languages use different grammatical methods to express the difference between the word used to designate anything and that which is used

---

1. In the original: "Moi seul" (*Rousseau, J. J.* Oeuvres complètes / Ed. Musset-Pathay, vol. 27. Paris, 1824, p. 3).
2. *The confessions of J. J. Rousseau: with the reveries of the solitary walker.* Translated from the French, vol. 1. London: Printed for J. Bew, 1783, p. 1.
3. Translator's note: i.e. in its own part, as a human being.
4. Part of the 30th verse of Satire III:
   Ego te intus et in cute novi
   (I know you even under the skin; *Lat.* Trans. F. A. Petrovsky).

to designate this precise thing. In Russian, it would be possible to express this by using, in the second instance, capital letters: table – means any table (as adequately expressed in the German language using the indeterminate article "ein"), Table, with a capital letter, means this is my table, personally familiar to me, unique, this Table, which possesses signs which are lacking in "tables generally". For example, on it there may be an ink spot. The ink spot cannot be a sign of a table in general terms, but it can be the inseparable sign of this particular table. Fonvizin, in *The Minor* (*Nedorosl*) reproduces the following scene:

| | |
|---|---|
| **Pravdin** | Door, for example, is what: a noun or an adjective? |
| **Mitrofan** | Door, which door? |
| **Pravdin** | Which door! This one. |
| **Mitrofan** | This one? It's an adjective. |
| **Pravdin** | Why? |
| **Mitrofan** | Because it applies to its place. In the pantry there's a door that hasn't been hung up for six weeks: so that is still a noun. |
| **Old Man** | So, for you, the word fool is an adjective, because it is applied to a foolish person? |
| **Mitrofan** | Yes, that's right.[5] |

Fonvizin's rationalist consciousness presents abstract thought as truth and concrete thought as a manifestation of foolishness.

Another point of view is, however, possible. We have already noted that, for Rousseau, in *Confessions* the carrier of truth is that "I" which is without a plural. Earlier, we gave the example of the use of proper names by Vladimir Solovyev as a child.[6] For the rationalist, the concrete world is merely an example for the illustration of general rules. In the fable, the relationship of text and morals is usually constructed according to this schema. The moral represents itself as the singular, logical interpretation of the sense of the tale. Significantly, Krylov, overcoming the rationalistic genre of the fable, created a much more complex system of relations between "text" and "moral". The moral in his works is not presented as an expression of abstract truth, but rather as the voice of the people, common sense.

Rousseau's audacious trick in declaring the superiority of the "atypical truth" and the value of Jean Jacques as a unique and individual personality paved the way for the reconstruction of the image of man in the novel and in the portrait of the subsequent epoch. These genres are not allegorical (in this sense, the lessons of Diderot's *Salons* are significant, in terms of their abject refusal of

---

5. Fonvizin, D. I. *Sobr. soch.* T. 1, p. 162. (Translator's note: translation my own.)
6. See this publication, ch. 7.

allegorism and their elevation of portraiture as the image of man in painting). They affirmed a new type of artistic consciousness: the hero is simultaneously exceptionally-unique and at the same time, is in some way connected to the reader and spectator in their shared features of similarity. The artificial behaves like the living. This is linked to a whole plethora of mythological subjects, dating back to antiquity at least, concerning the reanimation of the artificially created work of art.

Significantly the rationalist consciousness, especially that which is disseminated in school practice, always attempts to interpret the artistic text in its unitary form. Hence the theme of compositions of past eras "Onegin as a typical representative of the nobility" may have been substituted by "Tatyana, the Russian soul", but the general tendency to "streamline contradictions" and to reduce diversity to singularity has not changed. More and more we are hearing how, for example, the complexity and the contradictions of the image of Tatyana introduced in the lines:

She knew the Russian language badly,
[...]
And in her native tongue, I fear,
Could barely make her meaning clear.[7]

are reducing the "educational" value of the method.

It would, however, be too easy to attribute blame to school practice and to suggest that everything falls down to the teachers. Rather, the discussion must centre on the characteristic contradiction of art, which is simultaneously its strength and its weakness, and which cannot, in principle, be overcome because it is this which makes it possible for the artistic text to operate simultaneously with both common nouns and proper nouns.

---

7. Alexander Pushkin. *Eugene Onegin*. Trans. James E. Falen. Carbondale and Edwardsville: Southern Illinois University Press, 1990, p. 79.

# Chapter 17
# The phenomenon of art

The transformation, which occurs at the true moment of explosion, having been filtered by the lattice of the modelling of consciousness which converts the random into the regular, does not as yet complete the process of consciousness. This mechanism must also include the act of memory, which allows us to return once more to the moment preceding the explosion and to replay the entire process retrospectively. There are now, as it were, three layers of consciousness: the moment of primary explosion, the moment it is realised by the mechanisms of consciousness and the moment of its redoubling in the structure of memory. The last layer is the basis for the mechanism of art.

The positive philosophy of the XIX century on the one hand, and Hegelian aesthetics on the other, have affirmed in our consciousness the idea of art as a reflection of reality. At the same time, a diverse range of neo-romantic (Symbolist and decadent) ideas led to the widespread dissemination of the point of view of art as antithetical to life. This opposition was epitomized by the antithesis of freedom of creation and the servitude of reality. Neither view can be claimed to be true or false. They isolate and bring to a maximal point those tendencies, impossible in real life, which in real art are inextricably interconnected.

Art creates a fundamentally new level of reality, which is distinguished from the latter by a sharp increase in freedom. Freedom is introduced into those spheres which, in reality, do not possess it. The non-alternative achieves the alternative. Hence the growth in ethical values in art. It is precisely because of this greater freedom that art appears to fall outside of the moral sphere. It makes possible not only that which is forbidden but also that which is deemed impossible. Therefore, with respect to reality, art comes out as the domain of freedom. But the very sensation of this freedom presupposes an observer who looks upon art from *the point of view of reality*. Thus, the domain of art always includes a feeling of alienation. And this, inevitably, introduces the mechanism of ethical value. That very resolution, with which aesthetics denies the inevitability of the ethical interpretation of art; that very energy, which is expended on similar proofs, is the best confirmation of their stability. The ethical and the aesthetical are opposites and are inseparable as the two poles of art.

The relation between art and morals echoes the common fate of oppositions in the structure of culture. Polar origins are realised in an act of mutual conflict. Each of the two tendencies understands victory to be the complete destruction of their antithesis. However, such an interpretation presents victory as a suicidal option since it is determined both by reality and by the existence of its antithesis.

A sharp increase in the level of freedom in relation to reality makes art an experimental pole. Art creates its own world, one which is constructed as a transformation of non-artistic reality according to the law: "if, then ..." The artist concentrates the force of art in those spheres of life, where he experiences an increase in freedom. In fact, no differentiation is made whether the object of attention relates to the possibility of destroying the laws of family, the laws of society, the laws of common sense, the laws of custom and tradition or even the laws of time and space. In all cases, the laws which organise the world are divided into two groups: changes which are impossible and changes which are possible, but which are categorically forbidden (in this case, changes which are possible and not forbidden are not generally considered, they appear as the antithesis of pseudo-changes as opposed to authentic ones).

The character of Hoffmann *may* stretch up to the ceiling and then roll himself up into a ball again, just as the giant in "Puss in Boots" may be converted first into a lion and then into a mouse. Thus, for these characters, the transformation is an action. But these criteria do not work for Tolstoy's characters. Olenin does not experience a limitation of freedom because he is deprived of the kinds of transformations, which are possible for Hoffmann's characters, since these changes are not part of his vocabulary. However, the fact that the freedom available to old Yeroshka or Lukashka proves impossible for him becomes a tragedy for the character.

Each time, freedom is presented as a presumption, determined by the rules of the world, into which the work introduces us. The genius of art, in general, is a mental experimentation, which allows us to test inviolability of the various structures of the world. This also determines the ratio of art to reality. It verifies the impact of experimentation through the consequent expansion or limitation of freedom. Those plots (syuzhets) which represent the consequences of the rejection of experiment are considered to be derivatives. When a patriarchal society or any other form of idealisation of the immutable becomes the object of art, then, despite widespread ideas to the contrary, the stimulus for the creation of such an art is not a stable and motionless society, but a society which is embroiled in catastrophic processes. Plato preached the constancy of art in a period, during which the world of antiquity was irrepressibly embroiled in impending catastrophe.

The object of art, the plot of the artistic work, is always given to the reader as something that is already complete, prior to its narration. This past is illuminated at the moment when the work of art is transformed from a state of incompleteness to a state of completion. This is expressed, in particular, in the fact that the whole development of the theme is given to the reader as a past event which simultaneously appears as if it were in the present, and as a convention which simultaneously appears as if it were real.

The action of the novel or drama belongs to a past time in relation to the moment in which it is read. But the reader cries or laughs, i.e., he lives out the emotions which, outside of art, belong to the present. In equal measure, conventional emotions are transformed into real ones. The text fixes the paradoxical property of art, transforming the conventional into the real and the past into the present. Furthermore, herein lies the difference between the time of the development of the work and the time of its completion. The former exists in time; the latter is converted into the past which, in general terms, simultaneously represents a withdrawal from time. This fundamental difference in the spaces between the work and its completion makes it pointless to reflect on what happens to the characters at the end of the work. If similar reflections appear, what they testify to is the inartistic perception of the artistic text and are but the result of the inexperience of the reader.

Art is a means of acquiring knowledge and, above all, the knowledge of man. This position has been repeated so often that it has become trivial. However, what should we understand by the expression the "knowledge of man"? The plots defined by this expression have one common feature: they place man into a situation of freedom and investigate his behaviour in that situation. No real situation – from the most everyday to the most unexpected – can exhaust the entire sum of possibilities and, therefore, all of the actions which serve to reveal the potentiality of man. The authentic essence of man cannot, in reality, be revealed. Art transports man into a world of freedom and thereby elaborates his possible behaviours. Thus, any work of art generates a kind of norm and its violation or the establishment – at least in the domain of the freedom of fantasy – of another norm.

The cyclic world of Plato destroying the unexpected in the behaviour of man and introducing indisputable rules, itself destroys art. Plato reasons logically. Art is a mechanism of dynamic processes. In the Sixties, the British director L. Anderson produced the film *If*. The action of the film takes place in a college where young men experience complex conflicts between their destructive sexual, mercantile, and ambitious passions, which agitate them, and by the idiotic conventionalities imposed on them by society and incarnated in their teachers. The images, elicited by the passions burning in the souls of the characters appear on screen with the same measure of reality as authentic events. In the eyes of the spectator, the real and the unreal are hopelessly entangled. When two schoolboys, having skipped a lesson, enter a café and bring down to the floor a beautiful powerful waitress, the spectator experiences all the emotions of a witness to an erotic scene but at the same time the spectator is given to understand that all that occurs, in reality, is the purchase of cigarettes with what little money they have. Everything else is – *if*. The film finishes with a scene showing the arrival of parents for the weekend. On screen, the parents, a friendly crowd laden with flowers and gifts approach the school, at the same time, and with the same imitation of cinematic reality, the sons sitting on the roof of the school with machine guns, open fire in long bursts on their mums and dads. The external theme of the film is the problem of child psychology. But, at the same time, the question of the very language of art is raised. This question is *if*. With this question, an unlimited variety of possibilities are introduced into life.

All forms of artistic creation can be represented as varieties of mental experiment. The phenomenon which is the subject of analysis is incorporated into a system of relations foreign to it. As a result, the event takes place as an explosion and, therefore, is unpredictable in nature. The unpredictability (unexpected outcome) of the unravelling of events appears to constitute the core composition of the work.

What distinguished the post-folkloric work of art from the reality it reflected was the fact that it always had an end point. At the same time, the end point is the point from which the event may be viewed retrospectively. This backward observation seems to transform the random into the inevitable and all events are subjected to a second evaluation.

From this point of view, those structures which organise texts through a pointed title or a significant ending (or indeed both) are of particular interest. Of the many artistic values of these elements of composition, in this case, only one interests us: the ability of the text to change its content depending on the point of view of the reader. Thus, for example, the title of the tale *The Queen of Spades* or of the Chekhovian drama *The Seagull* changes for the reader (or the spectator) in proportion to his movement from one plot episode to another and the end requires a return to the beginning and a second reading. That which was organised by movement along the temporal axis, which is occupied by reading, is transferred into the synchronous space of memory. The sequence is substituted by simultaneity and this lends a new meaning to events. In this situation, artistic memory behaves in a fashion analogous to that which P. Florensky attributed to the dream: it moves in the opposite direction to the temporal axis.

A particular but interesting example are the serial articles in newspapers or periodicals. An extreme manifestation of these is, for example, *Eugene Onegin* by Pushkin or *Vasily Terkin* by Tvardovsky, in which one or the other chapter is published before the next chapter has been written or even thought of. Each new chapter places upon the poet the need to overcome his ignorance. Hence the characteristically dualistic position of Pushkin in *Onegin*: he is the author, who arbitrarily creates the history of his characters and at the very same time, he is the contemporary of these characters, the circumstances of whose lives he learns from stories and letters and from direct observations from real life. Hence it is, for example, that this is sometimes treated by scholars and in particular by this author, as an oversight on Pushkin's part, a casual error. In *Eugene Onegin* we read:

> Tatyana's letter lies beside me,
> And reverently I guard it still –

and elsewhere, already referring to Onegin:

> The girl whose letter he still kept [...],
> Where all was shown ... all unprotected ...[1]

If we add to this the paradoxical but, in reality, very deep statement of Küchelbecker in his prison diary that for a man who knows Pushkin as well as Küchelbecker knows him, it is obvious, that Tatyana herself is the poet[2] then before us occurs an exceptionally complex interlacing of the external and internal points of view. But, as background to this, there is a constant jumping between the reality of the text above and beyond the idea of author and the notion of the complete and unlimited authority of the author over his work.

Everything that has been said can be considered as a particular instance of the general law of the passage of the artistic text through an initially unpredictable semantic orbit. What subsequently occurs is a reconsideration of the whole of the previous history to the extent that what was not predicted is retrospectively reconsidered as the only possible option.

From a historical and cultural point of view, it is interesting to examine the different stages of art not in its evolutionary (historical) aspect, but as a unified whole. In the phenomenon of art it is possible to isolate two opposing tendencies: the tendency toward the repetition of that which is already known and the tendency toward the creation of that which is fundamentally new. Does the first of these theses not arise from a contradiction to the thesis that art, as the result of explosion, always creates a text that is initially unpredictable?

As a delimited case of the first tendency let us examine first of all not folklore and the crafted performance of a group of artists, working on one and the same work, but rather the repeated playing of one and the same tape recording of a musical or literary text. In this instance, we are not talking about a difference in interpretation or the result of the individual style of the executors. It is an

1. Alexander Pushkin. *Eugene Onegin*. Trans. James E. Falen. Carbondale and Edwardsville: Southern Illinois University Press, 1990, pp. 82, 204.
2. See: Küchelbecker, V. K. *Puteshestviye. Dnevnik. Statyi*. Leningrad, 1979, p. 99–100.

artificially created situation, which we may define as the reproduction of one and the same text.

Let us simultaneously note that it is precisely in this case, with unexpected clarity, that the difference between that which is art and that which constitute non-art may be manifested. It is highly unlikely that someone will decide to listen several times over to a radio broadcast of one and the same "news". The now deceased N. Smirnov-Sokolsky, in the 1950s, conversing with the young philologists of his day, asked: "What is the greatest bibliographical rarity?" And he himself answered: "Yesterday's newspaper: everyone has read it and thrown it away".[3]

Repetition of one and the same text by no means suggests, however, that one will obtain no information. Rereading the newspaper makes little sense because we expect to generate new information from the text which comes to us from outside of the text. However, in cases where we listen to one and the same recording repeatedly what changes is not that which is transferred but that which is received.

The structure of the human intellect is exceptionally dynamic. The idea that in the society of archaic folklore there were no individual differences and that changes experienced according to the calendrical cycle were one and the same for everyone, should be relegated to the stuff of romantic legend. The simultaneous existence of the parallel cults of Apollo and Dionysius, and the systematic entry of the most varied of ecstatic states into cults, which greatly expanded the boundaries of predictability, is sufficient to permit the rejection of the romantic myth of the absence of individuality in archaic society. Man became man when he realised himself as man. And this occurred when he noticed that the different members of the human race consisted of different people, different voices and different experiences. The face of the individual, as with individual sexual selection, was probably the first invention of man as man.

The myth of the absence of individual differences in the archaic person is analogous to the myth of the initial chaos of sexual relations in the first stage of human development. The latter is a result of the uncritical transference by European travellers of the ecstatic rites, which it occurred to them to observe

---

3. The newspaper, which is returned to the library and stored, has already lost its function as the carrier of news and is transformed into a historical source. In equal measure, there existed in XVIII century Russia, the practice of republishing a newspaper over several years for a second time attests to the fact that the psychology of newspaper reading was not yet formed and the newspaper still stored the traces of that which was not especially new, but which was "generally interesting" to read.

in the everyday behaviour of "savages". Meanwhile, the ritual gestures and the laws of everyday behaviour, in particular in relation to sexually imbued dances, represent the rituals of magic in everyday life and, consequently, and by definition must be distinguished from it. They must render permissible all that is prohibited. Consequently, in order to transform ritual behaviour into everyday behaviour, it is necessary to subject them to some form of decoding transformation.

Let us imagine that the researchers of the folkloric way of life, noting that demonic powers, magical characters as well as the deceased do everything with the left hand, might conclude that the creators of this mythology were the earliest left-handed people. Meanwhile, knowing the laws of folklore, even an alien could conclude from such a text that the human norm is to work with the right hand. Thus, even the constant storage of information is, itself, a form of transformation. The more constant a text is the more active will be the perception of the person interpreting it.

It is not by chance that the contemporary theatrical spectator sits quietly and, without interfering in the action, accepts the most terrible episodes and scenes, whereas in the ancient theatre, the action on stage provoked some exceptionally stormy behaviour amongst spectators. You may even have heard ancient legends of how Athenian spectators, excited by the actor's proclamations of love, threw themselves on their women.

An example of the excitatory action of an apparently neutral text is the following episode from *The Captain's Daughter*: "My father sat by the window reading the *Court Calendar*, which he received every year. This book has a great effect on him: he never read it[4] without agitation, and the perusal of it invariably stirred his bile. My mother, who knew all his ways by heart, always tried to stow away the unfortunate book as far as possible, and sometimes the *Court Calendar* did not catch his eyes for months. When, however, he did chance to find it, he would not let it out of his hands for hours. And so my father was reading the *Court Calendar*, shrugging his shoulders from time to time and saying in an undertone: "Lieutenant-General! ... He was a sergeant in my company ... a Companion of two Russian Orders! ... And it isn't long since he and I ..." At last my father threw the Calendar on the sofa ..."[5]

In all these cases the creative initiative belongs to the recipient of the information. The listener (reader) is therefore the authentic creator.

---

4. Let us focus attention on the fact that the discussion deals precisely with the rereading, and not simply reading.
5. A. Pushkin. *The Captain's Daughter*. Trans. Natalie Duddington. New York: The Viking Press, 1928, p. 5.

The archaic stage of the development of art is not as alien to creation as it is to art in its entirety. However, this artistic aspect takes a unique form. Above all, the two poles of traditional and improvised creation are separated. They may be opposed by genre or their opposition may be encountered in any one work. But in any event they are interconnected: the stricter the laws of tradition, the freer the explosions of improvisation. The improviser and the carrier of memory (sometimes these images are cast as "the fool and the wise man", "the drunkard and the philosopher", "the inventor and the savant") are interconnected figures; the carriers of inseparable functions. This duality, perceived of as a unique entity, has generated those concepts which attribute to folklore the fruit of improvisation on the one hand, and the embodiment of impersonal tradition on the other.

The archaic creation, many of whose features we can trace in folklore, is characterised not by a uniquely imaginary immobility, but by a quite different redistribution of the functions between actor and spectator. The archaic forms of folklore are ritualised. This means that in it there is no such thing as a passive spectator. To find oneself within the space of ritual (be it temporal, i.e., calendrical or spatial, if the ritual requires a specific conventional place) is already an indicator of participation. Vyacheslav Ivanov, in the spirit of the Symbolist tradition, sought to revive the collective unity of the actor and the spectator. However, these attempts too clearly reflected an imitation.

The fact is that the archaic ritual requires an archaic worldview, which cannot be recreated artificially. The confluence of actor and spectator implies the confluence of art and action. Thus, the child, not yet habituated to the adult perception of drawing, does not see a drawing but rather the act of drawing: not the result but the action. Anyone, who has had experience of observing how children draw knows that in many cases the process of drawing is more interesting to children than the result. In the process of drawing, the child gets excited, dances and shouts and frequently the sketch is torn up or is deleted by the child. We often see an adult trying to calm the child's excitement, saying: "It's already good, any more will spoil it". However, the child cannot stop.

This state of uncontrolled excitement into which the actor falls during the process of creation and which, in its ecstatic forms, according to many observations, ends in complete exhaustion may be compared with the state of inspiration in the later stages of the existence of art.

However, in the art of the "historical epochs" a separation between actors and audience occurs. If action in the sphere of art is always, *as it were, an action*, then in the art of the historical epochs it generates *a condition of co-presence*. The spectator, in art, must simultaneously act as a non-spectator in the real world: he sees, but he does not interfere, he is present, but he does not act, and in this sense he does not participate in the action being staged. The latter consideration is an important one. Mastery of any art, be it the gladiator's battle with the lion in the circus arena or cinematography, requires the non-intervention of the spectator in the artistic space. Action is substituted by co-presence which coexists simultaneously with presence in normal, non-artistic space and is its complete opposite.

Thus, the dynamic processes of culture are constructed as a unique pendulum swing between a state of explosion and a state of organisation which is realised in gradual processes. The state of explosion is characterized by the moment of equalisation of all oppositions. That which is different appears to be the same. This renders possible unexpected leaps into completely different, unpredictable organisational structures. The impossible becomes possible. This moment is experienced outside of time, even if, in reality, it stretches across a very wide temporal space. Let us recall the words of Blok:

> Yesterday wildly stares into tomorrow's eye.
> There is no present . . . [6]

This moment concludes by passing into a state of gradual movement. What was united in one integrated whole is scattered into different (opposing) elements. Although, in fact, there was no selection whatsoever (any substitution was made by chance) the past is retrospectively experienced as a choice and as a goal-directed action. Here, the laws of the gradual processes of development enter into the fray. They aggressively seize the consciousness of culture and strive to embed the transformed picture into memory. Accordingly, the explosion loses its unpredictability and presents itself as the rapid, energetic or even catastrophic development of all the same predictable processes. The antithesis of explosion and predictability is substituted by rapidity (dynamic) and slowness (gradual).

Thus, for example, all historical descriptions of catastrophically explosive moments, wars or revolutions, are constructed in such a way as to show the inevitability of their outcome. History, faithful to its apostle, Hegel, tenaciously demonstrates that, for it, the chance event does not exist and that all future events are secretly located in the phenomena of the past. A logical consequence of this approach is the eschatological myth of the movement of history towards its inevitable conclusion.

Instead of this model we propose another, in which the unpredictability of the extra-temporal explosion is constantly transformed in human consciousness into the predictability of the dynamics it generates and vice versa. Metaphorically speaking, the first model may present God as the great teacher who demonstrates

---

6. Blok, A. A. The Artist. In *Selected Poems*. Trans. Jon Stallworthy and Peter France. Manchester: Carcanet, 2000, p. 87.

with extraordinary skill a process previously known to him. The second may be illustrated by the image of a creator-experimenter, who is involved in a grand experiment, the results of which are unknown to him and therefore unpredictable. From this point of view, the universe is transformed into an inexhaustible source of information, like the Psyche, in which dwells the inherent self-growing Logos about which Heraclitus spoke.[7]

In its search for a new language, art cannot be exhausted, just as the reality it seeks to exploit cannot be exhausted.[8]

---

7. "No matter the path you travel, the boundaries of the Psyche you will not find; its Logos is so deep" *Fragment Geraklita/Materialisty Drevnei Gretsii: Sobraniye Tekstov Geraklita, Demokrita i Epikura. Red. M. A. Dynnika, M., 1955,* pp. 39–52 (Fragments of Heraclitus//The Materialists of Ancient Greece: A collection of texts from Heraclitus, Democritus and Epicurus/Ed. M. A. Dynnik. Moscow, 1955, pp. 39–52)
8. This position proceeds from the hypothesis concerning the linearity of the movement of our culture. Being located inside it, we cannot verify this thesis and we voice it as an initial presumption.

# Chapter 18
# The end! How sonorous is this word!

In 1832 Lermontov wrote:

> The end! How sonorous is this word!
> How many – how few ideas are in it...[1]

This "many – few" brings us to the very essence of the "problem of the end".

The behaviour of man is meaningful. This means that human activity implies some purpose. However, the concept of purpose unavoidably includes the notion of the end of an event. The human tendency to ascribe to actions and events an element of sense and purpose implies the division of a continuous reality into specific conditional segments. This is inevitably tied to humanity's desire to understand the object of its observations. The link between sense and understanding was emphasised by Pushkin in "Verses, composed at night during insomnia":

---

1. Lermontov, M. Yu. *Sobr. soch*, T. 2, p. 59. These lines are repeated by Lermontov in the poem "What good is life... Without adventure..." and in a letter to M. A. Lopukhina (the autographs are located in Pushkin's House and Public (National) Library in St. Petersburg). In the publications of both texts there is a small, but in reality, considerable, disagreement in the punctuation used. In the volume of letters, the words "many" and "few" are divided by a comma and a dash ("So many, – so few ideas in it" – VI, 415) in the second volume in the poem at this point there is only the dash ("so many – so few ideas in it" – II, 59). The semantic value of this difference is great. The dash transfers the sense of the simultaneous contrast, the dash and the comma a sequential enumeration. An examination of this difference presents one of the essential problems of Lermontovian semantics.
The Lermontovian contrast "many-few", of course, reflects a specific synchronic antinomy. However, in order to understand the sense of it, a further element of reasoning is required.
When speaking of the synchronic expression of two opposing ideas in a Lermontovian text, we need to fix upon a special feature of the poet's way of thinking. The linking of the two antinomies does, it seems, allow us to draw together the thoughts of Lermontov and Hegel. We refer, no less, to the notorious "unity of contradictions". However, we must immediately emphasise that the Lermontovian concept, which we named the "combination of contradictions", should not be compared with the notion of Hegelian unity. Rather, we are talking about the profound contrast between them. (The text referred to in this footnote was obtained in J. M. Lotman's archive as a fragment under the title "The combination of contradictions", written during his work on *Culture and Explosion* – T.K.). (Translator's note: English translation my own.)

I want to *understand* you,
I search for *sense* in you ...[2] (italics mine – J. L.)

That which is without end is without sense. Understanding is linked to the segmentation of non-discrete space. In this respect the attribution of value to reality, especially in the process of its artistic interpretation, inevitably includes segmentation.

Life – without beginning and end

...

But you, artist, solidly believe
In beginnings and endings.[3]

From the aforesaid, two essential consequences flow. Firstly, the sphere of reality is linked to the special semantic role of death in the life of man; secondly, in the realm of art, the dominant role of beginnings and endings are self-determined, especially the latter. The demonstrative rejection of the end – for example, in *Eugene Onegin* – only confirms this regularity.

The usual process of making sense of reality is closely linked to the transference to it of discrete articulations, in particular, literary texts.[4] Pushkin carried out an audacious experiment, when he introduced into poetry the non-discreteness of life. And so appeared the novel, categorically deprived of an ending. We see this also in Tvardovsky who renounces, in his poetry, the literary categories of beginning and end and instead contrasts them against an external living reality:

– We know: "The Book About the Soldier"
– And so, what of it?
– "Without beginning, without end"
It's hardly worth the "Affair".[5]

The purely literary problem of the ending is, in reality, analogous to the problem of death.

---

2. A. Pushkin. *Poln. sobr. soch.*, t. III. Moskva/Leningrad, 1948, p. 250. (Translator's note: English translation my own.)
3. Blok, A. A. *Sobr. soch.* T. 3, p. 301. (Translator's note: English translation my own.)
4. Lines from Baratynsky:
   And to give life, my lyre!
   I wanted your agreement
   (Baratynsky, E. A. *Poln. sobr. stikhotvorenii*, T. 1, p. 188).
5. Tvardovsky, A. T. *Sobr. soch. v 6 T.* Moskva, 1978, T. 3, p. 332. The homonymic rhyme *delo – delo* signifies, on the one hand, that which describes the thing – work, and on the other that which represents the thing – a bureaucratic term: a dossier for classifying documents. (Translator's note: English translation my own.)

The beginning-end and death are inextricably linked to the possibility of understanding the reality of life as something which may be comprehended. The tragic contradiction between the infinity of life as such, and the finite nature of human life, is only one particular manifestation of the more drastic contradiction between that which lies beyond the categories of life and death – between the genetic code and the individual existence of the organism. From the very moment that individual existence is converted into conscious existence (the existence of consciousness), this contradiction is transformed from a characteristic anonymous process into the tragic property of human life.

Thus, just as the concept of art is linked to reality, notions of text / text boundary are also inextricably incorporated into the problem of life / death.

The first stage of the aspect under analysis occurs in the biological sphere as the problem of "reproduction / death". The continuity of the reproductive process is antithetically linked to the discontinuity of individual existence. However, until this contradiction becomes an object of self-consciousness it, as it were, "does not exist". The unconscious contradiction does not become a behavioural factor. In the sphere of culture, the first stage of the battle with "endings" appears as a cyclical model, which is dominant in mythological and folkloric consciousness.

Thereafter (or more exactly, insofar as) mythological thinking gave way to the historical and the concept of the end assumed a dominant role. The need to reconcile the non-discrete nature of existence with the discreteness of consciousness (and the immortality of nature with the mortality of humanity) gave birth to the idea of the cyclical, and the passage towards linear consciousness stimulated the idea of death / resurrection. From this emerged the mythological idea of the regeneration of the old man through his son and the idea of death / birth. Here, however, an essential division also arose.

In the cyclical system, the notion of death / resurrection related to the survival of one and the same eternal deity. A linear repetition created the notion of the *other (* as a rule, the son) in whose image the dead person was seemingly resurrected by virtue of their similarity. Since, at the same time, the female element was considered to be non-discrete, i.e. immortal and eternally young, the new young hero asserts himself through sexual union with the female element (sometimes understood to be his own mother).[6] In this we see the ritual of the connection of the Venetian Doge to the sea or the rite, observed even at the end of the last century by D. K. Zelenin, during which the peasants rolled a priest about the field and urged him to imitate sexual union with the soil.

---

6. There are numerous examples of the marriage of the hero and the goddess in ancient mythology.

This ritual relationship of the mortal (but also rejuvenated) father-son with the immortal mother was transformed into a *fin de siècle* pseudo-scientific mythology, which gave birth to a substantial part of Freudian ideas. And, insofar as the general intellectual direction of the epoch was reflected in the transformation of ideas and fantastical theories into a secondary level of quasi-reality, which seemed to confirm them but was, in reality, itself produced by them, thus generating the illusion of scientific validation.

The linear construction of culture renders the problem of death a dominant one in the cultural system. Religious consciousness represents the path of victory over death: "death is conquered by death". However, culture is too deeply immersed in the space of humanity to limit itself to this method and to simply discard the problem of death as imaginary. The concept of death (the end) cannot be solved by simple negation insofar as it represents the point where the cosmic and the human intersect. This is what Baratynsky had in mind when he wrote, of death:

> When the world appeared, blooming
> With the equilibrium of savage forces
> To your omnipotent soul
> Fell the measure to control its growth

For such a consciousness, death becomes "the destroyer of all riddles" and the "the destroyer of all chains."[7] However, to understand the place of death in culture, it is necessary to interpret what is meant by these words, i.e. it is necessary to ascribe meaning to death. And this signifies the inclusion of death in a specific semantic range which determines a given selection of synonyms and antonyms.

The basis of reconciliation with death – if we exclude religious motivations – is its naturalness and independence with regard to human will. The inevitability of death and its links to ideas about old age and disease enable it to be included in a sphere of neutral value. Much more significant are those cases where death is connected to notions of youth, health and beauty – i.e. in cases of violent death: the connection with free will lends an optimum semantic loading to this theme.

Suicide represents a special form of victory over death, of overcoming it (for example, the deliberate suicide of the Lafargue). The complexity of meanings thus created relate to the fact that the situation must be perceived as contradictory to the natural (i.e. neutral) order of things. The inclination to preserve life is a natural feeling of every living thing. The possibility of referring to the natural

---

7. See Baratynsky, E. A. *Poln. sobr. stikhotvorenii.* T. 1, p. 138 (Translator's note: English translation my own.)

laws of nature and spontaneous feelings, free from theory, is a sufficiently valid reason to ascribe indubitable persuasiveness to the reflections based on them [i.e. laws and feelings]. This is precisely the position adopted by Shakespeare who, through the mouth of Sir John Oldcastle (Falstaff), declares: "Tis not due yet. I would be loath to pay him before his day. What need I be so forward with him that calls not on me? Well, 'tis no matter; honour pricks me on. Yea, but how if honour prick me off when I come on? How then? Can honour set-to a leg? No. Or an arm? No. Or take away the grief of a wound? No. Honour hath no skill in surgery, then? No. What is honour? A word. What is in that word 'honour'? What is that 'honour'? Air. A trim reckoning! Who hath it? He that died o'Wednesday. Doth he feel it? No. Doth he hear it? No. 'Tis insensible then? Yea, to the dead. But will it not live with the living? No. Why? Detraction will not suffer it. Therefore I'll none of it. Honour is a mere scutcheon. And so ends my catechism."[8]

Falstaff is a coward. But Shakespeare's objective genius forces us to listen, not to the muttering coward, but to the irreproachable account of the conception, which anticipates the doctrine of sensualist ethics. Centuries before, Falstaff exposes sensualist ideas which are more complete and more objective than those later presented by Franz Moore in Schiller. In Falstaff's monologue we are confronted with, not cowardice, but courage – the courage of a theorist who is not afraid to draw extreme conclusions from initial premises. The comic character is, here, elevated to that of ideologue and the conflict assumes the character of a collision of ideas. Each contains, within itself, a justification which is not only psychological but also logical.

The opposite position to Falstaff is realised in culture as the apology of heroism, the extreme example of which is heroic folly. The Arabic inscription on Shamil's medal in the Hermitage collection says: "Who sees consequences, achieves no great feats". In these words we see an entire philosophy of history. It causes us to recall the numerous apologies of heroic folly, all the way up to Béranger's *Fous*, which, in V. Kurochkin's translation, evoked an incredible response amongst the Russian populists.

The grand masterpiece of Michel Vovelle *La mort et l'Occident. De 1300 à nos jours*[9] demonstrates convincingly that the stability and limitation of the originating cultural code represents a stimulus for the creation of an avalanche of transformations which serve to convert and formalise the original content. It is precisely this that enables us to separate the idea of death from a primary range

---

8. Shakespeare, W. *The Complete Works*. Ed. by Stanley Wells and Gary Taylor. Oxford: Clarendon Press, 1986, p. 537.
9. See Vovelle, M. *La mort et l'Occident. De 1300 à nos jours*. Paris, 1983.

of values and to convert the notion of death into one of the universal languages of culture.

An analogous process also occurs in the sphere of sexual symbolism. The radical error of Freudianism lies in its ignorance of the fact that a language only becomes possible at the cost of the loss of immediate reality and the transformation of the latter into that purely formal sphere, which is "empty" and therefore ready to receive any content. By preserving its emotional (and always individual) reality, its physiological base, sex cannot become a universal language. For this to occur, it must be formalised and fully separated from sexuality as content as in the example of the baboon who recognises his defeat.[10]

The propagation of diverse variations of Freudianism that have invaded all layers of 20th century mass culture leads to the belief that they, least of all, rest on the spontaneous sensations of natural sexuality. They are, rather, witnesses to the fact that phenomena, once they have become language, irreparably lose their connection to extra-semiotic reality. Those epochs in which sex has become an object of the aggravated attention of culture coincide not with a period of growth but rather with its decline. From the field of semiotics of culture, sex reverts to the field of physiology, but this time as a tertiary metaphor of culture. Attempts to re-establish in physiological practice all those processes produced by culture, and above all the word, does not make culture a metaphor of sex as Freud asserts but rather makes of sex a metaphor of culture. For this, from sex, one thing only is required – that it ceases to be sex.

---

10. In a conflict of male baboons, the conquered baboon recognises its defeat by means of a gesture, which imitates the sexual post of the female.

# Chapter 19
# Perspectives

And so we note that explosions are an integral element of the linear dynamic process. We have already said that in binary structures such a dynamic is distinguished by a singular particularity. But what does this particularity consist of?

In ternary social structures even the most powerful and deep explosions are not sufficient to encompass the entirety of the complex richness of social layers. The core structure can survive an explosion so powerful and catastrophic that its echo can be heard through all the levels of culture. Nevertheless, where a ternary structure exists, the contemporary, and beyond this, historical, affirmation of the total destruction of any given order of the old system appears as a mixture of self-deception and tactical slogans. We are talking here not only of the impossibility of the absolute destruction of the old neither in ternary nor in binary structures, but of something much more profound: ternary structures retain certain values from the antecedent period and transport them from the periphery to the centre of the system. By contrast, the ideal binary system is represented by the complete destruction of all that already exists which is considered to be irremediably corrupt. The ternary system strives to adapt the ideal to reality, whereas the binary system seeks, in practice, to actualise an unrealisable ideal. In binary systems, the explosion penetrates life in its entirety. The ruthless nature of this experiment is not immediately apparent. First of all it attracts the most maximalist layers of society by virtue of its radicalism and a poetic subscription to the immediate construction of "a new earth and a new sky".

The price to be paid for such a utopia is only revealed at the next stage. The characteristic trait of explosive moments in binary systems is that they are perceived as unique and without equal in the entire history of humanity. They declare not the abolition of a specific layer of historical development but the very existence of history. In its ideal expression – this is the apocalyptic "time that will be no more" whereas in its actual realisation – in the words of Saltykov as he completed his *History of One City*: "The flow of history has been interrupted."[1]

The tendency to replace juridical principles with moral or religious one is no less characteristic of binary systems.

---

1. Saltykov-Shchedrin, M. E. *Poln. sobr. soch. i pisem: v 20 T.* Moskva 1937, T. 8, p. 423.

In *The Captains Daughter* there is a passage which attracts our attention from this point of view: Masha Mironova arrives in the capital in order to save Grinev who has fallen into disfavour. A remarkable conversation takes place between her and Catherine the Great (representing the State): "You are an orphan; I suppose you are complaining of some wrong or injustice?" "No, madam. I have come to ask for mercy, not justice."[2]

This theme, which Pasternak in *Doctor Zhivago* calls "the unprincipled heart", tormented Pushkin in the Thirties and he returned repeatedly to it. In *Angelo*, the hero – a strict moralist who falls into sin, realising his fall, shows himself the same inhuman principles he exercised when judging criminals:

> ... And the Duke said: "So, Angelo, tell me,
> What will it be? Without tears, or fear,
> He coldly replied: "Execute me ... "[3]

Nevertheless, it is not justice but mercy that triumphs:

> Isabella,
> With the spirit of an angel, forgave him ...

And the entire sense of the poem is condensed into the final line which is offset from the main body of the poem:

> And the Duke forgave him[4]

Finally, we find, in the same call for mercy, the sound of another Pushkinian verse:

> And forgiveness fell to the fallen[5]

Mercy opposes the Law which was the "hero" of the early ode to "Liberty".[6]

---

2.  Alexander Pushkin. *The Captain's Daughter*. Trans. Natalie Duddington. New York: The Viking Press, 1928, p. 207.
3.  Thanks to the graphic structure, the pause before the last verse sets the nature of the statement for the entirety of the poem.
4.  A. Pushkin. *Poln. sobr. soch.*, t. V. Moskva/Leningrad, 1948, p. 128. (Translator's note: English translation my own.)
5.  Ibid, t. III, 1948, p. 424.
6.  See the earlier version of this line:
    And mercy sang (III, 1034)
    This poem was connected to the preceding one:
    That following Radishchev, I glorified freedom (III, 1034), –
    connecting the ode to "Liberty" and "I have raised a monument to myself ... " as the beginning and the end of the journey.

In the antithesis of mercy and justice, the Russian idea, based on binary notions, opposes the Latin rules which lie at the heart of the law: *Fiat justitia = pereat mundus* and *Dura lex, sed lex.*[7]

More significant is the steady tendency of Russian literature to see the law as dry and inhuman in contrast to such informal concepts as forgiveness, sacrifice, love. Behind it lie the antithesis of State law, individual morality, politics and sainthood.

It is Gogol who, especially in his *Selected Extracts*, begins the tradition of contrasting the laws of the State with human morality. Although Gogol's advice to correct drunk peasants with admonitions of the type: "Ach, you, you dirty mug!" generated universal disapproval, even amongst Slavophiles, the very idea of constructing a non-juridical society of one form or another persisted in various forms throughout the entire second half of the 19th century. An attorney is invariably shown as a negative figure in both Tolstoy and Dostoevsky.

Judicial reform was, without a doubt, the fruit most reflected upon in the epoch of reforms and, nevertheless, suffered the most bitter attacks from both right and left. Political liberalism was set against utopia. Dostoevsky, through the mouth of Sonia, called upon Raskolnikov to get down on his knees and confess his sins to the people. Tolstoy in *The Power of Darkness*, together with Akim, tongue-tied but precisely for this reason proclaiming the truth which remains hidden from the "scribes and the Pharisees" declares conscience to be above the law and repentance to be above the court:

> *Several men approach and are about to seize him [Nikita].*

> AKIM: (*Shielding him with his arms*) Wait! Here, fellows, wait, y'see; wait, I tell you!
> NIKITA: Akulina, I poisoned him. Forgive me, for Christ's sake! [...]
> AKIM. O Lord! What a sin! What a sin!
> POLICEMAN: Seize him! And send for the village elder, and witnesses. We must draw up a document. Get up and come here.
> AKIM [to the Policeman]: But you, you know – Brass Buttons, y'see – just wait a bit, you know. Just let him tell the story, y'see.
> POLICEMAN [to Akim]: Look out, old man; don't meddle. I must draw up the document.

---

7.  "Let justice be done, though the world perish" and "The Law was severe, but this is the law." (Lat.) See the ironic quotation in Pushkin's poem "Tsar, wrinkling his eyebrows ...":
    "They hang by the neck,
    But the law is cruel ..." (II, 430)
    The comparison with the Latin proverb reveals the sense of the poem as an attempt at self-justification.

AKIM: What a fellow you are, y'see. Wait, I tell you. Don't fuss about the document, y'see. God's work going on here, you know. A man is repenting, y'see; and
you talk about a document, you know.[8]

The binary system equates evolution with explosions ("nature is nothing but
fractures", in the words of Mandelstam writing on Lamarck[9]). As has already
been said, in western type civilisations, explosion only partially ruptures the
layers of culture. Even where the rupture is significant, however, the historical
connection is not broken. In binary structures, moments of explosion rupture
the continuous chain of events, unavoidably leading not only to deep crises but
also to radical renewals.

In this way, in Russia, the reforms of the last third of the 19th century were
torn away by the simultaneous turn to terror tactics by both government and
democrats. The desire to halt history in fact forced it to leap. The opposing
parties agreed on only one point – an aversion to the "postepenovtsy".[10] As
such, the moral superiority of this or that activist of the opposing parties was far
from irreproachable in terms of the interests of the global structure. The global
structure is oriented towards levelling and survival through the mechanism of
justice. The 'party line' orients itself towards the truth (which is always 'its'
truth) whatever the cost. The extreme embodiment of the former is compromise,
of the latter – a battle to the bitter end and the complete annihilation of the
enemy. Therefore, a bloody battle and possibly defeat must precede victory.
Thus, victory is portrayed as the "the last and decisive battle" – the establishment
of the reign of God on earth.

The Holy Virgin, appearing before Savonarola, promised to intercede in the
realisation of his ideas, at the same time warning him: "But as you must realise,
this renewal and consolation of the church cannot take place without great tribu-
lation and much bloodshed, especially in Italy. It is precisely the latter that has
caused all these ills, through the pursuit of luxury, pride and the countless other
unspeakable sins of its leaders." The Madonna showed Savonarola a spectacle
of Florence and the whole of Italy overcome by rebellions and wars. And then
the Madonna showed Savonarola another globe:[11] "When I opened this sphere, I

8. Tolstoy, Leo. The Power of Darkness. Trans. George Rapall Noyes and George Z.
   Patrick. In *Great Russian Plays*. Ed. by Norris Houghton. New York: Dell Publishing,
   1960, p. 301.
9. Mandelstam, O. E. *Collected Works in 3 Volumes* [vol. 4 additional], 2nd edition.
   Washington, 1967, vol. 1, p. 178.
10. Translator's note: supporters of gradual development.
11. Is this not the source of the Voland's globe turning into a relief map in Bulgakov?
    The two-volume bibliography of Savonarola Pascale Villari, published in 1913 with
    a foreword by A. L. Volynsky, was without a doubt, available to Bulgakov.

saw Florence, covered in lilies, twisting over the uneven walls, stretching every-
where on their long stems. And angels, floating about the walls that surrounded
the city, looked upon them."[12] In theory, the miraculous utopian reincarnation of
humanity always originates with an expiatory victim, with the spilling of blood.
In practice, it is doomed to drown in blood.

Amongst the brilliant cohort of 19th century Russian writers who achieved
international acclaim, our attention somehow always slides to the solitary and
mysterious figure of Krylov. Recognised by readers from all layers of society, he
stands alone in the literary battles of his epoch. He has no need to idealise the
people, since he himself is a representative of the people. He is free of illusions.
His sober mind may not be entirely free from scepticism, but his principle passion
is sobriety. He does not believe in miracles, whosoever works them, whether it
be the Tsar or the people. He does not champion the peasant, although deep
down he is, undoubtedly, a democrat. There are times when he rises almost to
the level of prophecy. In his version (not intended for publication) of the fable
"Parnas" Krylov wrote:

> When in Greece the gods faced terrible moments
> That shook their very throne;
> Or, so to speak, in a much more simple tone,
> When the gods had passed out of fashion, they began
> To suppress the gods in many ways ...
> And the gods no longer feel like joking
> Their lives tighter by the year!
> Until finally, the declaration was given –
> 24 hours to clear out of Greece.
> But they were obstinate,
> They had to clean the temples;
> But this is not the end: let the gods peel away
> All that they have managed to accumulate.
> Heaven fordbid that you should be demoted from the rank of god.

It is true that the expulsion of the gods led to a situation wherein the new owner
of Parnassus "began to graze his donkeys there".[13] Neither old, nor new gave
Krylov any illusions. Krylov's pathos is tied to common sense, freedom from
illusions, and the authority of words and slogans. But Krylov's strength lies not
only in his destruction of illusions: perhaps more than anyone else during the

---

12. Villari, P. *Geralamo Savonarola and his Times: in 2 Vols.* Published 1913, vol. 2.
    pp. 251–252.
13. Krylov, I. A. *Poln. sobr. soch.* T. 3, p. 14. (Translator's note: English translation my
    own.)

entire history of Russian culture, no other person was able to so organically connect a genuine national character to the wider European culture.

Krylov, of course, was not the only representative (although he was the brightest) of this direction in Russian culture, which was as alien to Slavophiles as to Westerners, alien even to the very principle: "Who is not with us, is against us" – which is the primary principle of binary systems. In this sense, it is also necessary to mention the names of Ostrovsky and, more especially, Chekhov.

The aforesaid has direct relevance to the events, which are now taking place in the territory of the former Soviet Union. In terms of the questions we have investigated, the processes that we are witnessing may be described as the switch from a binary system to a ternary one. However, we cannot fail to note the uniqueness of the moment: the journey itself is thought of using the traditional concepts of binarism. In fact, two possible routes may be conceived of. One, which led to Gorbachev's loss of power, consisted in replacing reforms with declarations and plans and led the country up a blind alley fraught with the gloomiest of forecasts. The other – expressed in such diverse plans as the "500 days" and other projects for the rapid transformation of the economy – "fights fire with fire", explosion with explosion.

The mental crossover between the concept of explosion and evolutionary consciousness is, today, especially important insofar as all previous Russian culture, customary for us, was oriented towards notions of polarity and maximalism. However, self-knowledge is not an equivalent of reality. In the sphere of reality, explosions cannot disappear and the only real issue under discussion is how to overcome the fatal choice between stagnation and catastrophe. Furthermore, ethical maximalism has become so deeply enrooted in the very foundations of Russian culture that it is hardly possible to speak of the "danger" of the absolute assertion of the golden middle, still less to fear the levelling off of contradictions will put a brake on explosive processes. If forward movement – whose only alternative is catastrophe with unpredictable boundaries – nevertheless succeeds in overcoming the obstacle, with which we are currently faced, then the emergent order will hardly be a simple copy of the West. History does not know repetition. It loves new and unpredictable roads.

# Chapter 20
# In place of conclusions

The idea that the starting point of any semiotic system is not the simple isolated sign (word), but rather the relation between at least two signs causes us to think in a different way about the fundamental bases of semiosis. The starting point occurs not in a single isolated model, but rather in semiotic space. This space is filled with a conglomeration of elements whose relations with each other may be encountered in a variety of ways: they may emerge as a semantic collision, oscillating in the space between complete identity and absolute divergence. These multilingual texts simultaneously include both possibilities, i.e. one and the same text may find itself in a state of non-intersection in relation to a given semantic range and in a state of identification with yet another. This variety in the possible connections between semantic elements creates a multi-dimensional point of view, which can only be fully understood in terms of the ratio of each element to the other and all elements to the whole. Furthermore, it is necessary to keep in mind the fact that the system has a memory of its past states and an anticipation of potential 'future states'. Thus, semiotic space is simultaneously multi-dimensional in both the synchronic and diachronic sense. It benefits from fluid boundaries and the capacity to incorporate itself in explosive processes.

The system, passing through the stage of self-description, undergoes changes: assigning to itself clear boundaries and a considerably higher degree of unification. However, separation of the process of self-description from the state preceding it is possible only in a theoretical sense. In reality both levels continuously influence each other. Thus, the self-description of culture makes a boundary of the fact of its self-consciousness. The moment of self-consciousness defines the boundaries of cultures and the inclusion of governmental and political considerations has repeatedly added a dramatic character to this process. This may be compared with the fluid boundaries of language on a map showing their natural distribution in contrast to their clear articulation, for example, on a political map.

Earlier we spoke about binary and ternary cultural systems. Their journey through the critical line of explosion will be different. In ternary systems, explosive processes rarely penetrate all layers of culture. As a rule, what occurs in this instance is the simultaneous combination of explosion in some cultural spheres and gradual development in others. Thus, for example, we see how the fall of the Napoleonic Empire, accompanied by real explosion in the spheres of politics, government, and culture in its widest sense, did not affect property on lands sold off during the revolution (as 'national property'). It is also possible to point out that the Roman structure of municipal authority persisted despite numerous barbarian invasions and, whilst it has been transformed almost to the point of non-recognition, has, nevertheless, preserved its continuous succession to the present day.

This ability of culture, descended from the Roman Empire, to preserve immutability in the process of change and to transform immutability into a form of change has had a considerable influence on the fundamental characteristics of western European culture. Even the attempts to produce an absolute reconstruction of the entire 'living space' of society, such as Cromwell's socio-religious utopia or the explosion of the Jacobinian dictatorship, in fact, touched only upon very limited spheres of life. Karamzin also notes that when passions were high in the National Assembly and the theatre, in the streets of Paris close to the Palais royal life was merry and far removed from political life.

Russian culture, with its binary structure, characteristically features an entirely different self-evaluation. Even where empirical study reveals multiple and gradual processes, at the level of self-description we encounter the idea of the complete and unconditional destruction of existing developments and the apocalyptic generation of the new.

Marxist theorists wrote that the journey from capitalism to socialism would inevitably have an explosive character. This was based on the fact that all other formations were conceived within the framework of previous stages, whilst socialism initiates a completely new period, whose origins are only made possible by the ruins, rather than the bosom, of historical precedent. It was also noted that feudal and bourgeois orders arose first of all in the economic domain and it was not until later that they acquired a political and juridical form. However, a curious thing occurred: examples of the maturation of a new structure on the bones of the old were drawn from history, building on the cultural-historical space of the Roman Empire and its cultural heirs, whereas the theory of "socialism in one separated country" has been argued on the basis of the facts of Russian history in the current century, i.e. history with a distinctly binary self-consciousness.

Here, it should first of all be noted that the idea of the impossibility of the origin of socialism in the framework of capitalism diverged on the one hand from western social-democratic ideas, and on the other clearly resembled ideas which appeared periodically in Russian history. Apocalyptic words about "a new sky" and "a new earth" have, over the course of history, fed into many social and religious currents. However, in the West, these were, as a rule, peripheral religious movements, periodically floating to the surface but never, in the long term, becoming dominant traits of great historical cultures. Russian culture realises itself in the categories of explosion.

Perhaps the most interesting moment, in this sense, is that in which we now live. Theoretically, it is interpreted as the victory of real "natural" development over the unsuccessful historical experiment. The slogan of this epoch stands out as if it were an old rule of the physiocrats: *laissez faire, laissez passer.*[1]

The idea of independent economic development in Western Europe was organically connected to gradual development over time and the rejection of the idea of the "acceleration of history". In our situation, the same slogan presupposes the notion of government intervention and the instantaneous conquest of historical space into the most compressed periods – whether it be 500 days or any other period – previously dictated by history. Psychologically, here we see the same ideas proposed by Peter the Great "to overtake and surpass Europe" (in the period between the Battle of Narva and the Neustadt Peace Treaty) or the even more memorable "five year plan in four years". Even when we are talking of gradual development, we want to accomplish this using explosive techniques. This, however, is not the result of some lack of thought, but rather the severe dictates of a binary historical structure.

The radical change in relations between Eastern and Western Europe, which is taking place before our very eyes may, perhaps, provide us with the opportunity to pass into a ternary, Pan-European system and to forego the ideal of destroying "the old world to its very foundations, and then" constructing a new one on its ruins. To overlook this possibility would be a historical catastrophe.

*The author would like to thank V. I. Gekhtman, T. D. Kuzovkina, E. A. Pogosyan and S. Salupere for help in the preparation of this book.*

---

1. The slogan, directed against state intervention in the natural flow of economic processes, is more accurately defined as: "Don't interfere", "Let it go its own way".

# Afterword
# Around Culture and Explosion: J. Lotman and the Tartu-Moscow School in the 1980–90s

*Marina Grishakova*

Critics tend to view *Culture and Explosion* either as a synthesis of the whole Tartu-Moscow school's work (Deltcheva and Vlasov 1996: 148) or as the author's intellectual testament or confession (Emerson 2003: 210). There is a grain of truth in these definitions, though it is not without certain reservations that they might be accepted. Lotman's last book synthesizes his previous works, their key topics and concepts, indeed, yet its confessional character is not quite so obvious. On the other hand, it would be oversimplification to see the book as a result of the whole school's evolution. The polemics on the origins and significance of the Tartu-Moscow school in the late 1980s-early 1990s have demonstrated that what is currently termed a "school" was a virtual community rather than a monolithic whole. It brought together different approaches and research habits; though a common language was used to maintain mutual understanding and to promote professional research in the ideologically infected Soviet environment. In his article "On the problem of the genesis of the Tartu-Moscow semiotic school", Boris Uspensky offers two definitions of the "school": 1) the school as a corporative association unified by a certain program and presenting itself as a certain whole; 2) the "school" as a concept used by external observers to describe the activity of a group of scholars perceived from the outside perspective as a unified whole, which the members of the group do not claim themselves to be. The second definition pertains to the Tartu-Moscow school (Uspensky 1987: 18).

*Culture and Explosion* is not a mere summary of the previous work, however: it manifests a certain paradigmatic shift or "bifurcation point", where the developments of modern science and the author's personal evolution interestingly converge. As Caryl Emerson insightfully notes, further distancing from the "hard-wired structuralism" of the 1960–70s and a turn towards organic models are symptomatic of Lotman's work starting from the mid-1980s (Emerson 2003: 201). It is in the mid-1980s that the concept of "semiosphere" as an analogue for Vernadsky's "biosphere" and "noosphere", Bakhtin's "logosphere" or Uexküll's "Umwelt" appears in Lotman's articles (Lotman 1984; on "semiosphere" see e.g. Eco 1990; Mandelker 1994; Kull 1998; Alexandrov 2000; Andrews 2003). *Culture and Explosion*, with its key metaphor of "explosion", a burst of energy that renders the behaviour of the system unpredictable, seems to be a further step towards the realisation of this new, "poststructuralist" project whose development overlaps with a period of rapid and drastic changes in society (the "poststructuralist" refers not to poststructuralist theory or deconstruction but to the period in Lotman's biography marked by intensive interest in dynamic, non-linear, complex processes). Besides the emigration of certain members of the Tartu-Moscow semiotic school to the West in the 1980s and the fall of the "iron curtain" in the 1990s, which made possible stable contacts between Eastern Europe and the rest of the world and opened up an opportunity for East European scholars to move to western universities, I would single out the following important landmarks of this period of Lotman's biography: the book *Creation of Karamzin* (1986), polemics on the origins and significance of the Tartu-Moscow school (1989–1992), and *Universe of the Mind* (1990), a combination of revised articles from the earlier period and newly produced chapters. These landmark writings lead to *Culture and Explosion* (1992).

Polemics on the origins of the Tartu-Moscow school began with Boris Gasparov's essay "The Tartu school of the 1960s as a semiotic phenomenon" published in *Wiener Slavistischer Almanach* in 1989. The essay evoked a series of polemical responses in the Tartu newspaper *Alma Mater* and the Moscow journal *The New Literary Observer*. More recently, the materials contained in the polemics have been collected in two volumes (which partially duplicate one another): *J. M. Lotman and the Tartu-Moscow Semiotic School* (ed. by A. Koshelev. Moscow, 1994) and *The Moscow-Tartu Semiotic School. History, Reminiscences, Reflections* (ed. by S. Nekhlyudov. Moscow, 1998). The latter collection also contains essays on the reception of the Tartu-Moscow school in the United States, Great Britain, Italy, France, Germany and Hungary. Gasparov's account of the Tartu-Moscow school as a "utopian site" that emerged as a result of external pressure on the humanities and the "esoteric" theoretical language of the school as a manifestation of its alienation from the Soviet environment produced disagreement among the school's members. Without negating the opposition of the school to the Soviet official paradigm, some scholars, including Lotman, tended to view the semiotic language of the school as a means of mutual understanding and the very phenomenon of the school as a result of inner impulse rather than external pressure. Olga Revzina pointed out that the semiotic language of the school was simpler than the language of structural linguistics of the time, e.g. in its Hjelmslevan variety. On the other hand, the semiotic language was a basis for interdisciplinary collaboration and cultural openness that acted as a counterweight to the principle of narrow specialization and official pragmatism: Tartu-Moscow scholars were the "people of the word" by contrast with the Marxist "people of action" (Revzina and Revzin 1998).

The author of a recent essay on Lotman's reception in the West observes that, besides the fact that English translations of Lotman's works had been published when the heyday of structuralism was over, Lotman's unwillingness to employ politicised rhetoric (in the spirit of Marx's formula from the *German Ideology*: "The philosophers have only interpreted the world in various ways. The point is, to change it") or to take an open ideological stance for or against Marxism may have been another reason why his work remained outside the canon in both his own country and in the left-wing intellectual circles of the West in the 1980s (Blaim 1998: 333–334).

In the course of polemics on the destiny of the school, Igor Chernov noted that the study of prohibited or forgotten texts as well as contacts with writers, philosophers and defenders of human rights testified to the school's programmatic cultural openness (Chernov 1998: 91). I would add that the school inherited the Russian Formalists' interest in "marginal" or non-canonical texts and peripheral phenomena of culture. The school was interdisciplinary and international: besides Russian or Russian-speaking scholars from Moscow, Petersburg and Tartu, Estonian (L. Mäll, J. Põldmäe, P. Torop, P. Tulviste), Armenian (S. Zolyan, R. Papayan) and other theoreticians from different national backgrounds participated in its work. Publication of works by J. Mukarzovsky, G. Shpet, P. Florensky, A. Bely, O. Freidenberg, B. Yarho, U. Masing as well as notes in memoriam of Czech scholars Jiri Levy or Miroslav Drozda in *Sign Systems Studies* are clear symptoms of the school's broad cultural mission. No doubt, the school was a child of the political "thaw" of the 1960s, the period when disparate events and movements in various countries, despite the diversity of political and cultural contexts, manifested a striking similarity.

In his response to Boris Gasparov, Lotman made a programmatic statement: "I am not able to draw a clear line [to indicate] where historical description ends and where semiotics starts. There is no opposition, no rupture" (Lotman "Winter notes on summer schools"; Lotman 1994: 296). From this perspective, *Creation of Karamzin* is a paradigmatic book. It is a story of Karamzin's break with the circle of the Moscow Rosenkreutzers and his travel to Europe, where he met Kant, Herder, Wieland, Lavater and other prominent figures of the time and observed the events of the French revolution. As the details of this trip are unknown, data is scarce and the chronology questionable; a number of real names are hidden behind the initials. Lotman's research assumed the form of a semiotic investigation of lost traces of the past with the aim of reconstructing their hidden meanings and connections. I remember the impression of the scrupulous detective work that Lotman's course on Karamzin, which preceded the book and paved the way to it, produced. As the hypotheses were extended a bit further into the sphere of the possible and the style of the book was freer than in the canonical academic research of the time, the book was also a step towards a genre of intellectual bestseller or "theoretical fiction" employed by many theoreticians either as a testing ground for their hypotheses or as an intellectual game (Tynyanov, Shklovsky, Kristeva, Eco, Lodge and others). *Creation of Karamzin* is a story of self-creation, creation of oneself as another, new person, "Russian European". The theoretical framework to which Lotman's book refers is the theory of self-organizing systems and autocommunication where the subject and object of communication coincide and a "re-coding" or reformulation of the message in the course of communication is accompanied by the transformation of the sender-receiver himself (see e.g. Winner 1982: 55; Nöth 2006). The self-referential or self-organizing system is a basic, though implicit, conceptual metaphor of the book.

In the late 1980s Lotman became inspired by the works of Ilya Prigogine on self-organizing systems. Prigogine, a Russian Jew by origin, whose parents emigrated to Germany and later to Belgium in 1921, was awarded the Nobel Prize in chemistry for his study of self-organizing systems. Lotman's article "On the role of random factors in the evolution of literature" (published in *Sign Systems Studies* in 1989) was accompanied by the following authorial commentary:

> The present article was written and presented at the semiotic seminar in Tartu University in 1985. In 1986, the author became acquainted with Ilya Prigogine's works that produced an extremely strong impression on him. Prigogine's ideas not only extend our notions on the role of the random factors, but create a real basis for the mutual rapprochement of life sciences and the humanities since, in studying the irreversibility of time, they lay the foundations for a universal model of the historical (i.e. unrolling in time) process. (Lotman 1989a: 48)

Prigogine has shown that the states of non-equilibrium in chemical and biological systems that exchange matter and energy with the external world may increase the unpredictability of a system's behavior until the system reaches the bifurcation point, where a branching of the trajectories of development occurs. At this point the system has a choice of following one or the other path of development. Which new path is chosen involves an element of chance inherent in the oscillating behavior (the state of "fluctuations", in Prigogine's terms). As a result, the system either submerges in entropy or moves towards a new state of "order", i.e. a higher degree of complexity. These processes of self-organization are characteristic of both organic and nonorganic systems: the theory provides an interesting link between "nature" and "culture", unifying them in a common process of evolution, and demonstrates that the stable world of classical physics is rather an exception than the rule. Prigogine's theory also highlights a special role of time in the evolution and its irreversibility, which does not necessarily result in entropy, as it follows from the second law of thermodynamics. Disputed and contested by certain scientists, enthusiastically supported by others, Prigogine's works have had a stimulating effect on scientific developments and shed light on certain problems that had been previously neglected or insufficiently studied (see e.g. Rice 2007; Day and Chen 1993; McDaniel and Driebe 2008). In 1986, a discussion on Prigogine's work was organised by Lotman's semiotics research group, in which I worked at the time. My presentation on *Order out of Chaos* sparked a debate about the controversial aspects and invigorating impact of Prigogine's theory on the developments in science and the humanities.

The traces of Prigogine's influence on Lotman's work are at their most obvious in *Universe of the Mind* and *Culture and Explosion*. The articles "On the role of random factors in the evolution of literature" and "Culture as a subject and an object-for-itself" (Lotman 1989a, 1989b) may be considered as draft versions for the book-length revision of the author's previous conceptions. They were published simultaneously with Boris Uspensky's reflections on the perception of time as a semiotic phenomenon (Uspensky 1988/89) and are in many respects parallel to them. In his article on the role of random factors, Lotman refers to the Formalist (Shklovsky's – Tynyanov's) "seesaw" picture of literary evolution as the alternation of the role of "centre" and "periphery". From this perspective, any cultural or literary innovation seems to be a result of a mere recombination of already existing elements. The structuralist concepts of "language" (*langue*) or "code" also imply a high degree of predictability of the "encoded" message, although, according to Lotman, the passage from "code" to "text" already comprises a moment of probability or randomness. Introducing random factors that interact with regular, iterative processes and whose role is much more prominent in art than in science and technology, Lotman revises the Formalist theory of evolution. He underscores that a single, apparently insignificant, element may bring about considerable changes or even an "avalanche" of changes in the course of evolution. These ideas have been further developed in the third part of *Universe of the Mind* ("Cultural Memory, History, and Semiotics") where Lotman highlights the opportunity of their application to the study of historical processes that are neither wholly anonymous and unconscious nor entirely personal and conscious. History has its own "bifurcation points" with a sudden increase in unpredictability: "At these moments the movement of history should be pictured not as a trajectory but as a continuum that is potentially capable of resolving itself into any number of variants" (Lotman 1990: 233). The role of random factors is usually underplayed by historiographers: historical development is, *post factum*, construed as predictable and predetermined. The nodal point of evolution that surfaces a cluster of alternative opportunities is later considered as the outcome of a certain causal development due to the fact that the predominant path of development apparently cuts off other alternatives. On the level of interpretation, time is replaced by causation, irreversibility by determinism. These ideas form the theoretical background of *Culture and Explosion*.

Whether one accepts the usage of scientific models in the humanities or not, the point is that Prigogine's work stimulated Lotman's own reflections on the semiotic aspects of cultural evolution and this apparently allowed him to see many problems in a new light, while avoiding the straightforward transfer or naïve direct application of scientific models. No doubt Lotman was a scholar, working professionally in literary and cultural studies. Yet he was also a polymath. In conversations he sometimes mentioned his adolescent interest in entomology: it was obvious that his career choice might have been different. One of the bitter allegories he used to depict human life was a man sitting in a bathtub filled with eventually solidifying plaster. I think that it is due exactly to the combination of focused professional work and a broad epistemological horizon always present even in his narrow-focused notes or articles that allowed the avoidance of a petrification of concepts and ideas in Lotman's case.

Lotman's interest in semiotics and structuralism resulted from a sense of a deep bond between science and the humanities: both are part of human culture and their radical separation and isolation as closed systems may have a deteriorating effect on both. A similar opinion is characteristic of Prigogine's works: the resonance of Prigogine's theories was wider than the sphere of their initial elaboration and application.

In the early 20th century, the tendency toward mutual enrichment and cross-fertilization surfaced in different disciplines and areas of knowledge. One of the external manifestations of this tendency was a propensity for a structural, holistic and descriptive approach to dominate over the genetic one: in psychology and philosophy (Husserl, Brentano, Titchener, Gestalt psychology), linguistics (Baudouin de Courtenay, Kruszewski, Saussure, Jakobson), literary studies (Russian formalism, Prague and later French structuralism), mathematics, etc. (see e.g. Holenstein 1976). This structuralist trend produced very effective interpretations and proved to be very fruitful, though, in the long run, tended to evacuate itself in a series of purely technical procedures. Yet its role as a "holistic attempt at the interpretation of reality along the lines of philosophical argumentation" and "a specific *activity*, a *modus operandi* in reality itself" (Broekman 1974: VII) in the humanities has been groundbreaking.

The Tartu-Moscow school owes its appearance to developments in structural linguistics, machine translation and information theory in the 1950–60s (see Uspensky 1987; Shukman 1977; Seyfert 1983), yet the orthodoxy of structural linguistics was permanently questioned by the group of literary scholars. Juri

Lotman and Boris Uspensky were the leading figures in this group. Lotman's first article on structuralism was entitled "On the Delimitation of the Concept of Structure in Linguistics and Literary Scholarship" (Lotman 1963). The concept of a "secondary modelling system" and Lotman's account of the iconic nature of the work of art as well as the idea of the co-existence and mutual untranslatability of the discrete and continual texts in culture served as a means for further discrimination between linguistic and literary (artistic) structures. However, the concepts of structure, code and language inevitably imposed restrictions on the role of innovation in the system's development and tended to reduce it to the recombination of the pre-given elements of the system. From this perspective, the paradigmatic shift in Lotman's works of the 1980s was just a further step in his permanent effort to illustrate adaptation between the individual, extrasystemic factors and the holistic systematic approach to the culture.

Already in his early work, in the *Structure of the Artistic Text* (1970) and the articles of the 1960s–early 1970s, Lotman introduces the opposition of the "random" to "predetermined", "extrasystemic" to "systemic" factors in the rigid structuralist framework. In his theses 'The Place of Art among Other Modelling Systems' on the typological similarities and differences between art and game models (in many respects parallel to Huizinga's *Homo ludens*), Lotman argues: "The game is a unique reproduction of the combination of regular and random factors" (Lotman 1967: 135). Likewise, the combination and interaction of different languages introduces indeterminacy in the artistic construction. The artistic text is a set of complex and dynamic, constantly shifting, relationships between the elements belonging to various languages and levels of language. The elements of natural language become transformed by interaction with the elements of other semiotic series (the languages of different styles, movements and authors). At this time, Lotman, however, tends to view random elements as semiotically insignificant: they acquire significance only as elements of a system.

> A 'random' element of the speech may turn out to belong to the language of the other system. [ . . . ] It is characteristic that the randomness of a given *enchainement* of elements is not canceled altogether: being random and insignificant in one system, they are highly significant in another. (Lotman 1967: 144)

In the article 'The Problem of the 'Teaching of Culture' as its Typological Characterization", Lotman highlights a discrepancy between ideal self-images ("automodels"), grammars and rules of culture, and real cultural practices. The auto-models may serve as a means of the "additional regulation" of culture on its way to the systemic unity, as a means of potential change of existing cultural practices or as ideal images without any relation to practice. Obviously, cultural practices are not totally governed by rules and include an element of randomness.

However, while taking account of the apparently random elements of the semiotic system in his early works, Lotman tends to explain innovation in terms of transcoding (switching over from one code to another) and to consider the individual and unique as a point of intersection of various codes, as a result of interaction or creolisation of different languages. In the *Structure of the Artistic Text* Lotman argues that what seems to be "extrasystemic" or "nonsystemic" in the external world becomes "polysystemic" in art (Lotman 1971 [1970]: 96).

What makes Lotman's practical, applied-semiotic works (even of his early structuralist period) flexible enough is the fact that his scholarly "double vision", though system-oriented, always included a human agency or conscious author-ship of every "systemic" act. From this perspective, there is a clear similarity between Bakhtin and Lotman, despite their distinct positions on the intellec-tual map of the humanities. In his insightful essay, David Bethea has already demonstrated that Lotman's practical research on the semiotics of everyday be-havior shows how the "codes" or conventions of behaviour have been used for individual purposes to convey an individual message. Thus, Pushkin's duel is an example of "conventional behavior" endowed by individual meaning. In this case, convention is used as a "situational template" (Bethea 2000: 18).

Moreover, practical research reveals Lotman's awareness of the philosophi-cal and anthropological roots of structuralism and his familiarity with different scientific and philosophical traditions beyond structuralism, though not all of them have been explicitly manifested in his own work. The choice of books he recommended and lent me, when I started research on the semiotics of everyday behavior and literary biography, was symptomatic: on the one hand, scholars associated with Formalism (Vinokur's *Biography and Culture*, Tomashevsky's *Literature and Biography*); on the other hand, social anthropology (Erving Goff-man's *Frame Analysis*). Both Russian authors (Vinokur and Tomashevsky) un-derscore the creative aspects of biography and consider personal life as a partic-ular form of cultural creativity. In his treatise *Biography and Culture*, Vinokur explicitly draws on the German hermeneutic and phenomenological tradition. For instance, he refers to Dilthey's work and Spranger's book *Lebensformen* (Halle 1925) as his models. Vinokur argues that the everyday habits, family relations, intimate life and gossip that make the subject matter of the traditional biographical genre are actually external manifestations of the "real" life-story as a dynamic whole, an eventually unfolding part of the historical process, where external, social events become inner, biographical facts endowed with individual meanings. "There is no external or internal biography": the external reality is in-teriorized in the individual life-story, whereas the individual life-story becomes objectified as a dynamic part of the historical process. It is exactly this individual network of relations – a structural form, not a psychological content – that makes the main interest of a biography (Vinokur 1925: 25). Vinokur employs the notion of the "style of life" (cf. Spranger's 'Lebensform') that presumes perception and conscious construction of one's own behaviour as a certain expressive unity. He draws a parallel between the poetic and biographic styles, yet argues that they are not completely identical: poetry and biography come apart at the point where poetry assumes its own poetic form and creates a particular poetic world. A personal, individual component of behavior is prominent also in Erving Goffman's research. Goffman studied everyday communication to show how social roles and frames of behavior are activated or modified in individual performance. It is obvious that these sources were essential for Lotman's own conception of the "poetics of everyday behavior" to which the American New Historicists refer in their works (cf. Stephen Greenblatt's *Toward a Poetics of Culture*).

The displacement of emphases and the increasing role of the unique and individual become even more apparent in Lotman's aforementioned works of the 1980s to the early 1990s. The automatic "norm" may turn out to be a carrier of individual "content" and is susceptible of infinite modification or deviation through individual usage, which makes a stable norm itself an exception rather than a rule. Remarkable for its persistent attention to the phenomenon of explosion as a turning point in cultural development which breaks the predictable course of events and increases unpredictability in both human and nonhuman behavior, *Culture and Explosion* contains another persistent, though perhaps less noticeable motif: the difficulty of the "norm", "logic" and "order". Lotman often cited the Chestertonian dialogue of the anarchist and the police detective from *The Man Who Was Thursday* to prove there are two types of unpredictability: the unpredictability of the train crash and the unpredictability of the train's arrival in the station. From the romantic-anarchist perspective, the first is definitely more interesting and more valuable as an event deviating from the ordinary "prosaic" progression. From the "realistic" perspective of the police detective, there are innumerable invisible alternatives hiding under the surface of any recurrent progression. Taking into account all virtual obstacles that the train might have overcome and accidents that might have prevented the train from reaching the station, a "norm" is rather a miracle than a predictable regularity. This is not to infer that the turbulent situation of the early 1990s, the strange and apparently unpredictable course of Russian history, of which Lotman had always been an attentive observer, or his own rather frail physical condition and partial loss of sight, might have been projected into his account of the "norm" and "order" as exceptional states to strive for and to maintain while trying to overcome chaos, disorder and entropy (though these parallels are inevitable, of course). Rather, Lotman points at the co-existence of order and chaos as two mutually dependent states of culture and at the fact that maintaining the "normal" patterns of behaviour in certain conditions requires additional efforts. In Romantic culture, "rules" and "folly" are polar opposites. In medieval culture, the rules are manifestations of the highest, unattainable "norm" (such as knightly or Christian-ascetic behavior) that may look like "folly" from the commonsense point of view. Thus, the "norm" may become the highest expression of individual behaviour. On the other hand, a high degree of normativity may be perceived as perversion or deviation since misunderstanding, mistranslation or misinterpretation are part of the process of communication: absolutely predictable, normative behavior would make communication redundant and impossible.

In Lotman's late works, innovative or individual behavior, previously considered as a result of multiple encoding, is incorporated into the very development of a system as its inherent property emerging in states of instability. Individual behaviour does not mean "accidental" or "absolutely random", however: it includes a moment of conscious *choice* between alternative possibilities. Chance implies choice rather than occasional coincidence. "Biologists as well as philosophers have suggested that the universe and the living forms it contains are based on chance, not on accident" (Reid 1990: 127). From this perspective, chance and uncertainty are sense-generating factors that contribute to the continuation of evolution.

The publication of the English translation of *Culture and Explosion* is a pleasant event for all who happened to meet Juri Lotman and to observe the effect his radiant personality had on the surrounding world. I would like to thank Professor Irina Reyfman (Columbia University, New York) and Professor Angela Brintlinger (Ohio State University) for their help in searching out and identifying English translations of the Russian classics referred to by Lotman in this work.

# References

Alexandrov, Vladimir E.
  2000         Biology, semiosis, and cultural difference in Lotman's Semiosphere.
               *Comparative Literature* 52(N4), 339–362.
Andrews, Edna
  2003         *Conversations with Lotman: Cultural Semiotics in Language, Literature, and Cognition.* Toronto/Buffalo/London: University of Toronto Press.

Bethea, David M.
2000            Iurii Lotman in the 1980s: The code and its relation to literary bi-
               ography. In Arnold McMillin (ed.), *Reconstructing the Canon: Rus-*
               *sian Writing in the 1980s.* Amsterdam: Harwood Academic Publishers,
               9–32.

Blaim, Artur
1998            Lotman in the West. An Ambiguous Complaint. In J. Andrew, R. Reid
               (eds.), *Neo-Formalist Papers. Contributions to the Silver Jubilee Con-*
               *ference to Mark 25 Years of the Neo-Formalist Circle.* Amsterdam:
               Rodopi, 329–337.

Broekman, Jan M.
1974           *Structuralism. Moscow – Prague – Paris.* Dordrecht/Boston: Reidel.

Chernov, Igor
1998           Тартуская школа: извне и изнутри. С.Ю. Неклюдов (ред.).
               *Московско-Тартуская семиотическая школа. История. Вос-*
               *поминания. Размышления.* Москва: Языки русской культу-
               ры, с. 89–92.

Day, Richard H. and Ping Chen (eds.)
1993           *Nonlinear Dynamics and Evolutionary Economics.* New York/Oxford:
               Oxford University Press.

Deltcheva, Roumiana and Eduard Vlasov
1996           Lotman's *Culture and Explosion*: A shift in the paradigm of the semi-
               otics of culture [review article]. *The Slavic and East European Journal*
               40(1), 148–152.

Eco, Umberto
1990           Introduction. In: Y. M. Lotman, *Universe of the Mind.* Blooming-
               ton/Indianapolis: Indiana University Press.

Emerson, Caryl
2003           Jurij Lotman's last book and filiations with Baxtin. *Die Welt der Slaven*
               XLVIII, 201–216.

Holenstein, Elmar
1976           *Roman Jakobson's Approach to Language.* Bloomington/London: In-
               diana UP.

Kull, Kalevi
1998           On semiosis, Umwelt and semiosphere. *Semiotica* 120(3/4), 299–310.

Lotman, Juri
1963           О разграничении лингвистического и литературоведческого
               понятия структуры. *Вопросы языкознания* 3, с. 44–52.
1967           Тезисы к проблеме "Искусство в ряду моделирующих си-
               стем". *Труды по знаковым системам* 3. Тарту, с. 130–145.
1971           [1970] *Struktura khudozhestvennogo teksta.* Introduction by Thomas
               G. Winner. The Brown University Slavic Reprint Series. Providence:
               Brown University Press.

1971            Проблема "обучения культуре" как ее типологическая характеристика. *Труды по знаковым системам* 5. Тарту, с. 167–176.

1984            О семиосфере. *Труды по знаковым системам* 17. Тарту, с. 5–23.

1989a           О роли случайных факторов в литературной эволюции. *Труды по знаковым системам* 23. Текст – культура – семиотика нарратива. Тарту, с. 39–48.

1989b           Культура как субъект и сама-себе объект. *Wiener Slawistischer Almanach* 23, 187–197.

1990            *Universe of the Mind. A Semiotic Theory of Culture.* Bloomington/Indianapolis: Indiana University Press.

1994            Зимние заметки о летних школах. In: *Ю. М. Лотман и Тартуско-Московская семиотическая школа.* Москва: Гнозис, с. 295–298.

Mandelker, Amy
1994            Semiotizing the sphere: Organicist theory in Lotman, Bakhtin and Vernadsky. *Publications of the Modern Language Association of America (PMLA)* 109(N3), 385–396.

McDaniel Jr., Reuben R. and Dean J. Driebe (eds.)
2008            *Uncertainty and Surprise in Complex Systems. Questions on Working with the Unexpected.* Berlin/Heidelberg: Springer.

Nöth, Winfried
2006            Y. Lotman on metaphors and culture as self-referential semiosphere. *Semiotica* 161(1–4), 249–263.

Reid, Allan
1990            *Literature as Communication and Cognition in Bakhtin and Lotman.* New York/London: Garland.

Revzina, Olga and Grigory Revzin
1994            Некоторые сомнения по поводу статьи Б. М. Гаспарова. С.Ю. Неклюдов (ред.). *Московско-Тартуская семиотическая школа. История. Воспоминания. Размышления.* Москва: Языки русской культуры, с. 74–80.

Rice, Stuart A. (ed.)
2007            *Special Volume in Memory of Ilya Prigogine (Advances in Chemical Physics, vol. 13).* Hoboken, NJ: John Wiley & Sons.

Seyfert, Peter
1983            *Soviet Literary Structuralism. Background. Debate. Issues.* Columbus, OH: Slavica Publishers.

Shukman, Ann
1977            *Literature and Semiotics. A Study of the Writings of Yu. M. Lotman.* Amsterdam/New York/Oxford: North-Holland.

Uspensky, Boris
    1987            К проблеме генезиса Тартуско-Московской семиотической
                    школы. *Труды по знаковым системам* 20. Тарту, с. 18–29.
    1988/89         История и семиотика (восприятие времени как семиотиче-
                    ская проблема). Статья 1–2. *Труды по знаковым системам*
                    22. Тарту, с. 66–84. *Труды по знаковым системам* 23. Тарту,
                    с. 18–38
Vinokur, Grigory
    1925            *Биография и культура.* Труды ГАХН. Философский отдел,
                    вып. 2. Москва.
Winner, Irene Portis
    1982            *Semiotics of Culture: The State of the Art.* Toronto Semiotic Circle
                    (Monographs, Working Papers and Prepublications 1). Toronto: Vic-
                    toria University.

# Index

Made in the USA
Middletown, DE
06 December 2022

17070878R00133